bipolar
disorder
-the
ultimate
guide

bipolar disorder
disorder
-the
ultimate
guide

Sarah Owen
and
Amanda Saunders

ONEWORLD

OXFORD

A Oneworld Paperback Original

First published by Oneworld Publications 2008

Copyright © Sarah Owen & Amanda Saunders 2008

ISBN 978–1–85168–604–9

Typeset by Jayvee, Trivandrum, India
Cover design by Mungo Designs
Printed and bound in Great Britain
by TJ International Ltd, Padstow
Pathway of Care diagram on p.53 reproduced
by kind permission of Michel Syrett

Oneworld Publications
185 Banbury Road
Oxford OX2 7AR
England
www.oneworld-publications.com

Learn more about Oneworld. Join our mailing list to
find out about our latest titles and special offers at:

www.oneworld-publications.com

CONTENTS

With thanks ...   xi

A word from Paul Abbott   xvi

A word from Jo Crocker   xix

A word from Professor Nick Craddock   xxii

Introduction: Is this book for you?   1

CHAPTER ONE CAUSES, SYMPTOMS AND DIAGNOSIS

Q1.   What is bipolar disorder?   17

Q2.   Why has manic depression been renamed bipolar
       disorder?   17

Q3.   What is the difference between Bipolar I, II and III?   19

Q4.   What is cyclothymia?   20

Q5.   Is there an age or gender profile for people with
       bipolar disorder?   20

Q6.   What are the symptoms of bipolar disorder?   21

Q7.   What is depression?   22

Q8.   What is hypomania?   24

Q9.   What is a manic episode?   26

Q10.   What is psychosis?   29

Q11.   What is a mixed state?   30

Q12. What are the less recognized symptoms of bipolar disorder? 31

Q13. Are the symptoms of bipolar disorder linked to the symptoms of seasonal affective disorder? 34

Q14. Can bipolar disorder cause thyroid problems? 36

Q15. What causes bipolar disorder? 36

Q16. Is there an increased risk of bipolar disorder for other family members? 38

Q17. Is it possible to have genetic testing for bipolar disorder? 41

Q18. Is it possible for a child to suffer from bipolar disorder? 41

Q19. Are the symptoms of bipolar disorder different in children? 45

Q20. Is bipolar disorder ever diagnosed in the elderly? 45

Q21. Why is bipolar disorder often misdiagnosed? 46

Q22. What can someone do if they think a loved one might have undiagnosed bipolar disorder? 50

Q23. How is bipolar disorder usually diagnosed? 50

Q24. What happens once a diagnosis of bipolar disorder is made? 52

CHAPTER TWO **TREATMENT**

Q25. What is the most effective way to treat bipolar disorder? 57

Q26. Are there official treatment guidelines for bipolar disorder? 59

Q27. What is psychological treatment, such as cognitive behavioural therapy? 61

Q28. How can someone with bipolar disorder get psychological treatment? 70

Q29. What drugs are used in the treatment of bipolar disorder?   74

Q30. What does someone with bipolar disorder (or someone with a family history of bipolar disorder) need to know about antidepressants?   83

Q31. Does someone with bipolar disorder need to take medication for the rest of his or her life?   85

Q32. Will drugs encourage weight gain?   88

Q33. How can someone with bipolar self manage their treatment?   89

Q34. What is electroconvulsive therapy (ECT)?   95

Q35. What is transcranial magnetic stimulation?   98

Q36. How can the symptoms of seasonal affective disorder be effectively treated?   98

Q37. What is the best course of action if a child shows symptoms of bipolar disorder?   99

Q38. Does treatment need to be different for elderly people diagnosed with bipolar disorder?   102

Q39. What is an 'advance directive'?   103

CHAPTER THREE   **SUPPORT**

Q40. What professionals support someone with a bipolar diagnosis?   105

Q41. What is an advocate?   116

Q42. What role do family and friends play in the recovery of someone with bipolar disorder?   117

Q43. On a practical level, how can family and friends help someone with a diagnosis of bipolar disorder?   122

Q44. On an emotional level, how can family and friends help someone with a diagnosis of bipolar disorder?   123

Q45. If someone with a bipolar diagnosis feels suicidal, what is the best course of action?   126

Q46. What is the best way for a loved one to cope during the really tough times?   133

Q47. What support do mental health charities offer?   139

CHAPTER FOUR   **HOSPITAL CARE**

Q48. What are psychiatric hospitals like?   142

Q49. What is an 'informal' patient in a psychiatric hospital?   150

Q50. What does it mean if somebody is sectioned?   151

Q51. Are there different types of sectioning procedures?   154

Q52. Can someone refuse to be sectioned?   156

Q53. What are a person's rights if they have been sectioned?   156

Q54. Who looks after patients in a psychiatric hospital?   157

Q55. What is a 'nearest relative'?   162

Q56. How can friends and family support a loved one in a psychiatric hospital?   163

Q57. How can friends and family forge a good relationship with those who care for their loved one in a psychiatric hospital?   167

Q58. Do psychiatric hospitals allow smoking?   168

Q59. What happens when a psychiatric patient is well enough to leave hospital?   169

Q60. What are the pros and cons of being treated in a psychiatric hospital?   173

CHAPTER FIVE **LIFESTYLE CHOICES**

Q61. Can a healthy lifestyle lower the chance of relapse for someone with bipolar disorder and reduce the risk of developing it in the first place? 175

Q62. What is the link between stress and mood swings? 176

Q63. How can regular sleep patterns help control symptoms of bipolar disorder? 178

Q64. How does exercise affect bipolar symptoms? 182

Q65. Can complementary therapies help control bipolar symptoms? 183

Q66. What dietary changes can help control the symptoms of bipolar disorder? 188

Q67. What is the 'Mind Meal'? 193

Q68. Can nutritional supplements minimize the symptoms of bipolar disorder? 195

Q69. Can herbal remedies help control bipolar symptoms? 201

Q70. How does nicotine affect bipolar symptoms? 202

Q71. How does caffeine affect bipolar symptoms? 205

Q72. How does alcohol affect bipolar symptoms? 208

Q73. Can over-the-counter medications be harmful for someone with bipolar disorder? 211

Q74. Can prescription drugs taken for conditions other than bipolar disorder influence recovery? 212

Q75. How do recreational drugs affect those with a bipolar diagnosis? 213

CHAPTER SIX **LIVING WITH BIPOLAR**

Q76. What is the best way to explain bipolar disorder to other people? 218

Q77. What is the best way to explain to a child that their parent has been diagnosed with bipolar disorder? 223

Q78. Is a person with a bipolar diagnosis legally obliged to inform their employer? 225

Q79. What is the most sensible way for a woman with bipolar disorder to approach pregnancy? 229

Q80. Are those with a bipolar diagnosis entitled to any benefits? 230

Q81. What is a 'lasting power of attorney'? 231

Q82. What is the best way to make a complaint about any aspects of care? 232

Q83. Where can somebody with a bipolar diagnosis get insurance? 234

Q84. Is it ever unsafe for someone with a bipolar diagnosis to drive? 234

Q85. What well known people have/had bipolar disorder? 236

Q86. Can a diagnosis of bipolar disorder ever be a positive thing? 242

Q87. What does the future hold for bipolar disorder? 244

Extra resources 248

Recommended reading 264

With more thanks ... 266

Glossary 268

Index 273

With thanks ...

This book would not have been possible without the amazing people who came forward to be interviewed about their personal experiences of living with bipolar disorder. We thank each and every one of you for your courage, eloquence and willingness to share your most private, intimate experiences just because you wanted to help others who find themselves in the same boat ... We can't thank you all enough.

- Alison, 35, whose daughter Vicki, aged 15, was diagnosed with bipolar in 2006
- Amy, 26, care worker, who was diagnosed with bipolar in February 2005
- Ashley, 40, artist, musician and care worker, who was diagnosed with bipolar disorder in late 2006
- Carl, 49, motorcycle mechanic, who was first diagnosed with bipolar 27 years ago
- Dave, 33, personal trainer, who first noticed bipolar symptoms at the age of 24
- Debbie, 36, insurance claims handler, who was diagnosed with bipolar at the age of 22
- Doreen, 65, retired, whose mother Agnes was diagnosed with bipolar disorder at the age of 60
- George, 49, voluntary carer, who had his first manic episode at the age of 24
- Gill, 64, retired, whose son Neil was diagnosed with bipolar in 2002

- Ingrid, 37, IT officer, who remembers her mother being diagnosed with 'manic depression' when she was eight years old

- Jackie, 37, secretary, whose husband David, 36, has had rapid cycling bipolar for ten years

- Jane, 42, account manager, partner of Dave, who has had bipolar, for five and a half years

- Jayne, 38, full-time mother, whose own mother has had severe mood swings ever since she can remember

- Jo, 32, media executive, who lives with her partner Tom, 43, who was diagnosed with bipolar 12 years ago

- Jude, 28, teacher, who was first diagnosed with bipolar a year ago

- June, 55, retired teacher, whose daughter Laura was diagnosed with bipolar in February 2007

- Keith, 57, retired probation officer, who was diagnosed with bipolar in his early twenties

- Lesley, 34, town-planning consultant, who was diagnosed with bipolar in 2006

- Neil, 37, scientific officer, who was diagnosed with bipolar in 2002

- Paula, 36, dog groomer, whose ex-husband David had bipolar disorder

- Paul, 36, unemployed, who has had symptoms since adolescence, but who was diagnosed with bipolar disorder aged 36

- Rachel, 26, part-time student, who was diagnosed with bipolar at the age of 17

- Reka, 26, saleswoman, who has had symptoms of bipolar disorder since the age of 17

- Richard, 55, retired chief financial officer, who was diagnosed with 'manic depression' in 1981

- Sharron, 42, retired office manager, who was first admitted to a psychiatric hospital at the age of 21, but only diagnosed with bipolar disorder at the age of 30
- Sue, 52, retired care support worker, who was diagnosed with bipolar in her late thirties
- Tamara, 26, student, who was diagnosed with bipolar disorder in 2001

Some of the people we interviewed asked us to change their names. We hope that one day in the near future, no one with mental illness in their life will feel they have anything to hide. Until that day, we have, of course, respected each individual's right to privacy.

We would also like to thank all the people who gave up some of their valuable time to share with us their expert knowledge and opinions, provide useful information and answer infinite questions. In alphabetical order, enormous thanks go to:

- Clare Armstrong, NHS Practice Development Officer in Ayrshire and Arran, Scotland
- Jeremy Bacon, Groups and Self Management Director at MDF The BiPolar Organisation
- Lizzie Curtin, Publicity Manager, Oneworld Publications
- Shabir Dyer, pharmacist and natural health guru at Victoria Health
- Professor Guy Goodwin, W A Handley Chair of Psychiatry, Oxford University
- Ian Hulatt, Mental Health Advisor to the Royal College of Nursing
- Professor Steven Jones, Professor of Clinical Psychology, Spectrum Centre for Mental Health Research, Lancaster University
- Professor Peter Kinderman, Professor of Clinical Psychology at the University of Liverpool
- Julie King, ward manager of a psychiatric unit in Essex

- Juliet Mabey, co-owner of Oneworld Publications

- Susan McAuley, psychiatric nurse with 24 years' experience

- Ian Maidment, Senior Pharmacist, Kent & Medway Partnership NHS Trust, and Senior Lecturer, Kent Institute of Medicine and Health Studies, Kent University

- Tim McDougall, Consultant Nurse in Adolescent Psychiatry at Pine Lodge Young People's Centre in Chester

- Professor Richard Morriss, Professor of Psychiatry and Community Mental Health at Nottingham University

- Professor Alan Ogilvie, University of Oxford Honorary Research Fellow and Honorary Consultant Psychiatrist in Oxford, and CEO of Equilibrium – The Bipolar Foundation

- Fiona Slater, Editorial Assistant, Oneworld Publications

- Kate Smith, Production Manager, Oneworld Publications

- Michel Syrett, Editor of *Pendulum* magazine

- Dr Sara Tai, Clinical Psychologist and Lecturer at Manchester University

We would especially like to thank the hugely talented and supportive trio who agreed to write a foreword for the book, each representing a different viewpoint on bipolar:

- **Paul Abbott**, TV screenwriter, has written episodes of *Coronation Street* and *Cracker* and the dramas *State of Play*, *Clocking Off*, *Touching Evil*, *Linda Green* and *Shameless*. He has won numerous BAFTAs and Royal Television Society awards, as well as an Emmy and the Writer's Guild of Great Britain Award. He revealed that he has bipolar disorder during a radio interview in 2007.

- **Jo Crocker** is sister and PA to actor, broadcaster, director and writer Stephen Fry. Stephen, who was diagnosed with bipolar in 1995, wrote in his autobiography *Moab Is My Washpot*, 'Jo runs my life more efficiently and more sweetly than is credible, and knows

that were she not there I would be as a balsa twig in a tornado [...]
My life could neither have been led nor written without her.'

- **Professor Nick Craddock** is head of the Cardiff University
  Psychiatry Service where he specializes in diagnosis and treatment
  of bipolar illness. He is scientific adviser to MDF The BiPolar
  Organisation and is on the management boards of the
  International Society for Bipolar Disorders, the International
  Society of Psychiatric Genetics, and Equilibrium – the Bipolar
  Foundation. Further information about Professor Craddock's work,
  including how to help with research, can be found at
  www.cardiff.ac.uk/medicine/research/bipolar

A word from Paul Abbott

The first my family knew about me being a writer, or even wanting to be, was when they saw my photo in our local paper, aged 16, wielding the trophy I got that day for my story in the Lancashire Literature Festival competition. Their congratulations came instantly laced with discomfort and suspicion about me not being quite a full shilling, because I hadn't told a soul about this, nor for that matter, much about myself at all for a good long while.

It wasn't uncommon for one Abbott or another to be splashed across the Court Report pages, to reactions of tormenting laughter at being so thick as to get caught, at all! ... never mind the gimpish reputation it inflicted on the family name by making it into the bleedin' paper!

Being way down the pecking order in our big, chaotic family, I reckon I took up writing as a means of communicating without being contradicted. Truth being, I never consciously took up writing at all. I wanted nothing else but to be a surgeon in an outfit like Médecins sans Frontière. The writing thing crept up silently and *it* found *me*, like a latent self-defence mechanism rallying to jumpstart its host, having detected early warnings for the jet-black, depressive tailspin that was heading for me like thunder.

This wasn't the first time I'd done something bizarre and unpredictable. The last event was attempted suicide and being sectioned at the age of 15. Somehow, winning a writing competition was more embarrassing and inexplicable than a suicide slam. This heralded the beginning of the end of my relationship with the wider orbit of my family.

I hadn't deliberately kept secrets from anyone. But I had no clear memory of doing this. I don't mean amnesia – I remembered the anxiety of writing that story and rewriting with a mission, knowing I needed higher than average quality to stand a hope in hell of succeeding, or face scorching humiliation if I bodged the job in public. I couldn't fail. Mustn't. So I won, which was great. But to this day I don't know what possessed me to seek out combat of any sort, never mind a scrap on this scale.

Years later when I found myself doing something equally bonkers and 'out of character' it dawned on me that I had a regular, cyclical pattern for doing stuff like this behind my own back, seemingly without my authorization – those 'I swear, it wasn't me!' periods.

Actually, it was. It was the same me I'm no longer ashamed to recognize, the me I have learned to feel proud of and take credit for, the one winning regular BAFTAs and gongs for outstanding achievement. Then lifetime achievement awards I've received for maintaining high standards in my work which, in turn, racks-up the reputation of British drama in the outside world. I'm paraphrasing the prize giving eulogies here, not trying to show off! Point being – nearly all those BAFTAs and various prizes for outstanding achievement came from material I wrote during periods of manic propulsion, vivid cycles of accelerated behaviour that I now, but only recently, have learnt to come to terms with being *the way I am.*

After 20-odd years of this, I've obviously grown a fairly hefty CV. These ordinarily get updated by your agent or a PA so I don't need to be involved, but when I did look at it properly for the first time, it was like a shrink's X-ray, a disappointingly predictable, graphic demonstration of my bipolar phases – some more volcanic than most, but in stark black and white print, reveal a correlation between my mood swing cycles and achievements. During my last manic cyclone, I created and produced not one but two full primetime drama series – *State of Play* and *Shameless* – in a 12-month period. Proud as I am of both those titles, output like that isn't just 'not quite normal', it's as barking and demented, and as riddled with potentially dangerous consequences, as it can get in this Non-Full-Shilling Club!

I can only describe these manic cycles as some kind of protracted convulsions that can last weeks, months or sometimes years before I get to stop for a breather, look back and check out what the fuck I've been up to *this* time.

I can only dream of being as brave and clever as it might appear on the outside.

Having surprised myself by reaching my forties, I am now able to do this with a bit more admiration for the results I produce, and with a better understanding that all of this stuff comes from me – well, parts of me that ultimately form a full shilling, eventually! You can't blame me for loving the volcanics as much as I do on occasions. They're always odd. Same here!

Many bipolar people I know wouldn't sacrifice their illness. I don't have an opinion on this because I wasn't given the option of ownership in the first place. It belongs to me, and seemingly, me to it. We come as a pair. My wife Saskia and kids Tom and Annie might well tell you they could do without the 'fizziest' bits at both ends of the upsy–downsy daisy scale. But nowadays I can be frank about my state of order, and cool about them offering advice when a behavioural shipping forecast is suddenly required, which is, for me, inexpressibly comforting to be a task we share as a family.

I was delighted to be asked by Amanda and Sarah to contribute a foreword to this book, *Bipolar Disorder – the Ultimate Guide*. I'm pretty sure they regretted this the day we first met in London. They arrived armed with a dozen questions for me, but never stood a chance of airing a single one of them. I talked non-stop for a good two hours then waved them off. Only after they'd gone did I realize I didn't know what either of them actually sounded like! Well, they did ask!

This is the one book I wish I'd had in my pocket for each and every time when I've had to try describing myself and my oddness to anyone I love. It is quite possibly the most comprehensive and enabling guide I've come across to date, remarkably accessible, friendly and nourishing for anyone needing to know about people like me. Us.

A word from Jo Crocker

Jo who exactly? I hear you wonder – well, a fairly ordinary Jo, really, but I have an extraordinary brother. His name is Stephen Fry and in 1995 he was diagnosed with bipolar disorder. Some of you may be familiar with this. In 2006 he presented a two-part documentary *The Secret Life of the Manic Depressive*, in which he told his story of diagnosis and understanding of the condition woven throughout the stories of both well-known and not so well-known sufferers of the illness and the impact of the condition on them and their loved ones. Each and every personal account was heartbreakingly moving.

I have been Stephen's Personal Assistant for 20 years. He often introduces me as his Personal Sister which, I think, neatly sums up our sibling and professional relationship, both of which fill me with pride. The impact of the documentaries was perhaps naively and massively unexpected by me in terms of the public reaction via letter, email, telephone calls, text and posts to the forum on his website. My very small part in the two films (a discussion of his dramatic exit of a West End play and brief few weeks missing abroad in 1995 that led to his eventual diagnosis) had in turn a huge impact on me and my understanding of what I had always subconsciously known was different about my brother.

I should stress that Stephen's form of bipolar condition, cyclothymia, is thankfully relatively mild, and is described in *Bipolar Disorder* by Professors Guy Goodwin and Gary Sachs as a 'mood variation that typically takes place over many years with sub-syndromal mood depression or elation as a frequent feature of an individual's personal experience' (the science bit ...). Nonetheless, the impact of Stephen's disorder on our family and myself has been very real.

I was seven when I discovered my brother after he made his first suicide attempt. I remember the ambulance arriving, the family upset and finally, thankfully, Stephen returning home, stomach pumped and apparently restored. Stephen's story of his adolescent years and varied subsequent troubles is well documented, but looking back I can see that the impact of these testing times led to troubles of my own. The most trying on my parents must have been my phase of feigning illness at school so as to come home and demand attention from my poor mother, who had more than I could possibly realize to deal with and worry about at the time.

Much more positively it was during these years that I made up my mind to 'look after' Stephen, come what may, and of course I had no inkling that his spectacular career would allow me to fulfil this ambition to such great personal satisfaction.

His diagnosis allowed me to look back on the subsequent years of being in his close proximity assisting him (I shared his house in London in the late 1980s and early 1990s) and realize that I subconsciously and instinctively read his moods. I have to say, nothing hugely dramatic but the diary never lied about the enormous scale of personal and professional commitments he would undertake. I would, and still do, sternly point out when there is a full two weeks or more of engagements morning, noon and night. Most are unavoidable but some can be gently re-arranged for a later and less fraught time ahead.

I particularly worried when he was away for long periods alone writing or filming and we were out of physical contact, especially because I knew he was 'self medicating' in perhaps not the healthiest way (thankfully this is not the case now). I would find excuses to call him early in the morning with some daft reminder (that he was perfectly capable of remembering himself), just to check. Just to check ...

Watching the documentaries, it was a shock to learn that the condition is hereditary and can strike at any age, perhaps as the result of certain stressful triggers – which finally, hurrah, brings me to talking about this wonderful book, written by two such warm and compassionate cousins as ever you could hope to meet who both have close family members with bipolar disorder. Should I ever worry about myself or another close family member developing the condition, this book will answer any questions that I might have in the most friendly and uncomplicated style.

It really is *Bipolar Disorder – the Ultimate Guide* that stands as a unique and approachable reference book for those with the condition and their loved ones, who more often than not are their prime carers, who are most concerned for them and all aspects of their welfare.

So many of the truly remarkable letters from bipolar sufferers written to Stephen following the documentaries thanked him for 'being one of us' and those from their loved ones told movingly of how the programmes had helped them understand the condition more fully and got them talking openly about it for the first time. I thank Sarah and Amanda, Amanda and Sarah (they deserve equal billing) for writing this book for all of us who need to understand more about the illness and, armed and empowered with this knowledge, spread the word that bipolar disorder, indeed *any* mental illness, is not an embarrassment to be hidden behind closed doors.

Stephen answered the final question put to him in his film emphatically that he wouldn't change his condition 'not for all the tea in China'. I know how lucky I am that this is his response. I wouldn't change him either, not for all the Jimmy Choo handbags in the whole wide world. I hope Stephen will know, frivolous though it is, how much this truly means.

A word from Professor Nick Craddock

To improve the well-being of the millions of individuals whose lives are touched by bipolar disorder, there is an urgent need to increase understanding of the illness. This requires a major research effort to pin down the causes and triggers of bipolar disorder, in order that we can develop better approaches to diagnosis and more effective treatments that are tailored to the individual.

In addition, it is vital to help sufferers, family, friends, carers and the general public understand what bipolar disorder is, how it affects people and what is known about it. *Bipolar Disorder – the Ultimate Guide* does exactly that. It is written in a clear and accessible way, and provides a balanced and informative overview. I am delighted that Amanda and Sarah have written this book – I have no doubt that it will be highly valued by its readers and will contribute to increasing awareness of bipolar illness and reducing stigma. I will definitely recommend it to my patients.

INTRODUCTION

IS THIS BOOK FOR YOU?

If you've been diagnosed with bipolar disorder, there's no doubt that life has dealt you a challenging hand. The condition has been under the media spotlight recently, with a lot of emphasis on how it can boost energy and creativity in a positive way. There's a lot of truth in that, of course, but the reality of bipolar is often a much bleaker picture. The World Health Organization has identified bipolar disorder as one of the top causes of lost years of life and health in 15–44-year-olds, ranking above war, violence and schizophrenia. And new research from Edinburgh University has found that people with bipolar disorder suffer from an accelerated shrinking of the part of the brain that controls memory, face recognition and co-ordination. The truth is that when symptoms spiral out of control, living with this condition can be a complete and utter, seemingly never-ending nightmare – both for the person with bipolar disorder and for those who live with and love them.

If bipolar disorder is in your life, this book will be useful to you in three ways. First, it aims to answer all the questions – practical and emotional – that you will inevitably have. Second, it will offer hope because more has been discovered about bipolar disorder since the mid-1990s than was discovered in the 50 years before that. Also, there's increasing evidence to show that this sometimes debilitating condition can be kept under control with the right combination of psychological therapies, medication, support and lifestyle choices. However unpromising the outlook, it *is* possible to lead a healthy, happy life with a diagnosis of bipolar. Last, but definitely not least, this book will help end the stigma and feeling of shame that often come hand in hand with mental illness. There's no shame in breaking a leg or being diagnosed with asthma. Why the shame of bipolar? One day there will be none. This book is one step closer towards that day.

We want to stress, though, that this book has not been written just for those with a diagnosis of bipolar disorder. It is equally intended for their family and friends – the network of those who care for loved ones with the condition. Bipolar has a huge ripple effect. If you're a mother, father, husband, wife, partner, sister, brother, son, daughter or close friend, you probably suffer in silence from the loss, the unpredictability, the helplessness, the loneliness, the ignorance of others, the shame and the fear. This book will help you offer them your love and support in the most helpful ways possible, without losing your own sanity in the process. And if you're a blood relative, it will also show you how to minimize your own risk of developing the illness.

The bottom line? This book is the emotional equivalent of a good friend who's just researched all there is to know about bipolar disorder. It's brimming with useful, practical advice gleaned from the very latest research and the wisest individuals (psychiatrists, psychologists, psychiatric nurses, pharmacists, therapists) on the planet who have devoted their lives to making bipolar easier to live with. And the book has many other voices too – people with bipolar, and relatives of those with bipolar. Not impersonal 'case histories' or 'studies', but real people, real voices, all speaking out to tell the world what it's *really* like to live with bipolar disorder, helping to dispel the ignorance that often surrounds the condition.

Amanda is an editor and writer, and Sarah is a health journalist, with over 25 years' professional experience between us. First cousins, we share three close relatives with bipolar disorder (Amanda's mother, and Sarah's sister and late father). It's probable our late grandfather had bipolar too.

This book is dedicated to anyone whose life has ever been touched by bipolar disorder.

Amanda's story

Our family's bipolar fault line reached my mother when she was 51, and I believe you can trace the roots of it deep into her past.

We don't talk much about her early childhood, but I've heard enough to know it was desperately unhappy. Impoverished too: she was born and brought up in the grimy heart of 1940s Birmingham, with its Victorian slums of back-to-back houses. But poverty wasn't the worst part. My mum Irene and her younger brother Jim (Sarah's father) were ill treated and emotionally neglected by their parents. A few vivid and terrible details have filtered down to me ... the children were starved and had to scavenge in bins, they walked barefoot to school, they were left sitting outside pubs where their alcoholic parents drank all evening. And when my mum was 12, the family broke down – their mother abandoned them to start a new life with someone else, and then their father, struggling to cope, walked out on them too.

My mum's teenage years were spent first in a children's home, then with a series of foster parents. She was separated from Jim, who was fostered with an aunt, and their father disappeared from her life altogether. And despite the fact that they still lived in the same city, and would do for the next 20 odd years, my mum never saw her own mother again, even though Mum wrote letters begging her to visit. So she was all alone in the world – until a cold and rainy January evening, when (aged 16) my mother went to the Co-op youth club and first met my father, Gordon ... she's described how, as she hovered uncertainly in the doorway and saw the handsome, dark haired 19-year-old glance up from the pool table, it was as if her life only began at that moment. In fact I can't visualize my mother's face before then – I've never seen photos of her as a child ... maybe they're lost, or maybe none were taken. In the earliest picture I have, she's perched on my dad's lap at a New Year's Eve party, smiling up at the camera, a new engagement ring sparkling on her hand clasping his. When they married at Birmingham Registry Office in 1961, my mum just 18 years old, she was welcomed into my dad's loving family, and her rescue from the past seemed, at the time, to be complete.

And shall I tell you the most incredible thing about my mum? That despite her terrible upbringing, she was a fantastic mother. My brother Andrew was born in 1963, I followed in 1965, and together we had the happiest of childhoods. She once said to my dad, 'I have so much love to give ... there's no end to it', and she was right. We grew up in a neat semi-detached house in Sutton Coldfield, a quiet suburb of Birmingham, and I guess we fitted the description of an average suburban family – two hard working parents (Dad at a printing company, Mum in a department store), two kids at local state schools, a fortnight in a traditional English seaside town every summer (never 'abroad') ... But above all, my brother and I basked comfortably in the adoring gaze of both our parents, who encouraged us in everything we chose to do – when I said I wanted to take a degree in English, Mum helped me find my course at Leeds University, hiding the fact (as I later discovered) that she was miserable at the prospect of me leaving home. Andrew and I took this selfless love and support completely for granted, because we expected it as our right and because we knew nothing else. To us, our family just appeared to be like everyone else's on our leafy road – happy but ordinary. But to my mum, after the chaotic unhappiness of her own childhood, our cosy life must have seemed utterly extraordinary and wonderful. Of course I didn't realize any of this at the time, but now I'm so proud of her ... when I think of the model of motherhood she had to work with, our 'normal' upbringing appears nothing short of a miracle. How did she do it? I think she's amazing.

Did Mum have early bipolar symptoms during my childhood? I've tried hard to recall any mood swings or erratic behaviour, but none come to mind ... when I look back at those peaceful years, I can only see a calm, confident woman, always smartly dressed, running the complex logistics of family life with infinite care and organization. But bipolar disorder did show up on our family's radar when I was still at school and my mum's younger brother Jim returned to Birmingham from Kent. He was already ill, and spent most of his time in a psychiatric hospital, where my mother would visit him every week (until his death in 1987). She brought him back to our house for tea a couple of times, which as an insensitive teenager I resented because she would be upset afterwards. Also I was afraid ... partly because no one ever discussed Jim's illness with my brother and I (or even gave it a name), but also because I could sense my mum was afraid too. 'If your Uncle Jim turns up at the house when you're on your own,' she would say to me over and over again, 'don't let him in. Just tell him you have to go out.' It's so sad to think that she was frightened of her own brother, or his illness – and it planted an unwarranted fear and stigma about him in my mind. I wonder now if she was also afraid of developing bipolar disorder herself.

If so, then her fears were realized in 1993 when she was 51 – triggered by hormone changes during her menopause. During that spring and summer, my mum's familiar, loving personality changed ... she became suspicious, despairing and irrational, accusing my poor bewildered dad of having affairs and plotting to leave her, and finding hidden meaning in every irrelevant detail – the whole world, she declared, was whispering about her. In October, Mum was diagnosed with a depressive 'breakdown' and for a couple of weeks was admitted as a voluntary patient to a psychiatric unit. Antidepressants were prescribed for her, which initially seemed to work, so she came back home, quiet but rational. But within weeks her mood shifted again – at first we thought it was only the depression lifting, but she swung upwards even further, not just happy now but euphoric, rapidly shedding her inhibitions and culminating in a full-blown manic episode. At the time I was living and working in Bristol, 100 miles away – Mum had been sounding agitated on the phone, so I drove up to Birmingham for a flying visit one November day, when Dad was still at work. As soon as I arrived at their house, she began to unravel right in front of me. She flung her clothes, jewellery, shoes, family photos, all her most personal possessions, out of the bedroom window, then ran downstairs to hurl herself repeatedly against the living room walls, shouting that the IRA were coming to kill us. I tried to grab her arms and stop her, but she fought back, and I remember looking into those blue eyes I loved, and realizing she didn't recognize me as her daughter. One of her close friends rang in the middle of this – 'I'm brilliant, I'm feeling bloody brilliant!' my mum yelled down the phone before throwing it at me. Their GP turned up, but by then she was far beyond his help. She took him hostage in her bedroom, and in a ghastly parody of her engagement picture, sat on his lap and tried to kiss him. That evening, Mum was sectioned ... My dad, my brother and I watched helplessly as she was carried shrieking out of her house, and taken to hospital to be held down and medicated.

Eventually, after weeks of treatment, my mum returned home, but normality never really has. For the last fourteen years, she has swallowed a daily cocktail of mood-stabilizing drugs, including lithium, with partial success: the mania is kept at bay, the depression (mixed with agitation) is not. When she becomes depressed, irrational and paranoid, her typical behaviour pattern is to refuse all her medication. Sometimes she thinks she's dying of some mystery disease, so the drugs are useless ... At other times she believes the drugs are laced with poison because doctors want to kill her. 'It's too late,' she says over and over again. 'It's too late for me.' And then she'll spend days and nights anxiously pacing the house, unable to rest or sleep, eat or drink, and endlessly fixated on her imminent death.

Stopping the medication so abruptly only worsens her mental state, and during a particularly bad episode in 1998 she tried to kill herself. Since then she's been sectioned back into the psychiatric hospital 13 or 14 times (we've lost track), always during these phases, because her doctors fear she could try to commit suicide again. And as she grows older, the cycle of episodes is speeding up – she's been sectioned three times in the last 12 months alone.

Even when Dad knows that sometimes hospital is the best place for Mum (and as years have passed, he has come to accept this), he dreads it because he misses her so much. He can't even bear to go upstairs to bed, because she's not there – he'll just crash out on the sofa, with the TV blaring away for company, filling the silence of their house. The first few days are especially rough for them both; at first, as she struggles with her mood swings, she's often hostile and says hurtful things or orders him to leave because she believes she's going to die. But he still visits the hospital every day. He spends hours just sitting quietly with her, as close as she'll allow him, waiting for the bipolar cloud to lift from her mind, however long that takes.

Sometimes Dad opens up and begins to talk about how he feels, but then he'll stop himself and shake his head angrily and say, 'I shouldn't feel so sorry for myself … I have no right, I'm not the one who's ill – I'm not in hospital, am I?' He finds it hard to accept that his feelings are valid and that he does have the right to think about himself.

In between the mood swings and the hospital stays, when my mum is stable, we say she is 'well', but in reality of course it's a qualified 'well'. Yes, she's rational, but all her old self-confidence has gone, and she's nervous and emotionally fragile. She can see the negative effect that bipolar has had on her life and she resents it bitterly – she would 'press the button' to be rid of it in a heartbeat, and so would my dad. Both my parents live with enormous tension, always wondering what each day will bring. It can start well, but they don't know how it will end. One Christmas, we spent a great morning around my dining table, playing daft board games with my children: Mum was laughing, the kids were laughing, we were all happy. Twelve hours later, her mood had swung into the familiar drug-refusing depression and agitation, and my brother and I were struggling with her on my driveway, trying to 'persuade' her into my Dad's car so he could drive her back home to the care of her psychiatric team in Birmingham, who know Mum so well. Even after all these years, as we fought to close the car door so that Dad (tears streaming down his face as he pleaded with her) could lock it and drive away, we were still shocked at the speed of her mood change.

As I write this, Mum is stable again … But for how long? We don't know. No one does. It grieves me to acknowledge this, but bipolar undermines my relationship with her, and I tiptoe carefully through our conversations, editing what I say. I love her so much, but I can't share my worries with her. What if stress causes a mood swing? Even happy events can trigger episodes – she seemed to enjoy my fortieth birthday party, but the excitement of it threw her balance of mood into a tailspin, sending her back into hospital only days later. And I'm watching, always watching. Is she too quiet? Does she seem agitated? Why did she just say that? I can't switch this off ... It's just automatic. My dad and my brother look for tell-tale signs too, and we compare notes if we think an episode is brewing. There are warning clues we all recognize – Mum coming downstairs in the middle of the night to make herself a cup of tea, for example, which to anyone else would seem so ridiculously innocent, but we know always means trouble. Another warning sign is more poignant. She starts asking me and my brother if she was a good mother. When we answer 'yes', she'll reply, 'I don't believe you, because I'm a wicked person.' It's heartbreaking beyond words to hear this ...

I have been totally honest with my three children about bipolar disorder – so they've heard all about their grandma's illness, what the symptoms are, and why she sometimes goes to hospital. And they're completely cool about it. The great thing about telling kids is that they're still too young to have picked up all the old stereotypes about mental illness – as far as they're concerned, the brain is just one part of the body that can 'get sick', like any other part. They don't see a stigma. How fantastic it would be if the rest of the world felt the same.

Talking about bipolar disorder, and bringing it into the open, is one of the best forms of protection I can offer my children, who need to understand how to lessen their risk in the bipolar lottery of our family. If we all collude with the old taboos surrounding mental illness, how can we treat it effectively, and protect ourselves and those we love?

Sarah's story

My late father Jim was born in 1945 and grew up in Birmingham in extreme poverty. The only word I can use to describe his parents is 'dysfunctional' – Amanda has described what little we know about his and his sister Irene's neglected childhoods. Dad was a 'Barnados boy' for a while before being fostered by an aunt, although he never talked about his early years. He trained to be a chef and then married my mum in 1969. They moved from

London to the Kent coast and had two daughters – me in 1971 and my sister Rebecca in 1974. Sadly the marriage began to break down and, with hindsight, that was probably the catalyst for his first manic episode and later diagnosis of manic depression. Dad was working as a chef on a passenger ferry at the time and, years later, I discovered that he lost touch with reality in Germany, convinced he was a spy for the English government.

He was brought back home and all I can remember before he moved back to Birmingham months later are a few snippets of the effect the illness had on our family. At the age of six or seven, I came downstairs in the middle of the night to find a doctor sedating my obviously distressed father in our dining room. My mum hurried me back to bed, explaining that 'Daddy isn't feeling very well'. Another time, I remember him losing his temper and punching a hole in the dining room wall – my mother lifted my sister and me over the fence into our neighbours' garden. I wasn't frightened because his anger wasn't directed at anyone in particular and because there wasn't any obvious build-up to the outburst. One minute he was in his normal calm mood, the next minute he was shouting out and punching a wall. All I can recall about the aftermath of the event is being excited at the prospect of seeing the inside of the neighbours' house for the first time! By the time my sister and I were taken home, everything was back to normal and the incident was never mentioned again. In the summer of 1978, Dad had a few days off work and decided to organize a jumble sale in our front garden in aid of Save the Children fund. Mum was working at the time. He made hundreds of posters and we plastered them all over town. The next day, we set up several big tables in the front garden. Dad was so excited, infecting my sister and me with the feeling that something really amazing was about to happen. The trouble was we only had a few tatty old things to sell – two or three pieces of old crockery, a few old books and some half-used balls of wool. We spread them out over the tables, although Dad kept re-arranging them. I'll never forget the ear-burning shame I felt when I heard two ladies from down our road laughing at him. Another thing I remember was that he had a pair of the brightest blue and red shoes – sort of casual trainers, a bit like bowling shoes. He loved them, but my mum absolutely hated them, naming them his 'Joey' shoes after Joey the kangaroo. She did have a point ... They made his feet look enormous and looked ridiculous poking out from under seventies brown flares. Looking back, I suspect they were a symbol of his manic frame of mind.

My parents finally divorced, and Rebecca and I would speak to Dad once a week on the phone and visit him once or twice a year in a psychiatric hospital in Birmingham – it couldn't be more often because we didn't own a car and the train was expensive. The memories from those visits are indelible in my mind: a smoke-filled pool room; the smell of urine; horrible strong tea in Styrofoam cups; Dad wearing his pyjamas, stepping from side to side because of the medication he was on; squirrels climbing trees in the hospital grounds; Dad's friend Malcolm who thought he was Jesus; Dad's comfort items on a table – a transparent plastic lighter and a green packet of Wrigley's spearmint gum side by side on top of a black packet of JPS Superkings. Rebecca and I would clamour to sit on his knee in the common room or hold his hand as we walked around the hospital grounds. He was our dad and we loved him. I didn't think any of this was particularly strange. This was my normality. You don't question things as a child, you just accept them.

In December 1987, my dad was walking down a road in Birmingham and tragically knocked down by a drunk driver. He died the day before my sixteenth birthday. Since then I've mourned the years his premature death stole and I'm still mourning the years his illness stole. I can hardly remember my dad as a well man. It took me a long time and a lot of tears to get to this point, but now it gives me a lot of comfort to imagine how happy he must have been walking my mother down the aisle and holding his two new baby daughters in his arms. I can picture him teaching me how to ride a bike and sharing with me his love of word puzzles. I can conjure up an image of the two of us making cheese straws, and another time fish cakes, together. I can remember him cheering and thumping the living room floor with joy when Ipswich won the FA cup in 1978. Of course his neglected childhood and diagnosis of 'manic depression' as it was then called had a huge impact on him, but he did know happiness, as well as immense sorrow, in his life and I give thanks for the happy memories I have.

My sister Rebecca was diagnosed with bipolar disorder at the age of 22 – the catalyst for her first manic episode was, believe it or not, my wedding. We later discovered that an overwhelmingly happy event is often a trigger. There I was soaking up the Jamaican sun on honeymoon while my mother had doctors, social workers and policewomen round the house one evening, trying to persuade my psychotic sister to get into an ambulance to transport her to a psychiatric ward. I'll never forget visiting her for the first time in hospital. Rebecca had aged ten years in two weeks. I found it hard to reconcile the beautiful bridesmaid in my wedding photos with this girl – her skin pale, her eyes sunken and vacant, her fingers trembling as she tried to light a cigarette. How guilty I felt – and sometimes still feel – that I was the one fate had spared …

With hindsight, Rebecca had symptoms of bipolar disorder long before the official diagnosis. She was one of those children who always seemed to be getting into scrapes. She had obsessive tendencies – spending literally hours listening to the same pop records over and over again. She had a volatile temper. At school, she was labelled 'trouble' and left without a single qualification, even though she's very bright. My mum asked our GP if Rebecca could have the same condition as her father, but he said categorically that, no, manic depression wasn't hereditary. Yet things got progressively worse. The summer after our father's death, at the age of 13, she started bunking off school, drinking and smoking. She had relationships with a string of unsuitable boyfriends. She was brought home by the police for being drunk and disorderly a couple of times. At the time, perhaps not surprisingly, we all thought that her unruly behaviour was an expression of grief. She found it extremely difficult to cry about Dad's death, bottling up everything. Mum was at her wits' end. Rebecca was on a path of self-destruction and, it seemed, there was nothing anyone who loved her could do about it.

The year before Rebecca's first breakdown, fate dealt her two enormous blows. Her 19-year-old cat died. And then our nan, our mum's mum, to whom

Rebecca had always been very close, died from a stroke while Rebecca was at her side. At the time, Rebecca was working 100 miles from home, only returning for occasional visits and then for my hen party and wedding, which, it seems, turned out to be the final straw in her stress load.

In one way, the diagnosis brought relief because it helped to explain why Rebecca's life had been so turbulent. Yet naming the problem didn't really make the journey any easier. Since her diagnosis over ten years ago, I have witnessed my sister go to the depths of hell and back again several times. She has been sectioned four or five times and has made various suicide attempts (taken different combinations of pills and once thrown herself in front of a car). It seems like she's tried one hundred and one different types of medication with varying success. She's been psychotic, paranoid and as low as you can go – one winter she found it hard to get out of bed for weeks at a time. In 2003–4 she spent almost a year in a secure unit where she wasn't allowed in the garden or to have a cup of tea without permission; that was where we 'celebrated' her thirtieth birthday. My mum brought in a party tea and we laid it out on the pool table. I don't think I've ever felt as desperately sad in my entire life as I did while standing in that psychiatric common room eating Twiglets.

I have always loved my sister. She knows that. But it is only now, after hours and hours of research, interviewing experts, reading books, talking to people touched by bipolar and immersing myself in the bipolar world, that I really understand her. When I delve further into the subject, I understand more and more how huge the struggles are she's had to face; how hard her life really has been. In the past, I've envied sisters sharing secrets over lunch in restaurants and mourned the absence (both emotional and physical when she's in hospital) of mine. During the rough patches, she can be there, but not really there, and that makes me feel so sad and empty. I feel like I've lost her to the illness, that I'm grieving for her. I just miss her so much. I think that's why I've always felt so frustrated at the fact that she goes to the pub sometimes to drown her sorrows and blot out reality. I used to think – why can't she live a healthy life and then it's more likely she'll stay well? But now that I understand a bit more, I'm asking, how the hell has she survived through so much without drinking herself into oblivion?

There's no denying that bipolar disorder cast a huge shadow over Rebecca's twenties. She had to stop work – her job in a travel agency proved to be too stressful. Her relationships have never been straightforward or stable. But the decade that began with a thirtieth birthday in hospital is turning out to be more positive. Even though she suffered a set-back earlier this year and spent a couple of months in hospital, Rebecca's entire attitude towards her own well-being has changed. She's accepted that she does have a condition that needs careful controlling. She knows that she can't party every night of the week and deprive herself of sleep without suffering the consequences. She turns down invitations or requests because she knows she has to put herself first rather than say yes to please. She no longer forgets to take her medication. In other words, she's now taking responsibility for her own mental health.

In a logical sequence of events, I suppose, I've come to admire my sister. I admire how she's now managing to live alone in a really great flat. I admire how she copes with Christmas family get-togethers when all she really wants to do is hide under the duvet. I admire how generous and loving she is to my three sons when all she really wants is to have children of her own, but hasn't yet found the right relationship – probably at least in part because of her emotional instability. I admire how she's managed to pick herself up after a dark dark depression more than once. I admire how she has (reluctantly sometimes, I admit) come back down to earth after one of her incredible highs. I admire how she gets back up time and time again after being floored by this sometimes devastating illness.

I cannot tell you how much impact bipolar disorder has had on my mother, Rose's, life. Not only did she lose her husband to manic depression nearly 30 years ago, she has been my sister's main carer far beyond the 18 years of official childhood. Although Rebecca moved out of Mum's house a couple of years ago, my 57-year-old mum – who still has a full-time job – is there for my sister 24/7. On a practical level, Mum does Rebecca's washing, decorates the flat, helps sort out household admin and often takes her supermarket shopping as she doesn't drive. Yet from what Mum tells me, it's not the practical side of being a carer that she finds challenging, it's the emotional toll. Mum's the one who mood monitors and calls the key-worker if Rebecca stops taking medication. She's the one who can't relax if Rebecca's mobile phone is switched off for an afternoon, who phones the ambulance after a suicide attempt. And during the rough patches, my mum experiences guilt, frustration, helplessness, sorrow and exhaustion in equal measure. There is no love like the love a mother feels for her child. My mother is unequivocal proof of that.

I can't remember a time in my life when bipolar disorder hasn't caused my family pain. By writing this book, Amanda and I hope to turn those decades of pain into something infinitely more positive.

Amanda and Sarah's journey

Because of the geographic distance between us when we were growing up (Amanda in Birmingham and Sarah in Kent), we saw each other very rarely when we were children, and the six years' age difference between us seemed wider too. We last met as children in the winter of 1978, when Amanda was 13 and Sarah was seven, and both of us have happy memories of building a snowman together in Sarah's back garden.

Sarah saw Amanda's parents Irene and Gordon at her dad's funeral in December 1987, although Amanda was away at university. After that, the only link was the exchange of Christmas cards between Sarah's mum and Amanda's parents.

Fast forward to 1999, and Amanda's mum casually mentioned to Amanda (by now married with children) that Sarah and her husband had just had a baby boy. Husband? Baby? What had happened to the blonde seven-year-old cousin? On impulse, Amanda wrote a letter to Sarah, and a few days later, when Sarah phoned, the years and distance fell away. We clicked immediately.

The added dimension to this new friendship was discovering the shared experience of bipolar disorder. Amanda knew nothing about Rebecca's illness, and hadn't realized that her Uncle Jim's mystery illness from her childhood had been the same as her mum's. Sarah knew that Irene had been 'unwell' but didn't know it was bipolar. It was a shock to realize that three of our close relatives had all developed bipolar, but ultimately, the realization helped, knowing that our similar experiences could be a source of mutual support. Ever since that first phone conversation, whenever Irene or Rebecca goes through an unstable patch, we talk a lot on the phone. It is such a relief to be able to talk to somebody who *really* understands.

So although officially, the journey of this book started in October 2006 – when Amanda's mum had just been sectioned again, and Stephen Fry's brilliant two-part documentary *The Secret Life of the Manic Depressive* was aired on BBC1 – the journey really began when we reconnected.

And, if to begin with we were writing this book for our relatives with bipolar (and those who care for them), the purpose of the book has evolved. Now we also write it for ourselves. There's no longer a big brick wall dividing and protecting us from the possibility of bipolar. Before we began the research, we had neatly cordoned off our relatives into a bipolar box. In our minds, we had always blamed Irene and Jim's upbringing as the main reason why they both developed bipolar disorder. The early environment they had shared seemed the obvious culprit. Then, the divorce of Rebecca's parents, the death of her dad when she was 13 and the grief that she found impossible to express, seemed to confirm this view – Rebecca must have developed bipolar because of a difficult childhood, we thought. But, whilst their childhood experience was probably a big factor, we now know it's only one part of their bipolar profile. Through talking to experts such as Professor Nick Craddock, we've come to understand that genetics plays a much bigger part in bipolar disorder than we realized. We recently discovered that Irene's and Jim's father – our grandfather – had bouts of mental illness and probably had bipolar too. In fact his alcoholism was most likely a form of self-medication.

Yes, challenging events in their lives probably did nudge them further along the road to bipolar, but genetics played a huge part too. Stress alone, genetics alone or both stress and genetics can mean mental illness, which means that anybody, yes, *anybody* can suffer from bipolar disorder. We've spoken to men, women, young, old, rich, poor, teachers, cleaners, students, partners, mothers, fathers, sons, daughters. People just like you and us. Nobody is immune. There is no bipolar wall. There is no 'them and us', only 'all of us'.

Rebecca was diagnosed with bipolar at 22, Jim at 32, Irene at 51. It can strike at any time. How lucky we are to have come this far (Sarah is 36; Amanda is 42) with only a six-month bout of mild post-natal depression to Sarah's name. This realization means that we now live life differently. It may sound corny, but we are grateful for every single day we live without bipolar, for every single day Rebecca and Irene are well.

And our new-found knowledge has opened our eyes to yet another amazing realization – that we're also writing the book for our wonderful children: Amanda's Ben (13), Hannah (10) and Will (7), and Sarah's Harry (8), Jonah (6) and Luke (2). Because of our family history, our precious children have a greater risk of developing the condition than any old Joe Bloggs who doesn't have a relative with bipolar in sight. Yet, far from filling us with fear and foreboding, arming ourselves with information on their behalf has been an empowering experience. If we're lucky, our children won't be touched by bipolar. If we're unlucky, knowledge is power. We know that it's possible to live a happy and fulfilling life with a diagnosis of bipolar. With the right combination of medication, psychological therapies, support and lifestyle choices, the negative impact of bipolar disorder on a life is much smaller than once thought possible. And, as far as feeling ashamed is concerned, we genuinely would feel no more shame than if one of them had hay fever. We passionately hope that they and their friends would feel the same. Bipolar disorder will never be a dark shameful secret in our houses – we will talk about it openly and trust that others will follow our lead. If bipolar comes knocking on our family's door again, we're certainly not saying it will be easy, but we will seek help and support from all available sources and rise to the challenge in the wisest way possible.

And at least we'll have this book – the book we wish we'd had sitting on our bedside tables when Jim, Irene and Rebecca were diagnosed with bipolar all those years ago ...

CHAPTER ONE

CAUSES, SYMPTOMS AND DIAGNOSIS

Q1. What is bipolar disorder?

Bipolar disorder is a serious mental illness that's thought to be caused by an imbalance in the way brain cells communicate with each other. This imbalance causes extreme mood swings that go way beyond the normal 'ups and downs' of everyday life, wildly exaggerating the mood changes that everyone has. Someone with bipolar can have long or short periods of stability, but then tends to go 'low' (into deep depression) or 'high' (experiencing mania or psychosis). They can go into a 'mixed state' too, where symptoms of depression and mania occur at the same time.

Q2. Why has manic depression been renamed bipolar disorder?

'Bipolar disorder' is a relatively new term and has gradually replaced 'manic depression' as the official name for this condition. The term 'manic depression' was first coined in 1896 by Emil Kraepelin, a German doctor, and was widely used in the psychiatric world throughout the twentieth century, until the American Psychiatric Association renamed it in 1980 as 'bipolar disorder' – to reflect what it called the 'bi-polarity', or dual nature, of the illness (the highs and lows).

The move towards 'bipolar' has been reflected by the UK's largest charity for bipolar disorder, as Jeremy Bacon, Groups and Self Management Director explains: 'Our name changed from "The Manic Depression Fellowship" to "MDF The BiPolar Organisation" in October 2004, on our twenty-first anniversary, following consultation with our members – 60% favoured including "bipolar" in our title. The change also reflected the new terminology – people were being diagnosed with "bipolar" rather than "manic depression".'

Others have willingly embraced the new name too:

 I prefer the term 'bipolar' to 'manic depression' as bipolar sounds more medical and less scary. Manic depression seems to carry an undeserved stigma. I was speaking to someone I used to work with when I said my daughter had bipolar – she asked what that meant and I was able to explain. On a separate occasion that same day, I used the term 'manic depressive' to see if that was understood, and the reaction I received was of shock.

(Alison)

However, not everyone is as enthusiastic, including actor and writer Stephen Fry who presented the two BBC documentaries about bipolar disorder in 2006 – *The Secret Life of the Manic Depressive* – in which he openly talked about his own bipolarity. In the foreword to the book *You Don't Have to be Famous to Have Manic Depression*, which was published at the same time, he comments:

Bipolar isn't quite right – the condition isn't really just about two poles, there are mixed states in between. Besides, why not give it a title that names the effects?

Another writer with a bipolar diagnosis, Julie A. Fast, also dislikes the term bipolar disorder and suggests an alternative in her book *Loving Someone with Bipolar Disorder*:

 Bi-polar disorder is a bit of a misnomer. Yes, people with the illness do go up and down, but doesn't it seem as if they also go sideways or do little corkscrews as well? Maybe if it were called MULTI-polar disorder, people would understand the illness a little bit more.

We agree that the term 'multipolar disorder' describes the condition more accurately because there's so much more to bipolar than simply being up or down, at one pole or the other. In fact, at the time of writing, the psychiatric world is starting to recognize that the current labels used (such as Bipolar I and II) don't always reflect the wide range of bipolar symptoms. Yet the answer lies not in dispensing with the labels, says Nick Craddock, Professor of Psychiatry at Cardiff University, but using them as a starting point to decide how people are treated: 'We might move towards talking, for example, about "bipolar spectrum disorder" or a "continuum of bipolarity". That way, instead of lumping all people with bipolar disorder together, we will look very closely at each individual's unique experience of the illness and the underlying biological and psychological changes that are involved. Then we can get a full understanding of what's required to treat each individual effectively.'

In other words, experts will be less likely to focus on a concrete diagnosis in the future ('let's forget what the illness is called') and concentrate more on an individual's unique set of symptoms.

Q3. What is the difference between Bipolar I, II and III?

There are 'types' of bipolarity, known as Bipolar I, Bipolar II and Bipolar III.

To be diagnosed with Bipolar I, a person will have experienced at least one full manic episode in their lifetime, along with at least one major episode of depression. Around 1% of the general population is thought to develop Bipolar I at some point during their lives.

Bipolar II is diagnosed when someone's mood swings between major episodes of depression and periods of hypomania rather than manic episodes. The incidence of Bipolar II is estimated to be about 4–5% of the general population.

Bipolar III is not in the official rulebook, but is used by some mood experts in the United States to refer to hypomania that emerges only when a patient has been given an antidepressant.

In the US, Bipolar II and III are sometimes referred to as 'soft' bipolar.

Q4. What is cyclothymia?

If a person's depressive and manic symptoms last for two years but are not severe enough to qualify as bipolar disorder, they may instead be diagnosed with 'cyclothymia' which is a milder form of bipolar. According to MDF The BiPolar Organisation, 'cyclothymic disorder is characterized by frequent short periods of hypomania and depressive symptoms separated by periods of stability'. There is evidence that for some people with cyclothymia, the mood swings will worsen over time until they develop Bipolar II or Bipolar I. Confusingly, cyclothymia is also sometimes referred to as Bipolar III.

In terms of diagnosis, this is a tricky area because where do you draw the line between moody behaviour that's considered 'normal' and the kind of ups and downs that warrant a diagnosis of cyclothymia? Even the world's leading experts on mental health can't agree and probably never will. After all, what is normality?

Q5. Is there an age or gender profile for people with bipolar disorder?

According to Equilibrium – The Bipolar Foundation, bipolar disorder affects up to 254 million worldwide, 12 million in the US and 2.4 million people in the UK.

Gender

Unlike unipolar depression that affects more women than men, bipolar disorder affects equal numbers of men and women overall, although research
carried out at the Institute of Psychiatry at King's College in London does
show gender differences in the way bipolar tends to run its course:

- The researchers found that in early adult life (defined as 16–25),
  there were higher rates of bipolar disorder in men than in women.

- Throughout the rest of adult life (26 years and over), the rate of
  bipolar disorder was higher in women than men.

- Women are thought to have a higher chance than men of developing rapid-cycling bipolar disorder (in which changes in mood
  occur more rapidly), and mixed state (mania in which a low mood
  is predominant).

Age

In the mid-1990s, the average age of people being diagnosed with bipolar
was 32, but since then has dropped to under 19. The reason for this drop is
not known but is probably due to a number of factors, including an increased
awareness of the disorder among the public and mental health practitioners,
increased drug abuse, changing sources of life stresses and a huge jump in
the number of children diagnosed with bipolar disorder in the USA.

Q6. What are the symptoms of bipolar disorder?

People with bipolar often swing between depression and mania. But there's
no 'typical' pattern of symptoms. Every bipolar person is different, and the
length of time they spend at either extreme of mood (high or low) is very
variable – it can be days, weeks or months. And a person with bipolar can
have any number of episodes of highs and lows throughout their life. There
can be periods of normal mood in between the two extremes, but some
people can swing between depression and mania quite quickly without a

period of stability in the middle. More than four mood swings in one year is known as 'rapid cycling', and some people who rapid cycle can have monthly, weekly or even daily mood swings (sometimes called 'ultra rapid cycling').

According to the latest Diagnostic and Statistical Manual of Mental Disorders or DSM IV (the fourth version of a manual published by the American Psychiatric Association, which is used in the UK and US for categorizing and diagnosing mental health problems) the typical symptoms of bipolar disorder are depression, hypomania, mania and psychosis. Other 'unofficial' symptoms include anxiety, low self-esteem, libido problems and self-harm.

Q7. What is depression?

How many times do people say they're depressed about their job, their relationship or even the weather? Yet what does depression really mean?

The definition from DSM IV gives a list of common symptoms as:

- a depressed mood for most of the day
- a loss of interest or pleasure in almost all activities
- changes in weight and appetite
- sleep disturbance
- a decrease in physical activity
- fatigue and loss of energy
- feelings of worthlessness
- excessive feelings of guilt
- poor concentration levels
- suicidal thoughts.

Someone can experience either 'unipolar' or 'bipolar' depression. There are some differences between the two:

- In bipolar depression, the average duration of symptoms is three to six months, but in unipolar depression it is six to twelve months. The shorter the depression, the more likely it is to be bipolar.

- Compared with unipolar depression, post-natal depression is more common in bipolar disorder.

- The more episodes of depression you have, the more likely you are to be bipolar rather than unipolar. More than 95% of bipolar patients have recurrent episodes, versus unipolar patients, of whom two-thirds have recurrent episodes.

- The earlier the onset of the depression, and the more people in the family with bipolar, the more likely it is to be bipolar disorder (rather than unipolar depression).

And although mania or hypomania are the defining characteristics of bipolar disorder, people with a diagnosis tend to spend much more time depressed than manic during the course of the illness. In fact, it's been estimated that people with Bipolar I spend three times longer feeling depressed than manic and are depressed around a third of the time. People with Bipolar II have been found to experience an even higher proportion (50%) of time feeling depressed than manic.

Statistics aside, for those who experience depression in all its terrible, crushing reality, this is how it actually feels:

> I feel very detached and as if nothing is real. I feel like I am a camera and I'm watching every action, and everything is really slow. Then it just turns into this absolute nothingness ... I can't locate a cause, I just feel incredibly tired all the time, I sleep 22 hours a day, or I don't sleep at all, but I'm sort of on the edge of sleep. I don't want to eat, I don't want to move.
>
> (Tamara)

> What happens these days is that my body literally starts to give way ... suddenly walking to the shop becomes like climbing Mount Everest, and it's just ridiculous and I just can't do it. It's literally like somebody has pulled the plug on me. And there's this sense of impending doom, and my thoughts start to change drastically. I'll be

obsessed with death thoughts. I don't get suicidal, but my mind is full of anything to do with death or decay or waste, and it's like, 'Here it comes ... the winter of my mind'.

(Ashley)

For months on end I spend days and days shut in my room. I don't want to do anything. I don't want to see anyone. I hate everyone around me and hate myself more than anyone. I didn't speak to my dad for four years. It was a nightmare.

(Paul)

Sarah vividly recalls Rebecca's deepest depression, during the winter of 1999:

For a period of six or seven months, Rebecca cocooned herself in her bedroom under her duvet. Her life became TV and cigarettes – nothing more. And for much of the time the TV wasn't even on. The curtains were drawn, the shelves cluttered with mugs and ashtrays and the air smoky and stale. Rebecca stopped taking calls from friends and wouldn't have eaten if Mum hadn't brought up meals on a tray. It was impossible to connect with her during this time.

Q8. What is hypomania?

Hypomania is sometimes described as 'mania lite', and people who experience hypomania rather than full-blown manic episodes tend to be diagnosed as Bipolar II rather than Bipolar I. The World Health Organization calls hypomania 'a persistent mild elevation of mood (for at least several days on end)' and there is usually a heightened sense of well-being. A hypomanic person feels confident, creative, productive and full of energy, whilst the rest of the world seems sluggish and dull. One 12-year study found that people with Bipolar II are in a state of hypomania for approximately 1% of the time.

Hypomania begins with agitation and then just builds, and I become very impulsive, and create strange connections between things that don't exist. And sometimes I absolutely love it. I'm really active and productive. Sometimes I have energy in a way that other people just don't, and I get quite cross because I find them quite apathetic about things, whereas I will see something simple like a light on water which will completely light me up, and I just see the beauty ... you get ultimate clarity about things ... I've sat down and written essays and got really good marks, and I've written them when I haven't exactly been 100% stable. But I've just had the creativity to do it, and I read them back now and think, 'No way did I write that!' I write poetry and see connections between people and music. I guess sometimes it can actually be a gift.

(Tamara)

Normal daily life is not necessarily disrupted – in fact, a person with hypomania can put their extra energy, creativity and mild euphoria to good use. The artist with hypomania will create more pictures (Ashley painted 120 pictures in six weeks) or the hypomanic saleswoman (see Reka's story below) will smash through her quarterly target with ease. But the downside is that someone with hypomania can become easily irritated by other people, and disputes can erupt if they feel they're being challenged:

I'm very hypomanic. I get very excited; I think I'm very talented, better than everyone else. It's a beautiful feeling. All of my achievements, all of the good things in life, I've basically done when I've been hypomanic. If I'm high, I think I'm the best salesperson ever, and because of my great belief in myself I'd make really good deals ... It made me very confident – I'd walk around as if I owned the place. I'd see myself as an equal to the managing directors ... It caused a lot of friction with the management and the directors. And often I'd end up walking out.

(Reka)

And although some people (usually those with Bipolar II) will remain hypomanic, for others – if they don't recognize the warning signs – hypomania can herald an escalation into full-blown mania.

Q9. What is a manic episode?

According to the World Health Organization, manic episodes can last for between two weeks and four to five months if left untreated. Common symptoms of mania include:

- unnaturally high, euphoric mood
- inflated sense of self-importance
- extreme irritability
- incoherent, racing thoughts
- excessive, rapid speech
- easily distracted, can't concentrate well
- reduced need for sleep
- excessive risk-taking, such as extreme spending sprees, irresponsible sexual behaviour, or overuse of addictive substances such as alcohol or street drugs
- lack of inhibition.

One 12-year study found that, on average, people with Bipolar I were hypomanic or manic approximately 9% of the time.

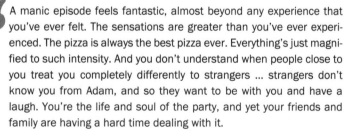

A manic episode feels fantastic, almost beyond any experience that you've ever felt. The sensations are greater than you've ever experienced. The pizza is always the best pizza ever. Everything's just magnified to such intensity. And you don't understand when people close to you treat you completely differently to strangers ... strangers don't know you from Adam, and so they want to be with you and have a laugh. You're the life and soul of the party, and yet your friends and family are having a hard time dealing with it.

(Neil)

A manic person will rush headlong into what seems like a great idea, acting on impulse with no thought to the consequences:

> In the grip of a manic episode, Tom would leap over things, climb trees, and jump out of windows. He thought he could stop traffic.
>
> (Jo)

> At the moment I can go high on a daily basis. Last night at 2am I was waxing the bathroom floor. I get up, pick up the dog I'm looking after for a friend, I then dig up a huge rose bush, then dig up a tree. Then I pick up a birthday present and go to the supermarket. I did actually rip our chimney breast out a few weeks ago. My husband Dave was a little bit shocked to say the least. We hadn't discussed doing it. The idea just popped into my head. The poor neighbours! I hadn't covered any furniture. They came round as they heard the banging. It took me two days. I was covered in soot. Me with a sledge hammer. 'Use the force', that's my favourite saying. Another time, I chopped down 18 trees at the end of the garden in one day. And when I was in my mid-30s I moved to Rhodes on a high and lived there for 18 months. I thought, 'I know, I'll be a holiday rep'.
>
> (Sharron)

Someone experiencing a manic episode usually has no insight into their condition and so has no idea of how difficult their wild behaviour can be for their family and friends, even if it causes terrible problems. One common problem is excessive overspending, which can lead to long-term financial difficulties:

> Whenever I'm high, I will spend anything that's going. It's led to so many problems in my marriage. When I was undiagnosed, my wife just assumed I was really selfish, especially as we haven't got a lot of money. I can easily go and blow £3 or £4k on a credit card. Electronic goods are my thing. It's making a big buy that creates excitement.
>
> (Paul)

> Credit card bills started arriving ... my husband had taken out about eight credit cards. And he owed in excess of thirty thousand pounds. The funny thing was that it must all have happened at the same time, because they all started demanding money at the same time. And then he left us within the week, just walked out. To this day, I have no idea what he spent it on.
>
> (Paula)

Another common problem someone in a manic state can experience is the delusion of grandeur:

> During one major high, I impulsively got on a flight from Newcastle to London and booked a room at the Park Lane Hilton. I got on the Tube, but it wasn't good enough for me. I felt like I deserved better. You think you're entitled to the best. Lots of friends call me Lord George. I thought I ought to have servants. In the hotel reception I was told that the room would be £315 per night, plus VAT. I was annoyed because I hadn't been told about the VAT on the phone. 'I'm terribly sorry, Sir, you can have a suite,' said the receptionist. 'This will do me nicely,' I thought. They sent me a valet who dry-cleaned and ironed my trousers. I bought all the chamber maids into my room and told them to have five minutes rest and a glass of champagne. Once, having lunch, I asked them to get me the chef. I had bought a bottle of fine expensive wine and offered him a glass. I went to Bond Street and found a fabulous tailor and got kitted out with clothes. I spent £2,000 in there. What a wonderful way to shop. I didn't need to carry the bags home because, when I got back to the hotel, all the clothes I had bought were hanging in the wardrobe. I rented a Rolls Royce with a chauffeur to get me round London. I stayed there for five or six days and spent over £10,000 on the credit card. I was having such a great time. I wish you could leave me on a high with an American Express card. It took me years to pay it back.
>
> (George)

Q10. What is psychosis?

Sometimes an episode of mania can become so extreme that the manic person experiences wild delusions, extreme paranoia and hallucinations. Losing touch with reality in this way is called 'psychosis'. It's not uncommon for the fun of mania to tip over into this state:

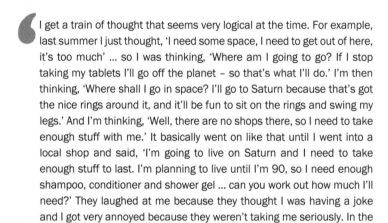

I get a train of thought that seems very logical at the time. For example, last summer I just thought, 'I need some space, I need to get out of here, it's too much' ... so I was thinking, 'Where am I going to go? If I stop taking my tablets I'll go off the planet – so that's what I'll do.' I'm then thinking, 'Where shall I go in space? I'll go to Saturn because that's got the nice rings around it, and it'll be fun to sit on the rings and swing my legs.' And I'm thinking, 'Well, there are no shops there, so I need to take enough stuff with me.' It basically went on like that until I went into a local shop and said, 'I'm going to live on Saturn and I need to take enough stuff to last. I'm planning to live until I'm 90, so I need enough shampoo, conditioner and shower gel ... can you work out how much I'll need?' They laughed at me because they thought I was having a joke and I got very annoyed because they weren't taking me seriously. In the end, they very tactfully said, 'It's going to take us a while to work out – if you come back next week we'll have it all worked out for you.'

(Sue)

Someone in the grip of a psychotic episode may think that the TV is sending them messages, or believe that other people are reading their mind or controlling them. A common psychotic belief is that they have superhuman powers, that they're a special being sent on a mission to solve the world's problems, and that there are forces of evil plotting against them.

It gradually gets worse and worse and worse, and then you get strange thoughts, like I quite often think I'm a special person – I'm somewhere between a human and Jesus. I'm better than everybody else, and I have these special insights that nobody else has. Then I start thinking that the devil is trying to get me, and that gets very frightening. And I start thinking that people are working for the devil and they're after me and trying to get me. Or sometimes I think that aliens are trying to get me, and that there are aliens disguised as humans. That gets very frightening. It just escalates. It starts off as being enjoyable, and then it goes over the edge and it's frightening.

(Sue)

It's also not uncommon for someone in a psychotic state to hear voices giving them instructions – even to harm themselves:

I had voices in my head telling me to take my tablets or drive my car into a tree – 'It will all be over' they kept saying. It was very scary ... sometimes they were outside my head talking to me and I couldn't work out whether they were real or not. I also had an evening of spiders running up my legs inside my jeans – I was convinced they were there. I'd never had that before. It was horrible.

(Debbie)

Psychosis doesn't need to occur for a diagnosis of bipolar disorder to be made, but it can often accompany a manic episode, especially if the mania is not treated effectively. Psychosis can also occur during a depressive episode.

Q11. What is a mixed state?

Someone with bipolar can experience a 'mixed state', when they have symptoms of mania and depression simultaneously – so they can be depressed and agitated at the same time, or 'tired but wired'. Any mix of the symptoms of mania and depression can occur at once – for example, someone may have racing thoughts, agitation, overactivity and unrealistic ideas, but feel worthless, guilty and suicidal. It's estimated that approximately two-thirds of those diagnosed with bipolar will suffer a mixed episode at some point in their illness. The people with Bipolar I who took part in the 12-year study spent an average 6% of weeks in a mixed or cycling state (where the polarity of episode was changing and symptoms of both were present). For people with Bipolar II, the proportion was just over 2%.

Amanda often sees her mother Irene in this mixed state, depressed and despairing, but also agitated and paranoid:

 I can only describe my mum's mixed episodes as despair on speed. There's none of the wild euphoria of mania, or the lethargy of depression. Her mood spirals downwards but she also becomes terribly agitated and restless, and can't even sit down ... just paces around for hours, as waves of paranoia and irrational fears overwhelm her mind.

It's a dangerous combination of moods, as someone in a mixed state has depression without the tiredness and demotivation that can go with it, whilst their agitation gives them enough energy to put suicidal thoughts into action.

Q12. What are the less recognized symptoms of bipolar disorder?

The 'unofficial' symptoms of bipolar disorder include anxiety, low self-esteem, libido problems and self-harm.

Anxiety

According to the US National Co-morbidity Survey, 31–42% of those with bipolar also suffer from anxiety disorders – an umbrella term used to encompass a wide range of symptoms, including excessive worrying, paranoia, a racing heartbeat, feelings of dread and fear, sweating, shaking, breathing difficulties and obsessive tendencies, such as collecting objects, repetitive actions and an inability to leave the house without making endless safety checks.

‘ Because of my condition, I can never judge whether I should be worried about something or not. I always try to question, would someone without bipolar be worrying or feel anxious about this? For example, we're refurbishing the house and I worry that the house looks like a tip. My husband doesn't seem to worry. Any stress at all is like a double stress. It makes me feel as though I'm the only person worrying in the world.

(Sharron) ’

‘ I don't feel I can teach well and I feel anxious a lot. That's why I've got a stammer at the moment.

(Jude) ’

‘ When I was first dating David, he was very paranoid. I didn't realize he was ill at the time, but he would phone at 3am to make sure I was on my own, and turn up at odd times. He was convinced I was married, and was trying to catch me out. He also has a lot of obsessive symptoms and collects things. I've since found out that this is typical bipolar behaviour. David will have 20 cans of the same deodorant in the cupboard, all with a millimetre of deodorant left, but I'm not allowed to throw them out in case he needs them. He will also buy lots of things exactly the same – shoes, shirts and trousers. When we moved, I had three bags of brown boots labelled 'Brown boots', 'More brown boots' and 'More bloody brown boots'!

(Jackie) ’

‘ I was hospitalized on two occasions when I was 22 after I'd had panic attacks, which I now recognize were tied in with me going hypomanic.

(Lesley) ’

‘ When Mum is low, she won't even go out of the front door, and is frightened to speak to anyone, let alone have any workman round the house.

(Ingrid) ’

Low self-esteem

Self-esteem is an individual's assessment of their own worth. Do they recognize their own qualities and talents or do they believe only negative statements about themselves? Those with a mental illness, including bipolar disorder, often have very low self-esteem, which can lead to a number of problems, including dysfunctional relationships and unfulfilled potential. Many fear revealing their true self to the outside world.

> I believe bipolar people wear this amazing mask outside the house. Most days it is possible to put on a mask for a certain amount of time and be normal. Some close friends I only told recently about my diagnosis said they never would have believed it.
>
> (Debbie)

> David's self-esteem was so low that he didn't believe that anyone would like him for himself, and so he had to create a persona.
>
> (Paula)

Libido problems

Some people with bipolar disorder experience a disrupted sex life. Problems include: a lack of libido during depressed periods, excessive libido during periods of mania, a general lack of affection because the bipolar symptoms can prevent a fulfilling and loving relationship, and the side effects of medication.

> Bipolar has had a huge impact on my sex life. First of all, you don't feel good about yourself, so you don't feel like sex. When I'm low, in my mind I'm wondering 'why does he want me, I'm just being used, why do I do this?' Then there's the other angle – when you're on a high, you just want sex all the time. It confuses the life out of your partner because they don't really understand. One minute you're refusing, the next minute you're all over them.
>
> (Sharron)

Self-harm

Sometimes referred to as deliberate self-harm (DSH), self-harm is a way of coping with distress. People self-harm in many ways, including destructive lifestyle habits, such as excessive drinking, taking recreational drugs and overeating. However, DSH is taken to mean self-harming in ways such as cutting, burning, scratching, taking overdoses and swallowing inedible objects. According to a report by the Mental Health Foundation, 100,000 people are referred to hospitals in the UK every year as a result of self-harm. Many of them have had traumatic, abusive childhoods and/or have psychiatric problems, such as bipolar disorder.

> I've self-harmed a lot. I used to cut the back of my legs using any surgical implement I could find – usually razor blades or scalpels. I wanted to cut myself open, turn myself inside out and put myself back together again feeling less stressed. I'd go through periods of doing that – anything from two weeks to one year.
>
> (Sharron)

> I do self-harm a fair bit. I cut my arms with a razor or a Stanley knife blade. I tend to do it when I'm feeling horribly anxious because it seems the only way to clear the anxiety. I know this sounds ridiculous, but because the anxiety makes me think something bad is about to happen, harming myself is the bad thing that happens, and then the anxiety goes because I can convince myself that nothing else bad will happen.
>
> (Paul)

Q13. Are the symptoms of bipolar disorder linked to the symptoms of seasonal affective disorder?

Seasonal affective disorder (SAD) is a type of winter depression that affects approximately one in 50, or just over an estimated one million people in the

UK every winter between September and April – particularly during December, January and February. A key feature of SAD is the desire to sleep more and eat carbohydrate foods. SAD seems to develop from inadequate bright light during the winter months, and is thought to be caused by a biochemical imbalance in the hypothalamus, the part of the brain that controls mood, appetite, sleep, temperature and sex drive.

DSM IV doesn't regard SAD as a separate condition, but as a seasonal pattern for depression and bipolar disorder. According to John McManamy in his book *Living with Depression and Bipolar Disorder*, people with mood disorders are far more likely to be affected by seasonal changes, with estimates of likelihood as high as 38%.

Many people diagnosed with bipolar disorder report symptoms of SAD:

About November, I can feel the symptoms coming on, and about March I begin to pick up again. And that's been pretty constant now for quite a good few years. I really collapse, and it's like there's an on/off switch in my brain, and it's 'goodnight'. And I just want to hibernate – for the first few weeks of that period I sleep and sleep and sleep and sleep. It was a running joke amongst my friends in my twenties. They'd just hammer on my doors and windows, and nothing was going to wake me. I'd be in bed 18 hours a day. And I can't go out. What I need to do is rest, massively. It's almost as if the rest of the year has caught up on me, as if I've burnt out my year's worth of energy.

(Ashley)

I have noticed over the years that Mum's high periods coincide with the fine weather from April to September and her low periods are usually from October through the winter months to April.

(Ingrid)

For info on how to treat the symptoms of Seasonal Affective Disorder, see question 36, p. 98.

Q14. Can bipolar disorder cause thyroid problems?

Situated at the front of the neck, the thyroid is a gland that produces the hormone thyroxine. This hormone is very important for many of the body's functions and also influences moods. It's been found that people with bipolar disorder quite often have abnormal thyroid function. The usual problem is that the thyroid gland doesn't produce enough thyroxine, leading to hypothyroidism, symptoms of which include slow body movements and speech, tiredness, weakness, poor concentration and memory problems (which can mimic depression). People with rapid cycling bipolar disorder may be particularly prone to problems with their thyroid gland. The problem is usually corrected by taking thyroid pills in addition to the usual medication for bipolar disorder.

In a chicken-and-egg situation, it's not yet known for sure whether bipolar disorder causes someone to be more prone to thyroid problems or whether having thyroid problems means someone is more prone to bipolar disorder.

Even more confusingly, taking the mood stabilizer lithium can cause low thyroid levels in some people, also resulting in the need for thyroid supplementation – see question 29, p. 74 for more information.

Q15. What causes bipolar disorder?

People often ask if mental illnesses are caused by either genes ('nature') or environment ('nurture'). Many research studies show that there's a tendency for bipolar disorder (along with other mental illnesses) to run in families. So is it all down to someone's genetic 'blueprint'?

No. All human characteristics are a combination of genes and experiences. And, it's now widely recognized that environmental factors can affect both the structure of our brain and our mood – both on a day-to-day basis and in the long term. Of course, all individuals differ in their life experiences and in the genes they inherit from their parents, so the relative importance of genes and environment will vary from person to person.

And having a genetic predisposition to bipolar disorder in the family doesn't mean somebody's destined to develop it. The best way of illustrating this is to look at studies of identical twins – if one twin has bipolar disorder, their genetically identical sibling has a 60% chance of developing the illness and a 40% chance of staying bipolar-free. If bipolar disorder was purely genetic, both twins would be diagnosed 100% of the time.

So if the cause of bipolar disorder can't be purely genetic, what environmental factors are in the mix?

- Upbringing may play a part for some people, such as the traumatic childhood shared by Amanda's mum and Sarah's dad.

- Stress – positive, as well as negative events – is known to be involved in triggering bipolar and other mental illnesses (see question 62, p. 176).

- The use of street drugs such as cannabis can also trigger bipolar and other mental disorders (see question 75, p. 213).

- Persistent lack of sleep can be a trigger (see question 63, p. 178).

- Hormonal changes, particularly for women going through the menopause as in the case of Amanda's mum, Irene.

Professor Nick Craddock at Cardiff University also explains that, in extremely rare cases, a head injury can be an external trigger for bipolar disorder: 'It depends on exactly what the injury is and what parts of the brain are involved, but head injury can bring on bipolar disorder in someone with a genetic susceptibility. That's because head injuries can cause damage to some systems in the brain that are involved in the condition.'

Q16. Is there an increased risk of bipolar disorder for other family members?

This is a question that looms large for us, as we consider the risk for ourselves and our children. At first glance, the straight answer is not an optimistic one. Yes, it's true that the children of someone with bipolar have a higher risk of developing the illness than the children of parents without bipolar. For the general population, there's a 1% chance of developing Bipolar I – and the risk increases to 5–10% if someone's mother or father has the condition. That's a big jump. There's also an increased risk of Bipolar II for children of a parent with bipolar, although not enough research has yet been done for an exact statistic.

My father was bipolar, though he was never actually diagnosed – he committed suicide. His mother spent 20 years in an acute psychiatric unit. And his father had 'shellshock' during World War 1 and was an alcoholic. Looking back, I wonder if there was more to it.

(Sharron)

Saying that, a more optimistic way of looking at it is that even with a 10% lifetime risk, there's a 90% chance that a child of a parent with bipolar *won't* develop Bipolar I during his or her lifetime. Amanda, Sarah and Amanda's brother Andrew – all children of a parent with bipolar disorder – are just three people who prove that point. And there are others ...

I really hope my daughter hasn't inherited my bipolar. She's nine. She doesn't seem to have the personality that goes with it. As a child I was already very impatient, very moody, I didn't listen to anyone, I did what I wanted to do. My daughter is very much more like her dad.

(Reka)

Unfortunately, though, the child of someone with bipolar disorder doesn't only inherit a higher risk of developing bipolar. Research at Manchester University found that the risk of them developing 'unipolar' depression is higher too. In fact, someone with a parent who has bipolar disorder is twice as likely to experience depression – this is because characteristics often shared by people with bipolar are also found in the children of parents with bipolar, even if they don't have bipolar disorder themselves, as Professor Steven Jones, Professor of Clinical Psychology, Spectrum Centre for Mental Health Research, Lancaster University, explains: 'We found in individuals with diagnoses of depression and also individuals with bipolar that there is a tendency towards a "ruminative" coping style (thinking over problems repetitively without moving to problem solving), and in people with a bipolar diagnosis this is also paired with a risk-taking coping style, particularly for dealing with negative mood ... And what we found in the children of bipolar parents was that they also showed a pattern of more rumination and more risk taking. Another thing that we found in the psychological research into people with a diagnosis of bipolar disorder is that instability seems to be a key characteristic, which is detectable in different ways. One reliable observation is that people with a bipolar diagnosis appear to have more unstable self esteem ... And what we found in children of bipolar parents again is that there was greater instability of self esteem, and also higher levels of negative mood.'

The research also looked at sleep patterns in the children of a parent with bipolar disorder, which found they reported poor sleep even when test results showed that they had in fact gone to sleep more quickly and had slept for longer than the control group (people who don't have a parent with bipolar). This would suggest that the children of a parent with bipolar need more sleep than the general population to feel refreshed – which in turn suggests that they might share the same vulnerability (to bipolar disorder being triggered by routinely disturbed or shortened sleep) as their parent with bipolar.

For other relatives of people with bipolar, it's likely that the chances of developing Bipolar I or II are less than the risk to children of bipolar parents but greater than the risk to the general population, as Professor Nick Craddock explains: 'The more and closer relatives with bipolar you have, the higher your risk for bipolar overall. If someone wants to know their risk in detail, they need to see a psychiatrist to discuss all the relevant issues. This allows the discussion to be tailored to the individual's specific risk factors and also their specific concerns.'

But, of course, risk is only half the story. Having an increased risk for bipolar does not automatically mean it will develop. Even if the genetic cards are unfavourably stacked, it's not necessarily inevitable. Far from it, in fact, as life events and lifestyle choices can make all the difference.

To explain the risk more clearly, Professor Craddock uses this analogy: 'If you're born with fair skin, you're more at risk of sunburn than someone with dark skin, but if you protect yourself (using sun protection cream, staying out of the midday sun, wearing a hat in summer, for instance) then you're far less likely to get burnt. And on the flip side of the coin, being born with dark skin means you have a lower risk, but does not eliminate the risk of sunburn altogether (if you spend time in the Australian outback with no protection, for instance). It's the same with bipolar risk. You can be born with a higher genetic leaning towards bipolarity, but if you protect yourself (generally making wise lifestyle choices), then you're far less likely to become unwell. And, similarly, if you're born with a low genetic risk yet don't protect yourself, you may become unwell with bipolar symptoms.'

Bearing this in mind, since finding out that bipolar can be triggered by lack of sleep, Amanda (a natural insomniac) has been going to bed earlier! And since learning that stress is a common trigger, Sarah (who leads the life of a working mother that can get pretty stressful) practices Reiki daily – a method of hands-on healing that helps create a feeling of balance and well-being. (Chapter 5 covers the best lifestyle choices in more detail.)

Of course, it's far from possible to control everything in life (parents divorcing, stress in childhood, bereavement, to name but a few). Luck plays a part in whether bipolar puts in an appearance or not. But it's reassuring to know that a high genetic risk doesn't necessarily mean that developing bipolar disorder is inevitable.

Q17. Is it possible to have genetic testing for bipolar disorder?

Every so often a headline in a national newspaper declares that the 'bipolar gene' has been discovered and that we're one step away from the definitive bipolar test. But it's not as simple as that ... There's not just one, or even just a few, genes involved in the development of bipolar disorder, but many.

In short, the answer is no, it isn't possible to have genetic testing for bipolar disorder. Although there's a great deal of research being done at the moment to understand the genetics of bipolar, the purpose of this is not to test people to see if they are personally at risk of developing it. Instead, the gene research is focused on trying to understand the brain processes involved in the illness, which will hopefully lead to more individualized and generally better diagnosis and treatment. For example, research by the Wellcome Trust Case Control Consortium (WTCCC) – a collaboration between 24 leading human geneticists who have studied thousands of DNA samples – has found new genetic variants for seven major disorders, including bipolar disorder. Professor Peter Donnelly, who chairs the WTCCC and is a Professor of Statistical Science at Oxford University, describes the research as a 'new dawn'. 'They have learnt more in the past 12 months,' he adds, 'than they have in 15 years, with major implications for treatment of bipolar' (see question 25, p. 57).

Q18. Is it possible for a child to suffer from bipolar disorder?

This is an extremely controversial subject area, to say the least. According to the Office for National Statistics, one in ten children between the ages of one and 15 in the UK has a mental health disorder, yet the medical profession is divided into two camps when it comes to diagnosing children with bipolar.

The 'yes' camp

A report from Harvard Medical School states that symptoms of bipolar disorder first appear in childhood or adolescence at least one third of the time. 'Childhood bipolar disorder is a real and serious illness that should be recognized and treated as early as possible,' says Dr Michael Miller, editor-in-chief of *Harvard Mental Health Letter*. In America, the number of children diagnosed with bipolar disorder has increased fivefold in eight years.

The 'no' camp

Until the 1990s bipolar disorder was exclusively an adult disease, only thought to affect people in their early twenties or older, and many psychiatrists are still reluctant to 'label' or medicate children. In fact, according to a report in the British journal *New Scientist*, one US paediatric psychiatrist says that only 18% of children referred for a second opinion actually have bipolar disorder. Similar results are reported by other specialists. In other words, more children are being diagnosed with bipolar, but many experts believe they're being misdiagnosed.

The middle ground

Professor Nick Craddock agrees that children can display signs of bipolar illness, but advocates a more cautious approach to giving a definite diagnosis: 'Although I believe it's impossible to diagnose children as young as two and three years old (which is increasingly seen in America) and that clear-cut bipolar in children is still uncommon, the number of cases does seem to be going up. This is probably due to a combination of the fact that we're more alert to the possibility and that there is a true increase, although we can only guess as to why this increase has happened. What I do believe is that we're coming to a point where we'll be able to identify certain behaviours in children that are indicative of a future likelihood of bipolar illness.'

The reason why it's so difficult to make a definite diagnosis in childhood is that every single person with bipolar disorder has a completely different experience of when and how the condition manifests itself. There is no typical pattern. For example, although Amanda's mum, Irene, didn't display any symptoms at all until she was in her fifties, Sarah believes with hindsight that some of her sister Rebecca's behaviour as a very young child were clues to a future diagnosis. When she was about six, Rebecca would sometimes say she had a 'speedo' and that when it was switched on she could do everything really fast. She hated school, partly because she found it so difficult to sit still and concentrate. She was always getting into trouble with the teachers.

Would a diagnosis in childhood have made a difference to Rebecca's experiences? We certainly don't believe that throwing medication at a problem solves everything, particularly because little is understood about how drugs can affect a developing brain. But at least if Rebecca had had a diagnosis, she might have been given support and understanding, rather than a label as naughty and disruptive. And though medical opinion is divided, many people have first-hand experience of symptoms showing up in childhood ...

 I suffered from depression at school and took my first overdose aged 11. The teachers just thought I had attitude problems and saw me as arrogant. I was always a strange child. I didn't mix or play games with others. I used to watch rather than join in. I felt like an alien who just couldn't fit in anywhere. Once, I went round all the ladies toilets and took all the taps off. I still don't know why I did it even now. Maybe it was a cry for help. I was diagnosed with bipolar disorder at the age of 30.

(Sharron)

 My symptoms probably started, looking back now, at the age of 12. I can pinpoint that's when my behaviour started to change. The first time I self-harmed – I'm a cutter – I was 12. When I was about 16, I was found by my teacher lying in the middle of a main road. I didn't know why ... I was diagnosed in February 2005 when I was 24.

(Amy)

My daughter Laura was always fighting with other children and in trouble at school. I was always being phoned and written to by the teachers. She wouldn't go to bed. She would throw things out of windows. When we were out shopping, she would always get into physical fights. She was generally very destructive, but there was literally nothing I could do to change it. I couldn't go anywhere with her. Looking back, I think these were definitely symptoms of bipolar at a very early age. I also believe that the behaviour left unmanaged led to more stressful conditions in her life, which in turn opened the door to bipolar, although she was also genetically susceptible due to my ex-husband's family history.

(June)

I was quite cross after my diagnosis at the age of 20, that someone hadn't picked it up sooner. I was completely off the wall at times. I was really miserable around the ages of 13 and 14. And as a child I could be quite hyperactive.

(Tamara)

My daughter Vicki's diagnosis at the age of 14 has been a positive thing, because she knows I'm looking into it all the time to help her. It makes her feel as though she's not abnormal. She can think, 'I feel this way for a reason ... I'm not weird or freaky, this is just the way my body works.' She does accept it. She's my little trouper ... I'm very proud of her.

(Alison)

Q19. Are the symptoms of bipolar disorder different in children?

The National Institute of Clinical Excellence (NICE) guideline states that for Bipolar I to be diagnosed in prepubescent children, a professional should use the same criteria as in adults, except that:

- Mania must be present.
- Euphoria must be present most days, most of the time (for seven days).
- Irritability is not a main reason to diagnose bipolar disorder.

The guideline also states that if a child experiences a major depressive episode and they have a family history of bipolar disorder, they shouldn't be diagnosed but monitored closely. Also, Bipolar II shouldn't normally be diagnosed in children because the symptoms haven't yet been officially defined.

Q20. Is bipolar disorder ever diagnosed in the elderly?

Late-life onset mania is relatively uncommon and the symptoms are slightly different – older people with bipolar tend to have shorter cycles and an increased severity of the condition. Martha Sajatovic, Associate Professor in the Department of Psychiatry at Case Western Reserve University School of Medicine, Cleveland says that of those who are diagnosed after the age of 50, only one in four have no past history of mood disorder. Of the rest, 30% have pre-existing depression and 13% have past mania.

I first remember Mum getting seriously depressed in the early 1980s when she was around 60. She had several long bouts of depression, sometimes lasting years rather than months, continuing up to when she died in 2003. She did have the 'highs' when she eventually came out of each period of depression, which probably only lasted for a few weeks before she settled down. The time between her bouts of depression varied, sometimes lasting a few months, other times a few years. Mum had all sorts of treatment. She was put on various antidepressants. She had several periods in hospital and had some courses of electric shock treatment which, although horrible, did seem to bring her out of the depressions. She was also put on lithium which she took for the rest of her life. My dad found it extremely hard to cope. Before Mum had her depressions, she was very outgoing and loved looking after everyone and Dad really never had to do anything in the home. Like many elderly people, he really couldn't understand mental illness and didn't see why she couldn't just snap out of it, so he was very impatient with her. He then became very demanding and expected me to be there far more than I could manage. It was particularly difficult as during one of Mum's stable periods they moved much further away from us (against everyone in the family's advice), which made it hard to visit very often once she again became depressed. Later on we persuaded them to move near to us which made life a little easier. We are convinced that Mum's illness was triggered by some personal problems in her early life which she kept hidden from us for many years and was scared of us discovering. We feel that it would have helped her enormously if she had been able to talk about her problems more. It is a very hard illness to cope with. I felt that I really lost my mum many years before she died as she was so changed. It was wonderful each time she came out of her depressions to have her back to normal, but we were always worried because we never knew how long it would last.

(Doreen)

Q21. Why is bipolar disorder often misdiagnosed?

It's hard to imagine living with any other type of chronic long-term illness without appropriate treatment, but there is, on average, an eight-year delay before a diagnosis is made for those with bipolar. In one national survey, 70% of people with bipolar disorder were initially misdiagnosed. And, on average, someone with bipolar sees four different doctors before the correct diagnosis is made. Andrea Sutcliffe, deputy chief executive of NICE, says: 'Bipolar disorder often goes unrecognized or misdiagnosed and more needs to be done to raise awareness of the condition and the fact that there are effective treatments.'

The trouble is, unlike a 'physical' condition such as diabetes, there's not a simple test to determine whether or not someone has bipolar. Often, the diagnosis is only made when a severe manic episode occurs – often involving sectioning under the Mental Health Act and a stay in a psychiatric unit (see Chapter 4). So why isn't bipolar diagnosed before such a desperate crisis point is reached? There are two main reasons:

1. Bipolar disorder is often diagnosed as depression

The first clue that someone has bipolar disorder is often a depressive episode. If someone seeks help from their family doctor at this point, and if no mention of previous mania or a family history of bipolar disorder is mentioned by the patient, the doctor is likely to make a diagnosis of and suggest treatment for depression. On the other hand, first experiences of mania are not always reported. A manic episode, especially in the early stages, often feels so enjoyable that the person experiencing it can't see what the problem is. Their family and friends may be alarmed and try to intervene, but for the manic person, feeling euphoric and invincible, it seems as if everyone else is trying to spoil their fun: 'Why should I go the doctor? There's nothing wrong with me!'

In fact, according to research carried out in Zurich, just over half of those diagnosed with depression have some form of bipolar illness. In other words, there's huge overlap between the two illnesses and it's extremely difficult for medical professionals to distinguish between the two during the depressed phase. 'What happens is that the person seeks medical attention for the depression, but sees the elevated mood as welcome relief so the medical professional only sees the depression and diagnoses accordingly,' explains Professor Nick Craddock. The result is that bipolar disorder is often misdiagnosed as depression. 'My own expectation over the next few years is that a lot more people than previously recognized will be diagnosed with a form of bipolar illness.'

In 1993, Amanda's mum Irene went through the all-too-common scenario of being misdiagnosed with depression, and others have had a similar experience:

I was only treated for depression for years. I would go to the doctor, get some antidepressants, take them for a while, stop taking them and then go back. I took a variety of antidepressants, long term, but things just weren't getting any better, the antidepressants just weren't working.

(Sue)

At 17 I was diagnosed with recurrent depressive disorder and only got my diagnosis of bipolar at the age of 22.

(Rachel)

My bipolar started at the end of 1981 following a period of stress at work. By 1984 nobody had really diagnosed it properly. The doctors thought it was depression and I was prescribed early antidepressants.

(Richard)

I was diagnosed with depression at the age of 20 and finally diagnosed officially with Bipolar II a year ago, when I was 33.

(Lesley)

The first two times I was in hospital in my twenties I was diagnosed with depression. Even though my dad has bipolar disorder, my psychiatrists didn't put two and two together.

(Carl)

After David had a car accident ten years ago, he was diagnosed with post traumatic stress disorder. At first he threw the antidepressants down the toilet. Then he was diagnosed with clinical depression and became suicidal 99% of the time. I knew what was wrong with him 12 months before he was diagnosed at the hospital because I went to the library and picked up a few books. I knew he had bipolar, but the professionals refused to listen to me.

(Jackie)

2. Bipolar sometimes gets misdiagnosed altogether

After my first major manic episode at the age of 24, I was diagnosed with schizophrenia which was way off course.

(George)

Five years ago I had a complete physical collapse for a few months. I couldn't function at all. I was just physically exhausted, could hardly get out of bed, or if I went to the shop I would have to fall into bed again afterwards. A specialist diagnosed me with chronic fatigue syndrome.

(Ashley)

Professor Nick Craddock explains why this kind of misdiagnosis happens: 'What we know is that lots of people are told they have schizophrenia or a personality disorder, and then it turns out they have bipolar disorder. It's not that suddenly things change completely. It's not that psychiatrists are stupid. It's actually that what we're trying to do is to use simple labels for something that's much more complicated.'

But he does believe that misdiagnosis will become less common in future. He says: 'As we understand more, we'll get a lot better at diagnosing and target treatments better.'

Q22. What can someone do if they think a loved one might have undiagnosed bipolar disorder?

The first step to recovery for someone with suspected undiagnosed bipolar disorder that's causing problems is an accurate diagnosis. If they are in the grip of an extreme mood swing, get immediate help – either call an ambulance and get them to A&E, or phone their family doctor and ask for help from the community mental health team. (There's more information about this in question 40, p. 105.) If they are relatively stable, try to persuade them to see their GP as soon as possible, accompanying them to the appointment if they allow it to describe any worrying symptoms.

Remember that the earlier they are diagnosed the better the long-term outcome will be, as Terence Ketter, MD, Associate Professor of Psychiatry and Behavioral Sciences at the Stanford University School of Medicine, explains: 'Early and accurate diagnosis is important in preventing disease-related episodes, which potentially lead to illness progression. It's much easier to treat patients who have had fewer than three episodes; after that bipolar disorder gets incrementally more difficult to treat. If we don't let episodes occur, patients can do exceedingly well.'

Q23. How is bipolar disorder usually diagnosed?

As discussed in question 21, a GP or family physician often only sees someone when they're experiencing the depressive symptoms of bipolar disorder, so it's very rare for a family doctor to diagnose bipolar disorder. Either he or she will misdiagnose the patient with depression or refer the patient to a psychiatrist who will review medical history, family history and compare symptoms with the official list in DSM IV. To gather a list of symptoms, a psychiatrist is likely to ask questions, such as the following:

Depression

- How sad do you get and for how long?

- Do you enjoy things?
- Can you imagine what your future will be like?
- Do you feel hopeless or helpless?
- Can you concentrate?
- Do your thoughts feel slow?
- Do you feel tired all the time?
- Do you sleep too much?
- Do you think about death and dying?
- Do you think about killing yourself?

Mania

- Do you have periods of high energy and productivity?
- How happy or angry do you get and for how long?
- Do you have times when you feel you're the best at everything?
- Have you ever got into trouble during these times by spending or borrowing too much money?
- Do your thoughts feel hyperactive?
- Do you sleep too little?
- Do you ever hear voices or believe you have magical powers?

Anxiety

- How much do you worry about things?
- Have you ever had a panic attack?
- Do you think people want to harm you?
- Do you ever self-harm?
- Do you hate social situations or avoid them altogether?

Mental health history

- Have you ever been hospitalized in a psychiatric unit?

- Have you ever been depressed or manic?
- Have you ever taken medication for a psychiatric condition?
- Have you ever seen a therapist?
- Do any family members suffer from psychiatric disorders?
- Did you experience depression or manic symptoms as a teenager or child?

Lifestyle

- What's your life like now?
- Do you work?
- How's your marriage/love life?
- Do you exercise?
- Do you eat well?
- Do you drink?
- Do you smoke?
- Do you take any prescribed or recreational drugs?

The psychiatrist will then give an initial diagnosis.

Q24. What happens once a diagnosis of bipolar disorder is made?

Once a diagnosis of bipolar disorder has been made, what happens next very much depends on the individual. The first factor involved is whether or not the person has insight into their own condition. This then determines a pathway of care – as brilliantly captured in diagram form by the editor of *Pendulum* magazine Michel Syrett. This diagram – on p. 53 – was originally published in the BBC booklet *The Secret Life of Manic Depression: Everything You Need to Know about Bipolar Disorder*.

PATHWAY OF CARE

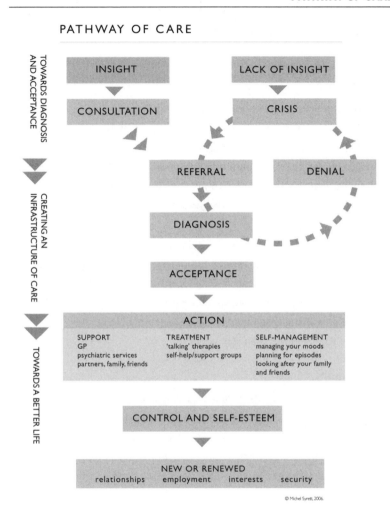

TOWARDS DIAGNOSIS AND ACCEPTANCE

CREATING AN INFRASTRUCTURE OF CARE

TOWARDS A BETTER LIFE

© Michel Syrett, 2006.

Below, Michel Syrett explains how his Pathway of Care diagram illustrates broad stages in the journey to managing bipolar disorder successfully:

Insight

'People with milder forms of the disorder, such as Bipolar II, often have the insight to recognize early symptoms, engage in consultation with their GP and agree to a referral to a psychiatric outpatient unit, which results in an accurate diagnosis.'

Lack of insight

'However, many people who develop a bipolar disorder have a distinct and potentially destructive lack of insight. The symptoms of the disorder are often only spotted with the onset of a crisis in a person's life, sometimes involving the police, a visit to an accident and emergency department or compulsory treatment under the Mental Health Act 1983. It is only then that they are referred to a psychiatric unit and diagnosed.'

Towards diagnosis

'Even then someone has to accept the diagnosis. Denial at this stage will lead into a cycle of crisis and re-diagnosis that, not confronted, can last decades. On the other hand, acceptance will lead to insight which will in turn lead to action and the creation of a self-management plan to help the person control the illness rather than vice versa.'

Life-long acceptance

Just as someone faced with a diabetes diagnosis pre-empts and controls their blood sugar levels, someone with a bipolar diagnosis needs to pre-empt and control mood swings for the rest of his or her life. And it's the 'incurable' nature of the illness that means some people find accepting the diagnosis extremely difficult, including Amanda's mum Irene and her family:

 When my mum was first diagnosed with bipolar in 1993, I don't think she or any one of us really understood what this meant in the long term. Each mood swing episode would last for a few days or weeks, and sometimes she would end up in hospital. But when she was stable again, and back home, she hated the bipolar diagnosis so much that she would go into denial, and think that the problem had been 'fixed' – and we would try to believe it too. It sounds so naïve now, looking back, but each time, we all so desperately wanted to think that Mum's illness was over. Eventually, as she struggled over the years with recurring mood swings, a realization sank in that for however long she might stay 'well' in between episodes, the bipolar was never cured, only managed. It was incredibly hard to face, but she, my dad and the rest of our family came to understand that you can't treat bipolar with denial.

People say once they're diagnosed they feel relief, but I've never felt relieved ... I felt really scared. I've always known you can't cure these things ... But somehow I wish there could be treatment without diagnosis. Because once you have a label like this slapped on you, it affects everything from insurance to driving licence. If you're honest about it and actually declare it, it's really hard to deal with.

(Tamara)

I was told over ten years ago by a psychiatrist that I suffered from manic depression but I dismissed it. Last year, I became manic but rejected the diagnosis again. My psychiatrist then explained that I had to accept the diagnosis in order to help prevent relapse, but I felt angry at myself for not being able to control it properly. Now I hope I can become fully stable on medication so I don't swing up and down so often, and that I can make bipolar disorder something I can live with.

(Jude)

At first I was relieved to have a diagnosis because it put a name to my problems. But on the other hand, having a diagnosis has added more of a strain. Although I'm diagnosed and getting treated, my behaviour is still very erratic. It felt like the diagnosis was an easy answer, but it wasn't. The diagnosis isn't the answer to all our prayers. It names the problem but doesn't solve the problem.

(Paul)

Others, though, experience relief when they are first diagnosed because they finally have an explanation for sometimes decades of inexplicable behaviour:

> It's early days, but I do feel relief from having the diagnosis. It's been a massive relief to realize that a lot of my behaviour has been completely normal for a bipolar person. And there's relief to know that I can get the right treatment.
>
> (Ashley)

> Laura was diagnosed with bipolar last February. I was very worried. We'd lost the person. When she's well and in a balanced state, she's a very sociable person and great fun. I would say she's like that one tenth of her life as it comes and goes. The rest of the time she's either up or down or aggressive. It was an enormous relief to give it a name.
>
> (June)

> The bipolar diagnosis has helped me, because it made sense of my previous feelings. I'm comfortable with it. It's not going to define me. It's just some aspect of me that probably made me who I am. Without the disorder, are you the same person? I don't think so.
>
> (Neil)

The important thing to remember, as Candida Fink and Joe Kraynak clearly explain in *Bipolar Disorder for Dummies*, is that a bipolar diagnosis doesn't define you: 'You're not bipolar, you *have* bipolar. This is a huge difference because language conveys powerful meanings. Always refer to your illness as something you're managing, not as a label that identifies you. People say "Pat is bipolar", but if Pat had cancer they wouldn't say "Pat is cancer". Always remember that you're not bipolar disorder but that bipolar disorder is something you have.'

CHAPTER TWO
TREATMENT

Q25. What is the most effective way to treat bipolar disorder?

It can't be said enough times that bipolar disorder is a lifelong condition like diabetes or asthma. The treatment for bipolar is, then, the management of a chronic illness, not a permanent cure.

This isn't necessarily bad news. So much more can be done nowadays to treat bipolar disorder successfully, to reduce or remove symptoms and help someone with a diagnosis to live a happy and stable life. According to Michelle Rowett, former Chief Executive of MDF The BiPolar Organisation, bipolar disorder is a highly manageable condition. 'With the right support and treatment, people with the diagnosis can lead positive and fulfilling lives,' she says. Plus, according to Equilibrium – The Bipolar Foundation, good treatment extends the life expectancy of someone with bipolar by six to seven years.

Currently, someone diagnosed with bipolar disorder in the Western world is typically prescribed medication (usually a mix-and-match combination of antidepressants, mood stabilizers, antipsychotics and anti anxiety drugs), and offered a form of psychological therapy and taught a range of self-management techniques. In hospital, they might also be given electroconvulsive therapy (ECT) or transcranial magnetic stimulation.

And even though in some cases it can take time and an element of luck to prescribe the right treatment, new research is radically improving how bipolar disorder is diagnosed and treated all the time. The research carried out by the WTCC (the Wellcome Trust Case Control Consortium, a collaboration between leading scientists) has cast light on the genetics of bipolar disorder, and will in time, according to Professor of Statistical Science Peter Donnelly, lead to 'more effective, personalized treatments'.

The key here is in the phrase 'personalized treatments'. The vision for the future shared by many scientists seems to be that rather than saying to someone, 'You have Bipolar I – here's the standard treatment for it,' a person's treatment will focus on their individual symptoms rather than their diagnosis.

Another growing school of thought is that the treatment of bipolar disorder should include *preventing* symptoms in high-risk people. Professor Richard Morriss, Professor of Psychiatry and Community Mental Health at Nottingham University, believes that it is possible to delay or reduce symptoms so that someone with a high genetic risk is more likely to develop the condition later in life – in their thirties rather than their twenties, for example, which will have huge, life-changing implications: 'Because you can identify a high-risk group (children of a first or second degree relative with bipolar – parent, sibling, aunt, uncle, for instance) it may be possible in the future to prevent or delay the full expression of the illness ... If we could identify and monitor closely people at risk – if we had good services, i.e. more supportive, less emphasis on drugs – at least there wouldn't be a long delay before diagnosis. Of course, it is difficult to know how much these things are pre-determined. But it would be great to delay or limit consequences. Then at least when symptoms arrive you have more experience, more maturity, you've achieved something, maybe met a partner, you're not involved in drugs, basically you're in a more stable part of your life. There are increasingly ways to identify high-risk behaviours – essentially identifying that people have something like cyclothymia. Then they could seek preventative treatment.'

Preventative treatment for those at higher risk of developing bipolar could include using psychological therapies, as Dr Sara Tai, Lecturer in Clinical Psychology at Manchester University, explains: 'There are a number of things we've identified that can help prevent potential signs of bipolar growing into full-blown bipolar. For example, it's natural for everybody to get low or to feel down sometimes. Those who mull and ruminate over why they're depressed are in much more danger of having mood swings, whereas those who think "What can I do to get over this?" are much less likely to get depressed. So that's a coping mechanism, a skill that anybody can learn, regardless of their natural tendencies. Another important factor is how people solve problems. You're not necessarily born with problem-solving skills, but you can learn them.'

Living a healthy life could also help protect someone who has a higher genetic risk of developing bipolar disorder – see Chapter 5 for advice on mental health protecting lifestyle choices.

Q26. Are there official treatment guidelines for bipolar disorder?

In England and Wales, treatment guidelines are issued by the National Institute for Health and Clinical Excellence (NICE), which was established in 1999 after widespread concern that treatment and care for a wide range of medical conditions was becoming a 'postcode lottery' characterized by random inconsistencies. The guidelines set the 'gold standard' for health care services – all NHS trusts are expected to comply and are regularly reviewed by the Healthcare Commission, the independent inspection body for health services in the UK.

The first NICE guideline for the treatment of bipolar disorder in England and Wales was published in 2006, and will be reviewed in 2010. Anyone with the time and/or inclination to view or download the full or summarized version for patients and their families can go to the NICE website or write to the head office – see Extra resources, p. 254 for contact details.

The guideline for the treatment of bipolar contains recommendations for:

- drug protocols for managing acute episodes of mania/hypomania, depression, 'mixed state' and serious behaviour disturbances
- use of ECT for severe manic or depressive episodes
- managing rapid cycling bipolar
- long-term management of bipolar after acute episodes, including drug and psychological treatment such as cognitive behavioural therapy (CBT)
- treatment of children and adolescents with bipolar disorder
- promoting a healthy lifestyle and relapse prevention
- physical monitoring of people with bipolar, with an annual health check up.

The guideline also sets out some general principles for working with patients and their families, including recommendations to:

- Establish and maintain good relationships with patients, families and carers (within the bounds of confidentiality). This includes:
  - respecting the patient's knowledge and experience of the illness
  - encouraging patients to involve their families and carers if appropriate
  - giving patients, families and carers information (including information on medication) at every stage of assessment, diagnosis and treatment
  - encouraging patients, family and carers to join self-help and support groups.
- Consider the needs of the patient's family members or carers, including:
  - the impact on relationships

- the welfare of dependent children, siblings and vulnerable adults

- carers' physical, social and mental health needs.

• Be accessible to family members and carers in times of crisis.

If NICE treatment guidelines are not followed – for instance, if psychological treatments or annual health checks are not offered – a patient or loved one can raise this with their GP, psychiatrist, CPN or other members of their community mental health team (see question 40, p. 105). Knowledge is power, and knowing what the recommendations are could be the first step towards getting them implemented.

It's also helpful to inform the Healthcare Commission if NICE guidelines aren't being implemented in a local area. The more information the Commission has, the better equipped they are to guide health trusts towards positive change – again, see Extra resources, p. 250 for contact details.

In Scotland, the Scottish Intercollegiate Guidelines Network (SIGN) performs the same function as NICE. They issued a bipolar treatment guideline in 2005, due to be reviewed in 2008. It follows broadly similar principles to the NICE document. For more details, email or write to SIGN via the details in Extra resouces, p. 255.

The Northern Ireland Assembly is (at the time of writing) still deciding its procedure for issuing treatment guidelines in the region.

And all around the world, clinicians refer to treatment guidelines from the World Federation of Societies of Biological Psychiatry (WFSBP) – a non-profit organization with members from over 50 countries.

Q27. What is psychological treatment, such as cognitive behavioural therapy?

More and more evidence is accumulating to show how important psychological therapy can be in the treatment of bipolar disorder. For example, a study published in the journal *Archives of General Psychiatry*, shows that patients with bipolar disorder who are taking medication improve faster and stay well if they also receive intense psychotherapy (a generic term which includes CBT as well as other therapies, such as family focused therapy). The study, led by David Miklowitz, Professor of Psychology at the University of Colorado, monitored patients who received nine months of intense psychotherapy, and others in a control group who received three psycho-educational sessions. During the course of the year, 64% of the patients who received intense psychotherapy became well, compared with 52% of the control group. The study also found that patients who received intense psychotherapy became well an average of 110 days sooner and were one and a half times more likely to be well during any month of the study year than the other patients.

So perhaps not surprisingly, the NICE guideline for the treatment of bipolar recommends psychological therapies, particularly as part of a patient's long-term treatment plan, and suggests the following after an acute episode:

- Individual structured psychological interventions, such as CBT should be considered.
- The therapy should be at least 16 sessions over a six to nine month period, and should:
  - include psycho-education, the importance of a regular routine and taking medication properly
  - cover mood monitoring, detecting early warning signs and strategies to prevent progression into full-blown episodes
  - enhance general coping strategies
  - be delivered by people who have experience of patients with bipolar disorder.
- A focused family intervention should be considered if appropriate. This should last six to nine months, and cover ways to improve communication and problem solving skills.

A huge number of experts in the field also believe that psychological therapies are an extremely important part of the treatment jigsaw. Professor

Steven Jones, Professor of Clinical Psychology, Spectrum Centre for Mental Health Research, Lancaster University, is one of them: 'Maybe ten years ago, there was a bit of an assumption that psychological approaches weren't really relevant to bipolar disorder – it was seen almost purely as a biological problem. I think that story is changing gradually, which is good.'

His colleague, Dr Sara Tai, Lecturer in Clinical Psychology at Manchester University, cautions that all therapies might not be equal: 'You have to be careful with the phrase "talking therapies". It doesn't mean you're just sitting there talking. In fact, it covers a wide range of interventions. It's true that some less evidence-based "therapies" might consist of nothing more than talking and befriending. But the type of psychological intervention that research shows really works is not just about talking, it's about getting people to become more aware of things and making changes in their life so they can understand how their symptoms have developed. It's not necessarily an easy process for people, not straightforward, but the results can be amazingly powerful. And as an added bonus, there aren't really any side effects in the same way that medication might cause side effects.'

The most common psychological treatments offered to those with bipolar disorder are: CBT; family focused therapy; counselling; and group therapy.

So how can they actually help?

Cognitive behavioural therapy (CBT)

The biggest buzzword in psychological treatment over the past ten years is CBT – cognitive behavioural therapy. Usually carried out by psychologists in one-to-one sessions with the patient, the theory is that thought, behaviour and mood all affect each other, which means it's possible to teach someone how to change their thoughts and behaviour in order to influence their mood.

The key to cognitive behavioural therapy is not about mental health professionals telling someone what to do, but about giving them the tools to monitor and control their own behaviour, thoughts and mood. Peter Kinderman, Professor of Clinical Psychology at the University of Liverpool, says: 'What this isn't doing is giving people advice, because you don't sit as a guru and say to someone either, "It is good in life to avoid going to parties – alcohol is a bad thing", or, "I can tell that *you* shouldn't go to parties and *you* shouldn't drink alcohol". What you say is, "When you notice yourself going high, bring yourself down, and when you notice yourself going low, do something about it". It's teaching people to respond to their own internal states in a way that they haven't done before.'

Research shows that CBT is particularly effective for patients with recurring depressive mood swings – here the therapy works on the idea that negative thinking is a bad habit, and that it's possible to learn techniques to break this habit. A patient gains more insight into their condition, learning to step back and look at the evidence for their negative thoughts, recognize these for what they are and then build up new positive ones. They intervene in their own automatic negative thinking about themselves and the world – for example, instead of the depressive train of thought that says, 'I'm hopeless, I can't do anything', the patient learns how to examine and challenge this thought, and recognize that it's not true.

And for those with bipolar disorder, research carried out in 2005 by Dr Dominic Lam and colleagues at the Institute of Psychiatry showed that CBT helps prevent relapse, when used alongside mood stabilizing drugs. The study recruited 103 people with a Bipolar I diagnosis who had frequent relapses, and split them into two groups – half were given CBT treatment as well as medication, and the other half (the control group) received only medication and no CBT. Comparing the two groups over the following 30 month period, results showed that:

- Only 44% of the CBT group experienced a relapse, compared with a 75% relapse rate of the control group.

- The group receiving CBT spent an average of only 27 days experiencing a bipolar episode, compared with 88 days for the non-CBT control group.

- Only 15% of the patients receiving CBT were hospitalized, compared with 33% in the control group, who did not receive CBT.

Research by Professor Jan Scott at the Institute of Psychiatry and Mary Taachi at the University of Newcastle has also shown that a shortened form of CBT can improve patients' regularity in taking lithium.

As well as the clinical research, there's also a lot of anecdotal evidence around to show that CBT is a good treatment for bipolar disorder:

> I've had a lot of CBT. It definitely works – and really it's the only thing that's ever worked for me.
>
> (Sharron)

> The CBT has really worked for me, but it's been a very long process. I've been trying to undo 20 years of learned behaviour.
>
> (Lesley)

> I started a course of CBT when I was in hospital for about nine weeks in 2001. It was on a weekly basis for about 50 sessions and I learnt a lot. I can identify the triggers much better.
>
> (Tamara)

So how does CBT actually work? For someone with bipolar disorder, the first stage of CBT is a short period of what's called 'psycho-education', giving them information on the cause, diagnosis, symptoms and treatment to help them get a real understanding of their illness.

This is followed by an extended period when someone records activities, behaviour and mood fluctuations in a 'mood diary'. This charts the impact of activities on mood, highlighting those that may trigger a mood swing. Another goal, as Professor Steven Jones explains, is to challenge the common trait in people with bipolar to identify personally with their internal experiences and not look for external reasons or activities as to why they may feel or react in a particular way: 'People within the bipolar spectrum seem to be more likely to explain how they are feeling as being to do with something about themselves, rather than something to do with what's going on in their environment. If a person is feeling slightly energized or more alert or aroused than usual, the tendency would be more to think, "I've got more energy, this is the real me", rather than to think, "Maybe I've had a bit too much coffee" or "I didn't sleep so well last night" or that there's some event coming up which is stimulating their interest. People come in and say, "I feel awful, it's come out of the blue, I've no idea why, this proves I've got no control over what's going on for me". And then you look back over their diary for the previous week and the person has been dealing with all sorts of significant and major challenges. Making those links with the person over time can help them detect these patterns earlier, and then they can take steps to deal with those.'

Another huge part of CBT for someone with bipolar is to detect early warning signs for the mood swings. 'What we try and do is to work quite hard to identify what we call early, middle and late signs, and recognize the early ones as early as possible,' says Professor Steven Jones.

So, before a depressive episode, the early warning signs might include:

- lack of energy
- insufficient/interrupted sleep
- feelings of anxiety
- negative thoughts
- low motivation/can't do routine tasks
- withdrawing from social/enjoyable activities
- less interest in food and sex.

And the early warning signs leading up to a manic period might include:

- the need for less sleep
- thoughts starting to race
- irritability
- heightened sense of self-worth
- feeling overexcited and restless

- 'goal directed' activities, often impulsive, such as chopping down all the trees in the front garden, applying for 20 new jobs in one week, suddenly redecorating the house
- overspending
- being more sociable than usual.

Yet not all early warning signs are the 'obvious' ones listed above. In fact, often they're very specific to each individual. When Amanda's mum Irene, for example, starts asking Amanda and her brother Andrew if they had a happy childhood, this is usually an early signal that a depressive mood swing is on the horizon. And when, in mid-conversation, Sarah's sister Rebecca starts casually referring to her plans to become a famous pop singer, this is a sure-fire sign that a manic episode is brewing. Other early warning signs can be just as random:

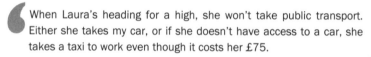 When Laura's heading for a high, she won't take public transport. Either she takes my car, or if she doesn't have access to a car, she takes a taxi to work even though it costs her £75.

(June)

When I'm starting to go manic, I start to think, 'Oh, I don't really have this illness, and I don't really need to take this medication'.

(Lesley)

I'm learning to recognize the early warning signs of a manic episode. I start to overbook gigs and take loads of work on and I'm out everywhere wanting to be sociable.

(Ashley)

So, once these early warning signs are spotted, what action does CBT encourage someone to take?

If the early warning signs point towards a looming depression, someone is advised to:

- take a positive goal-directed step, however small – for instance, sending an email or doing the washing up
- do something enjoyable – call a friend or go for a walk
- speak to a health professional, such as their doctor, psychiatrist or CPN
- take extra medication, as previously agreed with their doctor or psychiatrist.

If the early warning signs point towards impending mania, someone is advised to:

- reduce their daily task load
- engage in a calming activity, such as reading or soaking in the bath
- avoid stimulating activities
- take more breaks in the day
- ensure a good sleep routine
- take extra medication, as previously agreed with their doctor or psychiatrist.

Saying that, CBT certainly isn't a quick-fix option. Upward mood swings can sometimes kick in really quickly so there's very little time to spot the early warning signs. During this time, a person's insight can vanish and, of course, because going high can be so enjoyable, it's not unheard of for someone with bipolar to ignore the early warning signs even if they recognize them. But, as Professor Peter Kinderman explains, sensible protective steps can be taken beforehand to help combat this: 'Lack of insight is part of why CBT doesn't always work as well when people go high. The problems that you see with going high are often what the people themselves might not recognize as problems. Cognitive behavioural therapy is less easy then because you've got to persuade people to tell themselves to do something unpleasant – to not go out, not drink, not spend loads of cash, not go on eBay, all sorts of things that are really quite difficult for them to avoid doing. But it's not that difficult to set up a system beforehand where the person can protect themselves – so they could for instance phone up their bank and say, "Can you put a £100 limit on this credit card?" It's not difficult to do this when you're well, but it's very difficult to do this when you're high.'

Family focused therapy

Family focused therapy aims to foster good dialogue and improved communication within a family group, in this case the person with bipolar and their close family members. Educating family members in the causes, symptoms and treatment of bipolar, and encouraging more shared understanding of the condition, can lead each of them to understand the difficulties of others in relation to the illness, and help them all to develop coping skills and strategies to deal with the challenging situations the illness can create. Sarah and her mother, Rose, went to six family focused therapy sessions while Rebecca was in hospital in 2005:

Rebecca had been in hospital for nearly a year when we were offered family therapy once a week. Mum was worrying about how Rebecca would cope after having been in hospital for so long, and we were both concerned about what the future might hold for her. We talked lots of things through – how much we loved Rebecca, yet how frustrating we found her to live with and how difficult we found it to accept some of her life choices. Perhaps the most useful thing of all was that the therapist helped us see that while we continued to treat Rebecca as a child we weren't allowing her to grow up. We learnt that it was important for her to be allowed to make her own mistakes, as only then could she learn from them. And ultimately we learnt that however much we loved her and wanted to rescue her, we weren't responsible for her decisions. The idea was that Rebecca would join us for sessions after she left hospital, but she found the first one overwhelming and we all stopped going. It was a shame, but the timing obviously wasn't right for her. And even though Mum and I only had six sessions, it was really useful and tangibly changed our relationships with Rebecca, as we both took a step back and tried to treat her like an adult. It's no coincidence that Rebecca moved into her own flat a few months later.

Counselling

Here the patient talks about the difficulties and issues caused by their bipolar disorder to a counsellor, who listens supportively and helps the patient to acknowledge and accept the illness. Sometimes the counsellor is able to give practical advice and suggestions for ways of dealing with these challenges, but his or her main role is to listen. Bear in mind that anyone can call themselves a counsellor, which means that qualifications, training levels and experience can vary considerably.

Group therapy

People diagnosed with the same condition, such as bipolar disorder, can be invited to take part in group therapy sessions, which allow people to share the experiences of others with the same problems and realize that their experiences aren't unique. Mutual support and understanding, and the sharing of coping strategies, can also be very beneficial to group therapy members.

Q28. How can someone with bipolar disorder get psychological treatment?

Anyone with enough funds or private health insurance can seek private treatment from a clinical psychologist or professional counsellor. To find a good one, either get a list of suggestions from a GP, get a personal recommendation, or go via a professional body, such as the British Association of Counselling and Psychotherapy (www.bacp.co.uk, 0870 443 5252) or the British Association of Behavioural and Cognitive Psychotherapists (www.babcp.com, 0161 797 4484).

Alternatively, anyone diagnosed with bipolar disorder can ask their GP or their community mental health team (CMHT) for a free referral to a clinical psychologist. But, as with many health care services, the national availability of psychological treatment through the NHS is patchy. On the one hand, a report published in May 2007 shows the UK government acknowledges the value of psychological approaches for mental illness. On the other, the report *We Need to Talk* (produced by a joint project between the UK charities Mind, Rethink, the Mental Health Foundation, Young Minds, and the Sainsbury Centre for Mental Health) highlights that despite the government's good intentions and the NICE recommendations for more psychological treatments to treat mental illnesses, availability is still far from adequate. It says: 'It takes an average of six to nine months to receive psychological therapies, and waiting lists of up to two years are not uncommon. Waiting times of up to a year for assessment and two years for treatment have also been reported. One in four primary care organizations do not offer CBT.'

Dr Sara Tai, Lecturer in Clinical Psychology at Manchester University, agrees that it's nowhere near as easy to get psychological help as it should be: 'Currently, it's random around the country how many psychologists each trust employs. One trust near where I live doesn't have any psychologists at all. It cannot be possible that in a whole geographical area there are no patients with psychological needs or people who have problems that are 100% biological. Even where there are psychologists, there aren't enough. In the team I work in, there are six psychiatrists and one psychologist – part-time. That's the typical model of mental health care.'

This is a huge shame because evidence shows that the longer the wait between someone developing bipolar and receiving psychological treatment, the less effective the treatment is.

But at least there are encouraging signs of change on the horizon ... In October 2007, the UK government agreed to increase funding for psychological therapy, announcing that £170 million would be made available by 2010/11, with a target of 3,600 newly trained psychological therapists. Let's hope this investment will eventually widen choices, reduce waiting times and improve prognosis for anyone diagnosed with bipolar disorder in the not-too-distant future.

Online CBT

Computerised cognitive behavioural therapy (CCBT) can also be helpful, especially if face-to-face CBT is not easily available. Moodgym is an interactive online CCBT programme, designed for those with depression and run by the Australian National University in Canberra. According to its website, it aims 'to help users develop good coping skills in order to enjoy good mental health'. Registering for the programme is free at www.moodgym.anu.edu.au.

In the UK, an online CCBT programme has been developed for the treatment of mild to moderate depression by the Department of Health's *Improving Access to Psychological Treatments* programme. Called 'Beating the Blues', this CCBT package includes a 15-minute introductory video and eight interactive computer sessions, produces weekly progress reports (covering anxiety and depression ratings, and suicidal tendencies) which can be sent to the GP or other healthcare professionals. The programme is also available on CD ROM. (Another CCBT programme entitled 'Fear Fighter' has also been developed along the same lines, but for tackling panic, anxiety and phobia.)

Backing for the CCBT programmes has come right from the top – in November 2006, Professor Louis Appleby, the National Director for Mental Health (also known as the Mental Health Tsar) informed the chief executives of all health trusts that the recommended CCBT programmes should have been made available in every trust by 31 March 2007. Ask a member of the local CMHT for more information, or visit www.dh.gov.uk and search the site for 'Beating the Blues'.

Too many drugs, not enough psychology?

The frustrating thing about the poor availability of psychological treatment is that people with bipolar disorder and other mental illnesses are more likely to be prescribed drugs first, or even instead of, psychological therapies. In 2006, a record high of more than 31 million prescriptions for antidepressants were issued in the UK (a 6% rise from the previous year) – and some doctors may have prescribed these reluctantly, as the following section from the *We Need to Talk* report shows: 'According to an online survey by the

Mental Health Foundation, only 42% of people visiting their GP with depression were offered counselling by their doctor, although 82% would have been willing to try it. Another survey found that many doctors believe that they under-prescribe psychological therapies. Over half (55%) of GPs believe that talking treatments are the most effective way to treat mild or moderate depression, yet 78% have prescribed an antidepressant while believing an alternative would have been preferable.'

The result is that overmedication is a real risk for people with mental health conditions, including children. In July 2007, research revealed that the number of prescriptions given to children under 16 in England for depression and other mental illnesses had quadrupled in a decade – 631,000 prescriptions were written for children in the previous year, compared with 146,000 in the mid-1990s. There's some debate on how much the rate of childhood mental illness has actually gone up in recent years, but there's no evidence at all that it has risen four-fold. Dr Sara Tai, at Manchester University, sums up the situation like this: 'Our health service is heavily weighted towards psychiatry, rather than psychological interventions. It's the same in America. Did you know that drug companies in the US spend $11 billion a year on free gifts for medics? ... Of course drugs can help. But that shouldn't necessarily be considered as the first line of treatment. Whereas our whole system is pushed by diagnosis, particularly when you look at psychiatry, we should be treating the person not the condition. That's where medication really falls down – it treats the condition, the syndrome, the disorder, not the individual. Some of the people I work with learn to change their social factors or lifestyle and feel considerably better – no pill in the world is going to do that.'

That's not to say psychological intervention needs to be given instead of medication, but as collective expert opinion generally agrees, alongside it.

We like the way John McManamy, a writer with bipolar disorder, puts it on his excellent website (which is packed with up-to-the-minute research about the condition), www.mcmanweb.com: 'Clearly two therapies (medication and psychotherapy) together represent one of those rare cases where one plus one equals three.'

In other words, when it comes to treating bipolar disorder, medication alone is useful, psychological therapy alone is useful, but medication *plus* therapy is the most powerful solution of all.

Q29. What drugs are used in the treatment of bipolar disorder?

Most people diagnosed with bipolar disorder are automatically given a prescription for medication to help stabilize mood. And, it seems, there are a million and one different drug combinations a psychiatrist can choose from, depending on a number of factors, such as an individual's symptoms and previous mood patterns. The trouble is, a drug that works brilliantly for one person may not work for someone else, even if on the surface their symptoms appear to be similar. Or, side effects caused by a medication may be terrible for one person and non-existent for another. Often a number of drugs need to be taken at the same time, and some drugs can interact with each other. Finding the right combination is challenging, as Professor Guy Goodwin, W A Handley Chair of Psychiatry at Oxford University, explains: 'The medicines primarily used to treat bipolar disorder have been studied under the controlled conditions of clinical trials. They have been shown to be effective at a particular dose in the majority of patients, and to produce negative effects (or not to work) in a minority of others. So when you prescribe any medicine to someone, all you know as a doctor is its average predictable effects. For the patient this seems like trial and error, which it is, but the advantage of the trials done to establish the drug mean that the odds of it working are quite favourable. Dosing is difficult because the human liver (and gut) is a wonderfully variable thing and the level of any drug in the blood varies ten-fold for any dose given by mouth. Indeed, the different ways a drug is metabolized in the body will contribute to different responses to the same dose. In an individual patient, it's wise to start with a low dose, go slowly, but build up to the highest well tolerated dose possible. That way you should always be giving enough, but not every doctor or patient seems to have the patience to follow that principle.'

Broadly speaking, there are four main types of medication for treating the symptoms of bipolar disorder:

- mood stabilizers (also sometimes called antimanics), which aim to treat both the highs and the lows
- antipsychotic drugs (also sometimes called neuroleptics), which are mainly used to bring mood down from the highs of hypomania, mania or psychosis
- antidepressant drugs to lift mood out of depressive mood swings
- sleeping pills and anti anxiety drugs, such as benzodiazepines.

The tables on the following pages provide a round-up of these four groups. Generic names are given first, with popular brand names in brackets. Potential benefits and drawbacks are also listed, but these are by no means exhaustive – for a more detailed explanation of the uses and side effects of each drug, refer directly to the drug manufacturers' leaflet or speak to a psychiatrist, psychiatric pharmacist or GP. Some of the bigger mental health charities, such as Mind and MDF The BiPolar Organisation, also provide useful information about medication (see Extra resources, pp. 251–3).

Mood stabilizing/antimanic drugs

Lithium is probably the most well known and widely used of the mood stabilizing drugs. It can successfully treat mood swings without acting as a sedative, and has also been proved to reduce the risk of suicide.

- Lithium is a naturally occurring salt, so should only be used for anyone with a history of heart, thyroid, epilepsy or kidney problems after a careful specialist review of the risks and benefits.
- Family history may help decide if lithium can be prescribed – there's evidence that the response to lithium may be similar between family members, so if it works well for one family member with bipolar disorder, it may work well for another.
- Baseline and six monthly renal (kidney) tests are recommended.

Table 1 MOOD STABILIZING/ANTIMANIC DRUGS

Generic name (& common brand name)	Potential benefits	Potential drawbacks
Lithium carbonate (Priadel, Camcolit, Liskonum, Lithonate) Lithium citrate (Litarex)	Reduces frequency of cycles Antidepressant effect Reduces suicide risk Can be taken long term	Kidney problems Hypothyroidism Increases need to urinate Thirst & dry mouth Tiredness Stomach problems Blurred vision Rashes Muscle tremor
Carbamazepine (Tegretol)	Effective against rapid cycling Can be taken long term Effective for people who can't take or don't respond to lithium	Nausea Dizziness Drowsiness Skin rashes Headaches
Sodium valproate (Epilim) Valproate semisodium (Divalproex, Depakote)	Effective against rapid cycling Can be taken long term Greater range between beneficial and toxic levels than lithium	Weight gain Drowsiness Nausea Shaking Unsteadiness Risk of liver damage
Lamotrigine (Lamictal) (not yet licensed in the UK for treating bipolar disorder)	Reduces low mood swings Good for tackling long term depressive symptoms	Skin rashes Headache & fever Double vision Dizziness Nausea Stomach problems

- Someone taking lithium should also have frequent and regular blood tests (usually every three months). Lithium levels must be monitored very closely because there is a very narrow range between beneficial and toxic levels.

- Levels of lithium in the blood can rise if someone becomes dehydrated.

- Lithium should only be used in early pregnancy after a careful specialist review of the risks and benefits.

- Anyone wanting to come off lithium should not do so suddenly (as the risk of relapse is very high) but gradually, in consultation with their doctor or psychiatrist.

- Regular blood tests are also recommended for people taking carbamazepine.

- Someone taking valproate needs to have regular liver function tests.

Taking lithium? Take note ...

Before anyone starts taking lithium, they should have a blood test to monitor their thyroid function, followed by a thyroid function test every six months. This is because the drug can cause hypothyroidism – a condition where the thyroid gland doesn't produce enough of the hormone thyroxine, which controls the way the body uses energy. Symptoms of hypothyroidism can include slow body movements and speech, tiredness, weakness, poor concentration and memory problems. It can also increase the risk of depression, causing further complications for someone who already has bipolar disorder.

The risk of developing hypothyroidism when taking lithium is fairly high – one research study tracked a group of 713 people who took the drug over a 15 month period, and found that over 10% developed the condition. Women were at greater risk than men – 14% of the female participants developed hypothyroidism compared with only 4.5% of the men, and for women aged between 40 and 59, the figure was 20%.

Amanda's mum Irene's experience is typical of these results:

 Two years after starting on lithium, my mum developed new symptoms – she felt continually exhausted, had difficulty concentrating and her movements and speech became more sluggish. At first we thought it was the side effects of other medication, but a blood test for thyroid function eventually diagnosed hypothyroidism. Since then she has taken thyroxine drugs daily, and probably will for the rest of her life, as hypothyroidism is a chronic condition. So on the one hand, lithium can create extra problems. But, on the other, the risk of hypothyroidism has to be weighed up against the potential positive effects of lithium – Mum took lithium for a number of years and during that time it worked well for her. And for some people, lithium is literally a life saver.

Table 2 ANTIPSYCHOTIC DRUGS/NEUROLEPTICS

Generic name (& common brand name)	Potential benefits	Potential drawbacks
Haloperidol (Dozic, Serenace, Haldol)	Lowers mood May reduce cycling	Neuromuscular effects (uncontrollable movements) Drowsiness Dry mouth Weight gain
Chlorpromazine (Largactil)	Lowers mood May reduce cycling	Neuromuscular effects (uncontrollable movements) Drowsiness Weight gain Dry mouth Blurred vision Dizziness Constipation Nausea

Olanzapine (Zyprexa) [atypical]	May reduce cycling Also has antimanic effect Good for treating moderate to severe mania	Drowsiness Dry mouth Weight gain Oedema (puffy feet and hands) Low blood pressure Blood sugar levels raised/decreased Sensitivity to sunlight
Quetiapine (Seroquel) [atypical]	May reduce cycling Also has antimanic effect	Drowsiness Dizziness Dry mouth Weight gain Changes to heart rhythm Possible cataract risk
Risperidone (Risperdal) [atypical]	May reduce cycling Fewer neuromuscular side effects than other antipsychotics Also has antimanic effect	Weight gain Increased levels of the hormone prolactin (can cause breast enlargement, lactation and menstrual problems)
Clozapine (Clozaril, Denzapine, Zaponex, Leponex) [atypical]	Effective for persistent mania and psychosis Fewer neuromuscular side effects than other antipsychotics	Low blood pressure Risk of reduction in white blood cells Dizziness Drowsiness Increased or irregular heart rate Weight gain Blurred vision Dry mouth Headaches

Antipsychotics/neuroleptics

- Antipsychotics are divided into two groups – older (or 'typical') antipsychotics such as haloperidol and chlorpromazine, and the new generation of antipsychotics (more commonly known as 'atypical') such as olanzapine, quetiapine, risperidone and clozapine.

- Most atypicals have fewer side effects overall, and are usually the first choice, although the older antipsychotics are better for people who can't take or don't respond well to the typical antipsychotics.

- Clozapine runs a 3% risk of causing a reduction in white blood cells, so weekly blood tests are usually recommended for the first 18 weeks of treatment and fortnightly after that.

- Both typicals and atypicals can encourage weight gain, with a risk of developing type 2 diabetes, though this is more common with the newer atypical drugs.

- A rare but potentially life threatening side effect of neuroleptic/antipsychotic drugs is neuroleptic malignant syndrome, or NMS. Symptoms usually appear within two weeks of starting treatment and include high fever, sweating, muscular rigidity, unstable blood pressure and delirium.

Antidepressants

- SSRIs are the most commonly used type of antidepressant in the UK and are simple to take (usually as one daily dose).

- Risk of overdose from SSRIs is low.

- SSRIs should not be stopped abruptly, as there's a risk of relapse and unpleasant withdrawal symptoms.

- Concerns have been raised by some experts that SSRIs could increase the risk of suicide for anyone under the age of 18.

- Tricyclic antidepressants and venlafaxine may be effective for resistant depression.

Table 3 ANTIDEPRESSANTS

Generic name (& common brand name)	Potential benefits	Potential drawbacks
Selective Serotonin Reuptake Inhibitors (SSRIs)		
Paroxetine (Seroxat) Sertraline (Lustral, Zoloft) Citalopram (Cipramil) Fluvoxamine (Faverin, Luvox)	Antidepressant Anti anxiety Less likely to cause manic switch than tricyclics	Agitation Nausea Decrease in libido (sex drive) Can increase the effect of alcohol
Other types of antidepressants		
Venlafaxine (Effexor)	Antidepressant Less likely to cause manic switch than tricyclics	Headaches Nausea Insomnia Decrease in libido (sex drive) Anxiety High doses can cause high blood pressure
Mirtazapine (Zispin, Remeron)	As above	Drowsiness Increased appetite Weight gain Dizziness
Reboxetine (Edronax)	As above	Dry mouth Constipation Insomnia Increased sweating Vertigo Urinary problems

Generic name (& common brand name)	Potential benefits	Potential drawbacks
Trazodone (Molipaxin, Desyrel)	As above	Headaches Dizziness Drowsiness Nausea Weakness Weight loss Dry mouth Constipation Diarrhoea Hypertension Blurred vision

Tricyclic antidepressants

Amitriptyline (Tryptizol, Elavil) Clomipramine (Anafranil) Imipramine (Tofranil) Lofepramine (Gamanil) Doxepin (Sinequan, Adapin) Protriptyline (Concordin, Vivactil)	Good for resistant depression	Can trigger mania Dry mouth Blurred vision Constipation Drowsiness Dizziness Nausea Tiredness Weight gain Headache Can increase the effect of alcohol

- Caution is needed when prescribing antidepressants if treating someone with bipolar disorder, as occasionally these can trigger a switch into mania. To prevent this, mood stabilizers should be prescribed at the same time. See question 30, p. 83 for more information.

Table 4 BENZODIAZEPINES/ANTI ANXIETY DRUGS/SLEEPING PILLS
(sometimes also called 'benzos' or tranquillizers)

Generic name (& common brand name)	Potential benefits	Potential drawbacks
Diazepam (Valium)	Reduce anxiety	Over sedation
Lorazepam (Ativan)	Aid sleeping	Slowness of thought
Clonazepam (Klonopin, Rivotril)	Can also reduce mania	Confusion Light-headedness
Oxazepam (Serax, Serenid, Alepam)		Risk of dependence or addiction
Zopiclone (Zimovane)		Dangerous if combined with too much alcohol

Benzodiazepines/anti anxiety drugs

- These drugs are usually only prescribed in the short term, as dependence can develop very quickly.
- Driving and operating machinery is not recommended, as the effects from taking a drug the night before can continue into the next day.
- Occasionally, these drugs can cause aggression.

Q30. What does someone with bipolar disorder (or someone with a family history of bipolar disorder) need to know about antidepressants?

Antidepressants treat the symptoms of depression. Most research on anti-depressants has been done in people with unipolar depression (people who have never had a manic episode). Little research has been carried out on the use of antidepressants for people with bipolar disorder. What is known is that taking antidepressants without a mood stabilizer may trigger mania and/or worsen the course of bipolar illness. So it's extremely important that someone with bipolar disorder doesn't take antidepressants alone, but together with mood stabilizing medication. This also means that anyone with a family history of bipolar disorder going through a depressive episode is unwise to take antidepressants without a mood stabilizer. Why? Because of their genetic susceptibility, there's a chance their low mood could be 'bipolar in waiting' and that taking antidepressants could trigger a full-blown manic episode. Unbelievably, though, regardless of family history, this is an all-too-common occurrence, as Amanda recalls:

> When Mum had her first breakdown, she was diagnosed with depression and given a course of antidepressants – even though she was treated in the very same psychiatric hospital where her brother Jim (Sarah's dad) had been sectioned with bipolar only a few years earlier. Her family history just wasn't considered, which seems an incredible oversight. Within weeks of starting on the anti-depressants, her first manic episode struck, and knowing what we know now, the link seems so obvious. Would Mum have developed bipolar without the trigger of antidepressants? It's impossible to say. We'll never know. What we do know is that the manic switch she experienced after taking the anti-depressants was fast, out of control and terrifying for her to experience and for us to witness.

Sarah – in spite of the fact that her father, sister and aunt have had diagnoses of bipolar disorder – was offered antidepressants in 2002.

> About a year after I'd had my second son, I found that I was completely physically and emotionally exhausted. I wasn't sleeping or eating properly. I cried a lot. My GP referred me to a psychiatrist who diagnosed post-natal depression and prescribed antidepressants. Luckily I didn't ever get the pills because the turning point came for me when I finally admitted to myself that I needed to ask for help. I got through my low patch with extra sleep, good food and lots of support from family and friends. I did keep the prescription for a while, though, in case my mood slipped down again. I didn't have a clue that taking

antidepressants, with my family's medical history, could have triggered mania. Of course I'll never know what would have happened, but I think it's shocking that I was given them without my genetic family tree entering into the equation.

The really important point here is that anyone who has a family member with bipolar disorder and who is seeing their GP because they're feeling depressed needs to emphasize their family background so that it can be taken into account if any medication is prescribed.

Q31. Does someone with bipolar disorder need to take medication for the rest of his or her life?

Few people like the idea of taking medication, especially in the long term. It's a reminder of being ill, and the side effects may be unpleasant. When first diagnosed with bipolar disorder, Amanda's mum, Irene, did not want to take pills indefinitely, as Amanda explains:

 For Mum, the pills were a hated symbol of the illness. So for a couple of years, she waged a secret war against medication, by trying to cut down on the doses – skipping a morning pill, taking one tablet instead of two, sometimes flushing the whole daily dose down the toilet – in the belief that the less tablets she swallowed, the less ill she must be. Inevitably, this led to more mood swings and hospital stays. Eventually Mum came to acknowledge the need for long-term medication and these days she'll even take her pills in front of us, instead of hiding them, although she's always keen to ask the psychiatrist if any can be reduced. I do understand that it's been a hard road for her to accept this, especially as the medication won't prevent every mood swing, so she still experiences several mixed state or depressive episodes a year. And she's from a generation for whom being 'on pills' was, sadly, regarded as shameful. But she does now see that without any drugs, her illness would disrupt her life to an even greater degree. Despite the drawbacks, 'managed' well is still a better alternative.

The other problem can be that when the drugs are working and someone is feeling well, they can think, 'I'm feeling fine now – so that must mean I don't need these drugs any more!'

David was medicated, and within two weeks he was a lot better, but then he decided it was nothing to do with the medication and got rid of it all. He was medicated probably about 12 times, and every single time he would only take the medication for about two weeks.

(Paula)

The reality usually is, though, that feeling fine means that the drugs are controlling the symptoms, not that the illness has vanished. Also, if the drug treatment that's causing a patient to stay well is stopped suddenly, they are more likely to feel worse and suffer a relapse. A sudden break in medication can also trigger very unpleasant withdrawal side effects.

The key to good mental health in the long term, then, is acceptance. As someone with diabetes accepts that they have to take insulin every day for the rest of their life, someone with bipolar disorder is wise to do the same.

I would say compliance is key, in terms of taking the drugs and following appointments, because I think mental health professionals listen better to you when you're compliant than when you're not, and I think you can play the game … If you take the drugs and it doesn't work out, and they have the confidence that you are taking them, then I think you come from a position of power.

(Neil)

That's not to suggest that people should just automatically agree to take drugs they're prescribed without question or discussion. In an ideal world, new medication (or changes to existing medication) needs to be agreed between the patient and their prescribing doctor or psychiatrist together. Useful points to discuss include:

- which symptoms need managing
- whether there's an alternative to taking the drug (e.g. psychological therapy)
- what benefits the new medication may provide
- any possible side effects
- how new drugs may interact with other drugs already being taken
- how long the medication is being prescribed for
- when the drugs schedule will be reviewed again.

This means the patient can make an informed decision to accept (or refuse) treatment. It is worth bearing in mind, though, that someone who persistently refuses to take prescribed medication and becomes a risk to themselves or others could be sectioned into hospital (see Chapter 4) so that doctors can treat them against their will.

If someone with bipolar (or a member of their family) has a concern about any aspect of their medication, they should discuss it first with their doctor or psychiatrist, or seek the opinion of a psychiatric pharmacist.

Some of the mental health charities offer information on psychiatric drugs – see the Extra resources section, p. 248 for their contact details.

Forgetting to take medication

Another potential problem is forgetting to take medication. In the best-case scenario, everyone follows the dispensing instructions to the letter and takes the right doses at the right times. But, of course, everyone's human and mistakes are made, particularly when someone is unwell. If medication has been forgotten, it's essential not to panic and/or take a double dose. Speak to a doctor or pharmacist as soon as possible about what action to take – it may depend on the type of drug being prescribed. Lithium in particular should *not* be taken as a double dose.

If forgetting to take medication happens regularly, the best thing is to be prepared – when a prescription is dispensed, ask a pharmacist for their advice on what to do if doses are missed. Practical measures can be taken to back this up. Why not try:

- pinning a medication chart up on the wall, with drugs labelled into daily doses
- linking a medication schedule with other routine daily tasks – making the first cup of tea of the morning, or cleaning teeth at bedtime, for example
- getting a plastic pill container with sections divided into days of the week and times of the day, so that it's easy to see what needs to be taken when.

Q32. Will drugs encourage weight gain?

There's plenty of evidence to show that some of the drugs prescribed for bipolar disorder do cause weight gain. Sarah's sister Rebecca has gone from a skinny size 10 to a size 16 since being diagnosed with bipolar disorder ten years ago – and she's not alone, although some doctors can be keen to play this down:

> I've always done loads of sport, and yet I put on three stone in weight, which made all my self-confidence just fall away. I'm only 5 ft 4, and that's a huge amount to put on. And people don't look at you and say, 'Oh, you've got an illness, and the drugs are making you fat', people just think all those horrible things that are associated with weight ... you know, like a slovenly attitude. You're just so bloated the whole time, and you see that they are judging you on that, and it becomes another issue in itself. And doctors won't acknowledge that drugs can cause weight gain either. They'll just say, 'It must be you', or they'll sometimes talk about 'slight' weight gain. But that's just rubbish.
>
> (Tamara)

But according to Ian Maidment, Senior Pharmacist, Kent & Medway Partnership NHS Trust, and Senior Lecturer, Kent Institute of Medicine and Health Studies, Kent University, honesty is the best policy: 'Some of the new antipsychotics in particular do appear to cause weight gain. And the way I explain it is that they affect part of the brain which controls what we eat. And so these drugs make people think, "I want chocolate and I want it now." It's a real drive to eat more food, and it's really hard to over-ride. So weight gain may be a problem ... The important thing for people is that they are aware of the side effects, so it's not unexpected. When I speak to people, I like to be totally honest and say, "This is what may happen – this is what the evidence suggests", because if I was on a drug, I would want to know exactly what the side effects may be.'

The obvious solution (eat less, exercise more) is easier said than done, but is possible, particularly if it's not too late for the 'prevention' rather than 'cure' approach. If it's too late for prevention, the NICE guideline for the treatment of bipolar states that if a patient gains weight when receiving drug treatment, mental healthcare professionals should:

1. Review the patient's medication.

2. Consider:

    *   giving dietary advice
    *   advising regular aerobic exercise
    *   referring the patient to weight management programmes in mental health services
    *   referring the patient to a dietician.

Q33. How can someone with bipolar self manage their treatment?

'Self management' is not an alternative to drug or psychological treatments for bipolar disorder, but a way of gaining more control over the illness. Many of its underlying principles are similar to those used in psychological therapies, such as CBT. As Jeremy Bacon, Groups and Self Management Director for MDF The BiPolar Organisation (the UK's leading bipolar disorder charity) explains: 'It's about using those times when you are well to prepare for those times when you're less well, such as looking for warning signs that people (from past experience) can identify as potential triggers for setting off episodes. The idea of self management isn't to say, "this will cure you" – the idea is learning more about your bipolar individually, how it affects you and what can set you off, and being aware of your warning signs.'

MDF The BiPolar Organisation runs three-day self management training courses in different locations across the UK, led by trained facilitators who themselves have been diagnosed with bipolar. Open to anyone who has a diagnosis of bipolar disorder, the only other criteria for taking a place on the course is being a member of the charity. Joining the MDF is easy and inexpensive (with a reduced rate for unwaged members), and as well as a means of accessing the self management courses, is in itself a positive step towards learning more about bipolar disorder and taking control of the illness (see Extra resources, pp. 251–2 for their contact details).

So what can attending an MDF self management course offer? Jeremy Bacon explains: 'It's giving people three days when they can take time out, and bring into focus how this condition has affected them individually. It's not a three day lecture on bipolar. It's very group based, with a lot of interactivity. And it all comes together at the end, so people have a clear understanding of their bipolar, their triggers, their warning signs, their support networks, and what they can do to minimize the risk of relapse, but also what they can do, in terms of an action plan, if things start to go wrong. It's providing people with a platform so that they can empower themselves.'

The content can vary depending on the facilitators, the participants and the latest developments in the bipolar world, but the course is usually made up of six modules, which loosely cover:

1. The principles of self management, and also the aims and objectives of the course

The opening session often includes a discussion about personal expectations of the participants, and the nature and impact of bipolar disorder.

2. Triggers for episodes of illness, and also the warning signs that can precede these episodes

This module often covers common triggers and how they are very individual to each person. This is the essential key to self management – people learning to recognize their individual triggers for illness and also the early warning signs of illness that these triggers may prompt. The earlier that signs can be recognized, the greater the chance for intervention to prevent a full-blown relapse into illness.

3. Coping strategies and self medication

During this session, participants often discuss what coping strategies can be used in response to the warning signs and why they can be very effective in preventing relapse, as outlined in question 27, p. 61 (on cognitive behavioural therapy, which uses similar principles).

This aspect of self management is backed up by research – a study carried out by Dominic Lam and colleagues at the Institute of Psychiatry in 2001 looked at people who used coping strategies when manic warning signs started to appear. Only 12.5% of people eventually suffered a relapse into a full-blown manic episode, compared with 45.5% of people who didn't use these strategies.

4. Support networks and action plans

This session looks at how support networks can act as a safety net, how to use reliable people to spot early warning signs and how to apply coping strategies, or take further action if the coping strategies don't work. The network can include a number of people – for example, a partner or other close family member, a good friend, a CPN or a psychiatrist. It's then recommended that they are written into an action plan, which identifies what someone with bipolar should do if the coping strategies don't prevent a relapse.

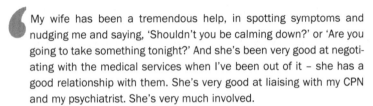

My wife has been a tremendous help, in spotting symptoms and nudging me and saying, 'Shouldn't you be calming down?' or 'Are you going to take something tonight?' And she's been very good at negotiating with the medical services when I've been out of it – she has a good relationship with them. She's very good at liaising with my CPN and my psychiatrist. She's very much involved.

(Keith)

5. Strategies for maintaining a healthy lifestyle and drawing up an advance directive

This session focuses on lifestyle choices that can influence mental health, because there is strong evidence that making healthier choices can help prevent bipolar relapse (see Chapter 5 for lots of information on diet, exercise, sleep, nutritional supplements, and avoiding stress, caffeine, alcohol, nicotine and recreational drugs).

There's also an explanation of how to draw up an advance directive – a legal document stating what treatment a person with bipolar does not want to receive in the future. (See question 39, p. 103 for more details.)

6. Complementary therapies and finalizing action plans

The final session looks at complementary therapies (such as, acupuncture, homeopathy, massage, meditation, reflexology, reiki and yoga) and how they can help someone with bipolar reduce the risk of relapse. (See question 65, p. 183 for more information.)

So does self management work?

Research carried out by MDF The BiPolar Organisation shows that people who have attended the self management courses say they:

- feel more positive about past experiences in their life
- feel more positive about themselves
- find their concentration has improved
- experience less suicidal thoughts.

The research also demonstrates that there tends to be a larger gap between relapses of both manic and depressive episodes.

Comments from participants include:

- 'I feel more in control of my psychiatrist – he found that my advance directive was the highest level of insight he had ever come across in a patient.'
- 'It's spring, I'm normally in hospital now.'
- 'Everyone had some constructive input to make, and it was wonderful to be able to draw upon the combined wealth of experience of the participants. There was a common purpose – to get well and keep well.'

Many people who have been on a self management course talk about how it was a positive turning point in their lives:

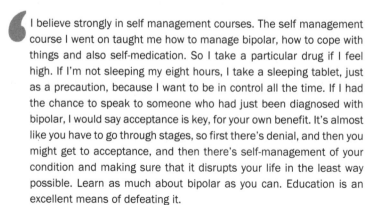

I believe strongly in self management courses. The self management course I went on taught me how to manage bipolar, how to cope with things and also self-medication. So I take a particular drug if I feel high. If I'm not sleeping my eight hours, I take a sleeping tablet, just as a precaution, because I want to be in control all the time. If I had the chance to speak to someone who had just been diagnosed with bipolar, I would say acceptance is key, for your own benefit. It's almost like you have to go through stages, so first there's denial, and then you might get to acceptance, and then there's self-management of your condition and making sure that it disrupts your life in the least way possible. Learn as much about bipolar as you can. Education is an excellent means of defeating it.

(Neil)

These positive personal testimonies are backed up by a 2007 report from the Cochrane Library (a collection of databases containing independent healthcare evidence), which reviewed 11 research studies into self management training for people with bipolar. Their review concluded that self management, in helping to identify early warning signs of bipolar episodes, had several beneficial effects – less frequent bipolar relapses, lower rates of hospitalization and better 'functioning' in normal life for those who took part in the training.

The NICE guideline for the treatment of bipolar also recognizes the importance of self management and directs mental health care professionals to advise patients on its usefulness. However, the challenge at the moment is finding enough course places to fill the need, as nationally the availability is, yet again, patchy. In the longer term, MDF The BiPolar Organisation is aiming to work closely with local health trusts and attract funding from them, hopefully increasing the number of courses, so that self management becomes a front line option for bipolar treatment as soon as people are diagnosed.

Also, the UK mental health charity Rethink has run a pilot scheme on self management, and is planning to make more self management resources available in the near future – visit www.rethink.org or see Extra resources, p. 254 for details.

Online self management

In the future, there may be the possibility of online self management, which at the time of writing is being researched and piloted at the Black Dog Institute in Sydney, Australia. The research study has participants logging into a mood monitoring programme every week to answer multi-choice questions about their mood – these answers generate 'scores' which are monitored by researchers, who pick up on worrying or suicidal signs and contact the participant's doctor if necessary. The aims of the programme are to help the participants to understand their mood swing triggers better, to develop coping strategies and to help them take their medication more regularly. The research project's lead investigator Dr Caryl Barnes says: 'Potentially, this type of online help can supplement traditional health care which is already stretched to meet community needs.'

For more information, visit www.blackdoginstitute.org.au (or go to Extra resources, p. 261).

Q34. What is electroconvulsive therapy (ECT)?

Electroconvulsive therapy (ECT) is a controversial treatment, to say the least. The phrase itself conjures up alarming images from the fifties and sixties of conscious and terrified patients tied to beds in dingy hospital rooms with live electrodes forcibly applied to their heads by doctors more intent on control (or even punishment) than effective treatment. Broken bones were not uncommon, as the electric currents could cause patients to thrash about, despite their restraints, and sometimes more than 100 ECT treatments could be administered to one person, causing severe memory loss and speech impairment.

Thankfully, the reality of modern ECT is rather different. Perhaps most importantly of all, a patient is treated in an operating theatre and is unconscious under a general anaesthetic. 'Paddles' containing electrodes are placed on the scalp, and instead of the steady stream of electricity that used to be given, modern ECT uses a high frequency electrical pulse, which stimulates the brain to induce an epileptic seizure, or 'fit'. It's not fully understood how or why inducing a seizure can help stabilize mood, but it's thought that it somehow boosts the chemicals used by nerve endings in the brain to communicate with each other.

Because the patient has usually been given a muscle relaxant too, there is no thrashing of limbs or broken bones – at most just a mild twitch shows when the electrical pulse is passing through the brain. The procedure lasts for under a minute and a course is typically between six and 12 treatments over a two-week period. Such is the 'respectability' of modern-day ECT that it's now recommended in the NICE guideline for the treatment of bipolar. However, the guideline does state that it should only be used for severe and prolonged mania/psychosis or for severe depression, when other treatment may have failed – so ECT is far from being a routine treatment for most people with bipolar symptoms. And despite the changes in how it's administered in the twenty-first century, there are still divided opinions on its use and effectiveness. A survey by UK charity Mind, which looked at 418 questionnaires from people who had previously received ECT treatment, reported that:

- 40% of respondents complained of permanent memory loss and 36% of difficulty in concentrating.
- 73% of respondents felt they had not been given any information about side-effects.
- 43% of respondents felt the treatment was 'unhelpful, damaging or severely damaging'.
- 66% would not agree to ECT treatment in the future.

Other reported side effects from ECT include headaches, nausea, aching muscles and feeling confused and distressed for some hours afterwards. It's worth remembering, though, that the Mind survey was largely based on less recent experience – only one-third of the respondents in the survey had received ECT in the last five years. And, as Mind itself acknowledges, ECT does work extremely well for some people, relieving their symptoms when all else has failed. And there are many personal stories testifying that ECT can be extremely effective:

 Four lots of ECT treatment pulled me out of depression very quickly after only one week. There's a lot of misunderstanding around, but it really helped me. The only thing is that you get buzzy for two minutes when you come round. And the only memory loss I had was about what had happened in hospital – but that wasn't a bad thing. There were no headaches, no significant memory loss and no other effects at all. As far as I'm concerned, the whole experience of ECT is totally trivial ... Having ECT is no less disconcerting than having a filling. The actual thing itself a non-event. Of course, years ago there were no anaesthetics or muscle relaxants as there are today – that's why there's so much misunderstanding surrounding the subject. But it's just not like that now. Forget the usual media rubbish. ECT definitely works on depression. My consultant psychiatrist told me that it's saved many lives. I think it's saved mine!

(Richard)

In 2005, junior doctor and *Daily Telegraph* columnist Max Pemberton told his readers how he had refused to participate in giving a patient ECT, but two years later wrote: 'I was surprised by the amount of correspondence the column generated. What surprised me most was what the letters said. Certainly there were a few condemning the practice, but I was overwhelmed by letters from people wanting to tell me how ECT had helped them, how it had saved them when they were in the quagmire of despair and all other treatments had failed.'

It would seem that ECT provokes a black and white response – and that those for whom it works are fervent supporters. The bottom line for anyone being offered ECT (or for their family) is to ask for as much information as possible, so they can weigh up the risk of side effects against the potential benefits. Then they can make an informed choice based on their own individual circumstances. If someone decides that they don't want to receive ECT in the future, when they may not be able to make their wishes clearly known, the sensible step would be to declare this wish in an advance directive (see question 39, p. 103).

In the UK, the Mental Health Act 2007 introduced new safeguards for the use of ECT – the treatment may not be given to a patient who has the mental capacity to refuse consent (except in an emergency). ECT can only be given to a patient without mental capacity to give or refuse consent if this is not in conflict with an advance directive – i.e. if the patient has not specified beforehand that they don't want to receive this treatment.

The Act also states that a second opinion from another doctor has to be obtained before ECT treatment can be administered to patients under 18.

Q35. What is transcranial magnetic stimulation?

Transcranial magnetic stimulation (TMS) is a new therapy which uses pulses of magnetic energy to induce electrical currents in the brain. TMS is currently being linked with a number of possible uses, including treatment for depression, hallucinations, anxiety disorders, migraine, epilepsy and tinnitus, and seems to have fewer side effects than ECT, as well as being less invasive, as the following description in the March 2004 issue of *Technology Review*, published by the Massachusetts Institute of Technology, explains: 'A doctor typically holds a powerful magnet over the frontal regions of the patient's skull and delivers magnetic pulses for a few minutes a day, over the course of a few weeks. The treatment alters the biochemistry and firing patterns of neurons in the cortex, the part of the brain nearest the surface. Preliminary research indicates that the treatment affects gene activity, levels of neurotransmitters like serotonin and dopamine, and the formation of proteins important for cellular signalling – any of which could play a role in alleviating depression. What's more, magnetic stimulation seems to affect several interconnected brain regions, starting in the cortex and moving to the deep brain, where new cell growth may be important in regulating moods.'

There is some evidence that magnetic stimulation over the left prefrontal cortex of the brain can help treat depression, and that stimulation over the right hand prefrontal cortex can relieve mania. However, the use of TMS is far from widespread, and although several research studies have shown promising results for unipolar depression, further research is needed to assess the effectiveness of the therapy for treating bipolar disorder.

Q36. How can the symptoms of seasonal affective disorder be effectively treated?

Light therapy can be a very effective treatment for seasonal affective disorder (SAD) – around eight out of ten SAD sufferers find that sitting next to a light box for ten minutes every day during the darker winter months relieves symptoms within four to ten days. Most light boxes use special fluorescent bulbs rated at 10,000 lux. Research shows that morning treatments work better, so place the box on the breakfast table or next to a computer for use at the start of the day. For a 28-day free trial, visit www.sad.uk.com or call 0845 095 6433.

A word of warning, though. Some research suggests that too much light can cause hypomania and mania occasionally, especially during the spring and summer months when more light is available naturally – so use a light box more sparingly when the typical SAD season is just beginning or about to end.

Cognitive behavioural therapy or counselling may be helpful, and there is some evidence that the right diet can also make a positive difference. Dieticians recommend that people with SAD symptoms eat fruit, vegetables and nuts to raise energy levels and take vitamin B and D supplements to boost serotonin levels, which enhances mood. Also, taking exercise outside – even on a dull day – can help.

Contact the SAD Association, PO Box 989, Steyning, BN44 3HG, or visit its website www.sada.org.uk for more information and advice on treating symptoms of SAD.

Q37. What is the best course of action if a child shows symptoms of bipolar disorder?

As worrying as the situation might seem, don't jump to conclusions and start panicking if a child seems to be showing symptoms of bipolar disorder. Take things step by step.

Step 1: Prevent things getting worse

Regardless of the frequency and severity of symptoms, making positive lifestyle changes can help prevent the situation from deteriorating. These include encouraging him or her to:

- eat a healthy diet that's high in nutrients and low in sugar, artificial additives and junk food

- follow a good sleep pattern (going to bed and getting up at the same time; getting enough sleep; avoiding getting overtired)
- get plenty of exercise
- avoid stressful situations and family conflict
- feel good about themselves with plenty of praise
- get extra help to cope with the ups and downs of life, maybe from a child psychologist (contact The British Psychological Society on 0116 254 9568 or at www.bps.org.uk) or a play therapist (call 01825 712312 or see www.playtherapy.org.uk).

Step 2: Get a proper diagnosis

Because the symptoms are so many and varied, bipolar disorder is notoriously tricky to diagnose, and often goes undiagnosed or gets misdiagnosed. This is particularly true in children. It goes undiagnosed because children with bipolar are often written off as naughty, bad, defiant or difficult. And it gets misdiagnosed because bipolar behaviour overlaps with so many other childhood conditions, including attention deficit hyperactivity disorder (ADHD), depression, panic disorder and obsessive-compulsive disorder to name but a few. In fact, research from Harvard Medical School found that up to 30% of children originally diagnosed with ADHD eventually receive a diagnosis of bipolar disorder.

Remember that there's an increased chance of bipolar disorder developing if it runs in the family (see question 16, p. 38) so a relative with a diagnosis should act as a warning light. Regardless of the genetic link, stress can also be a trigger, so any bipolar symptoms that appear or get worse after bereavement, trauma or parents' divorce should be noted.

Speak to the school nurse or the child's GP about any concerns, as they can refer the child to a psychologist or psychiatrist if necessary. An official diagnosis can then be made.

Step 3: Choose treatment wisely

Clinical Psychologist and Lecturer at Manchester University Sara Tai says: 'Although our system is heavily weighted towards psychiatric treatments, psychological intervention should be considered first for children because we don't know what effect drugs will have on a developing brain. Psychological intervention can be highly successful if used at an early stage when problems first arise. The key is treating the individual child's behaviour, not the condition.'

If medication is considered as a last resort, it's worth bearing in mind the advice of co-author of *The Bipolar Child*, Demitri Papolos: 'We want to state clearly that, given the accumulating knowledge in the field of research and the reaction of the children in our study, [...] bipolar disorder should be ruled out before any of the stimulant drugs or antidepressants are prescribed.'

Why? Giving bipolar children stimulants or antidepressants can throw them into manic and psychotic states, causing violent, paranoid and suicidal tendencies.

'In coming years we are likely to develop better ways to define the mood problems of children,' says Dr Michael Miller, editor-in-chief of *Harvard Mental Health Letter*. In the meantime, some experts recommend prescribing mood stabilizers – often several drugs in combination – for children with a diagnosis of bipolar. In the UK, medication is much less likely to be prescribed.

For an extremely small minority of children and teenagers with bipolar, treatment in a psychiatric unit may be an option, either as an informal patient or (very rarely) under a section order. In the UK, the 2007 Mental Health Act introduced new safeguards for children in psychiatric hospital care, aimed at ensuring they're treated in an environment suitable to their age. This echoed a commitment made by the UK government in 2006 that no children under the age of 16 should be treated in an adult ward. Anyone whose child is being considered for hospital treatment should refer mental health professionals to this legislation and ask that an age appropriate environment is provided.

Step 4: Work as a team

The NICE guideline for the treatment of bipolar states that when planning the care of children and adolescents with bipolar, parents and other loved ones should be involved in developing care plans so that they can give informed consent, support treatment goals and help ensure that suggested treatment is carried out. But the guideline also states that children and teenagers should be offered separate individual meetings as well as joint meetings with family members.

Step 5: Gather information

There are two brilliant books about bipolar disorder in childhood – *The Bipolar Child* by Demitri Papolos MD and Janice Papolos and *Intense Minds: Through the Eyes of Young People with Bipolar Disorder* by Tracy Anglada. Both are available from www.amazon.co.uk The first is a comprehensive yet easy-to-read round-up of the latest research into early onset bipolar disorder. The second is a moving collection of first-person accounts describing what it's like to live with this condition as a child, plus a practical guide for parents on how they can help.

Q38. Does treatment need to be different for elderly people diagnosed with bipolar disorder?

The NICE bipolar guideline states that people older than 65 should be treated according to need rather than age, although also recommends when treating this age group that professionals:

- use medication at lower doses
- are alert to the increased risk of drug interactions
- address any other medical conditions.

Martha Sajatovic, Associate Professor in the Department of Psychiatry at Case Western Reserve University School of Medicine, Cleveland agrees that treatment should be tailored to the age group. For example, she says that lithium, the most extensively studied medication for bipolar disorder in the elderly and an effective mood stabilizer in older adults, should be prescribed at a dose reduced by one-third to a half of that given to younger patients and the dose should not exceed 900 mg/day.

Relatives of someone with late onset bipolar disorder who need help finding the right kind of care (such as care at home, sheltered accommodation or a nursing home) can contact Grace Care, the leading Independent Care Adviser in the UK at www.any-care.co.uk or on 0800 137 669.

Q39. What is an 'advance directive'?

2007 saw the introduction in England and Wales of the Mental Capacity Act, which was drawn up by the Department of Health, 'to empower and protect people who may lack capacity to make some decisions for themselves, for example, people with dementia, learning disabilities, mental health problems, stroke or head injuries, who may lack capacity to make certain decisions'. The Act has five key principles:

- A presumption of capacity – every adult has the right to make his or her own decisions and must be assumed to have capacity to do so unless it is proved otherwise.

- Individuals are supported to make their own decisions – a person must be given all practicable help before anyone treats them as not being able to make their own decisions.

- Unwise decisions – just because an individual makes what might be seen as an unwise decision, they should not be treated as lacking capacity to make that decision.

- Best interests – an act done or decision made under the Act for or on behalf of a person who lacks capacity must be done in their best interests.

- Least restrictive option – anything done for or on behalf of a person who lacks capacity should be the least restrictive of their basic rights and freedoms.

In line with these principles, the Mental Capacity Act recognizes the legal status of an 'advance directive' (also sometimes called a future directive), in which someone can state in advance, i.e. before illness or injury makes them unable to make their wishes known to health professionals, what treatment they *don't* want to receive if they become mentally incapacitated in the future. Rather confusingly, an 'advance statement' is where someone can say in advance what treatment they *do* want to have. An important difference between the two is that advance statements are not legally recognized by the Act, so these treatment preferences can be ignored by mental health professionals. The UK mental health charity Mind, amongst others, is campaigning to change this.

Although an advance directive can be given verbally, it's sensible to write it down, ideally with the name, address, date and signature of the person preparing the directive, and with a sentence stating that they fully understand what they are doing and that they are legally competent to write their own advance directive. The particular circumstances and the treatment that a patient wants to refuse (or, in the case of an advance statement, to request) need to be mentioned specifically, so there's less room for doubt or misinterpretation later on. Giving reasons for the choices expressed in the advance directive also adds credibility.

It is also a good idea for the directive to be witnessed by a doctor (who can confirm that the person was fully capable of making decisions when the advance directive was written) or an advocate (someone, usually a volunteer, who supports someone with a mental health condition to communicate their needs – see question 41, p. 116). Copies need to be sent to the person's GP, any mental health professionals they are dealing with, and to their family, ideally to their legally defined 'nearest relative' – see question 55, p. 162 for more details.

It's worth noting that an advance directive has no legal status if the person who wrote it is later sectioned in a psychiatric hospital under the Mental Health Act, when treatment can be given without consent.

Contact the Mind Legal Advice line on 020 8519 2122 for help and advice on drawing up an advance directive, or an independent advocacy service may be able to help (see question 41, p. 116).

CHAPTER THREE
SUPPORT

Q40. What professionals support someone with a bipolar diagnosis?

Although it has been estimated that up to three-quarters of people with bipolar disorder don't receive the best possible care, there are literally thousands of dedicated individuals working in the mental health sector. In an ideal world, they are available to provide support whenever it's needed, although the degree of involvement will very much depend on the phase of the illness and the person's recent history. A 32-year-old man who's living with a partner, working, self-managing his moods and who hasn't been in hospital for four years is going to need less support than a 19-year-old who's living alone, unemployed, unstable and recently out of hospital, for example.

So who makes up the team of mental healthcare professionals?

General practitioners (GPs)

A GP is a family doctor who sees patients with every ailment under the sun. In the UK, research shows that for every thousand patients a GP sees, around 230 have psychiatric symptoms. The first health professional involved in the care of someone with bipolar disorder is often a GP. Professor Richard Morriss, Professor of Psychiatry and Community Mental Health at Nottingham University who has run courses for GPs on psychiatry, says that a GP's role is slowly changing: 'Not so long ago, bipolar disorder was completely off the map for GPs. They were taught that, on average, only six of the 2,000 patients on their list had bipolar disorder. But even if you take the most conservative estimate (of bipolar affecting only 1% of the population), that figure has got to be wrong, let alone if you take the broader view that around 5% of the population has it. So, generally, bipolar just wasn't really a priority for most GPs, who have so many other things to do. Also, there's no doubt that unless a GP makes a point of putting mental health at the top of his or her priority list, it's difficult to diagnose bipolar disorder in a ten-minute consultation. That's because, of course, a GP is rarely presented with the entire picture. However, there are signs that things are changing. Since the NICE guideline was published in 2006, bipolar disorder is more widely recognized in the healthcare system in general and this has filtered down to GP level. Also, the Department of Health has introduced a system where GPs' practices get extra money by earning QUOF (Quality and Outcomes Framework) points. Most of these points are earned by monitoring their patients' weight, cholesterol, heart disease and smoking, but GPs can also be incentivized for monitoring people taking lithium and for creating a list of all patients with a serious mental health problem. Things like that help to put bipolar disorder on a GP's busy agenda.'

A GP's role is crucial for several reasons:

- Everyone in the UK has the right to access a GP – when problems arise, they're likely to see a GP first.

- Even in a ten-minute consultation, a GP has a chance to run through what's called an 'index of suspicion', asking questions that can help to build up a picture of overall mental health. The index of suspicion for bipolarity should be high when the depression is episodic and/or there is a family history of bipolar illness or its counterparts, such as alcoholism, drug abuse, uncontrolled episodes of rage and/or violence, suicide attempts, postnatal depression, psychiatric hospitalizations for depression or psychotic states.

- A GP can refer a patient to other health professionals who can offer specialized help.

- Once a diagnosis is made, a GP can prescribe medication and alter dosages.

- If someone is taking lithium, the NICE guideline recommends that their GP provides a health check-up every year, reviews lithium levels every three to six months, takes a blood test to monitor thyroid and kidney function at least every 15 months and checks blood pressure annually.

- A GP is key in monitoring the physical health of someone with bipolar as a diagnosis can increase the risk of other conditions, such as heart disease, obesity, diabetes and thyroid problems. In fact, the NICE guideline recommends that someone with a bipolar diagnosis has an annual physical examination to check glucose levels, weight and waist measurement, smoking status, blood pressure and cholesterol (in people over 40). At the time of writing, Professor Morriss says that only 40% of GP practices earn QUOF points this way, but remains optimistic that the figure will grow, particularly if patients know their own rights. 'Why not ask your GP for an annual physical health check, referring to the recommendations in the NICE guideline,' he says.

There's no doubt that a GP or family doctor can be the cornerstone of support for someone with bipolar.

I'm very lucky that I have a supportive GP. I had a blip four weeks ago. I got very depressed to the point where I was suicidal. My GP was fantastic and helped bring me back up very quickly with the right medication.

(Amy)

The community mental health team (CMHT)

If a GP is concerned about someone's mental health, they are likely to refer them to a community mental health team (CMHT), which is usually made up of between eight to 16 people. The team is responsible for the well-being of people with mental health problems, not just when they're acutely ill but on an on-going basis. Even when someone with bipolar is stable, they are entitled to continuing support. And rightly so: if someone has been in hospital in the previous 12 months, they have a 50% chance of an acute bipolar episode in the next 12 months. Today, thanks in part to the NICE bipolar guideline, much of the CMHT's work is about preventing relapse.

The team usually includes a senior consultant psychiatrist, junior psychiatrists, a clinical psychologist, community psychiatric nurses, social workers, pharmacists, occupational therapists and support workers. They tend to work from day centres, out-patient departments and GP surgeries; sometimes they have a base in a clinic, or they see people at home. Someone with bipolar only usually meets the members of the team involved in their care, one or two at a time. Every so often there will probably be a 'review' meeting where the person with a diagnosis and the members of the team directly involved in his or her care review the situation.

Psychiatrists

Psychiatry is the study of mental disorders and their diagnosis, management and prevention. The most senior member of a CMHT is the consultant psychiatrist, who has the overall responsibility for the care and assessment of all patients and prescribes treatments. In the UK, qualifying as a psychiatrist usually takes five years of general medical training, plus two further years on a post graduate foundation course, followed by up to six years of training in psychiatry. This is split into core and advanced training, and involves passing both parts of the MRCPsych examination. Junior psychiatrists, known as SHOs (senior house officers) or registrars, are still in training.

In the UK, a GP refers a patient to a psychiatrist via the National Health

Service (NHS), or there's always the option to go private. Take care when choosing a psychiatrist privately – go by personal recommendation if possible or contact the Royal College of Psychiatrists (RCP), which is the main professional body for psychiatrists in the UK, for a list of practising psychiatrists in different areas. Always ensure that the psychiatrist is properly qualified and affiliated to the RCP. (See Extra resources, p. 254 for contact details.)

If medical insurance is used, there may be a list of approved psychiatrists offered by the insurance company – try to find out if any specialize in treating bipolar disorder.

In the USA, it's common to ask for a 'preferred-provider' list from an insurance company. Or there's a list of recommended professionals on the Depression and Bipolar Support Alliance – see www.dbsalliance.org. Ensure he or she is 'board certified' which means they've passed a rigorous set of exams, indicating mastery in the speciality of psychiatry. To check the credentials of almost every licensed physician in the US, see the American Medical Association website at www.ama-assn.org.

Psychologists

Someone diagnosed with bipolar disorder may also see a clinical psychologist – either during a stay in hospital or as part of a general treatment plan. Clinical psychologists typically take a three-year degree course, followed by another three years at doctorate level and two to three years in between spent in on-the-job training. Psychologists use non-medical treatments with an emphasis on psychological therapies such as CBT and group therapy.

See question 28, p. 70 for more information about getting any kind of psychological therapy in the UK.

In the USA, a qualified psychologist can be found via the American Psychological Association at www.apa.org – simply type in a zip code in the 'Find a psychologist' section. For links to state licensing boards for psychologists, visit: www.m-a-h.net/hip/stateboards.htm

Care co-ordinators

In most cases, one member of the team (often a CPN or a support worker) is assigned the role of a care co-ordinator – their job is to get to know the person well and to ensure they're getting the help they need. The care co-ordinator is responsible for co-ordinating the care of the person to make sure all their mental health needs are met. They also need to make sure that someone with bipolar has a clear plan about how they're going to be helped – a care plan.

Community psychiatric nurse (CPN)

CPNs, also known as mental health nurses, support those with mental illnesses when they're not in hospital. Tim McDougall, Nurse Consultant in Psychiatry, says that a CPN's role, like a GP's, is going through big changes. 'Traditionally a CPN's role was very medical and they worked with the illness and the management of symptoms. But this model of care was very much based on what people can't do. These days, CPNs deal more with what people can do, and their work is much more about prevention and self-help rather than just medication, medication, medication. We've realized now that when it comes to managing disorders like bipolar, one size doesn't fit all. Now we ask, what needs to be in place to assist recovery?'

This new holistic, needs-based approach improves outcomes for people with mental illnesses in several ways:

- CPNs can help someone with a bipolar diagnosis understand their prescribed medication – how and when to take it, potential side effects and the consequences of missing or stopping medication. If there is a problem, a good CPN will pass on the information to the psychiatrist in his or her team and negotiate a treatment change.

- One important area of a CPN's work is risk management. Someone with bipolar can often be vulnerable and at risk of harmful behaviour and suicide. That should be central to a CPN's thinking, with regular risk assessments being made.

- CPNs can listen while someone talks through their problems and can offer people with bipolar disorder increased support during significant events in their lives, such as losing a job or following the death of a close family member or friend. They can talk through financial problems, work dilemmas, parenting issues, and deal with contributing factors rather than the aftermath of a crisis.

- CPNs generally have more contact with service users than any other professional group, so they are well placed to recognize the early warning signs that most people experience for several days or weeks before becoming seriously unwell. One of the most important roles of a CPN is noticing these signs and helping to prevent relapse by getting help early.

- CPNs are key in improving physical healthcare, which is important because people with bipolar disorder are more likely to be overweight, smoke heavily and be physically inactive. The NICE guideline recommends that nurses promote healthy living and arrange annual health checks.

- A CPN's work now involves family members a lot more because it has been recognized that loved ones themselves need support. A CPN is in a good position to offer that – in terms of practical advice and emotional support. In fact, a CPN is the link between family and medical help in the chain of support.

- Some nurses have received extra training in particular problems and treatments, such as eating disorders or behavioural therapy – they are called nurse therapists.

The above list is the gold standard, with a CPN maintaining daily contact when someone's acutely unwell, being available during unstable periods and seeing someone monthly during the maintenance stage. In reality, though, a CPN's role, like the role of the community mental health team in general, largely depends on the area of the country where they're based. We speak regularly on the phone about how Irene and Rebecca are doing and know without a doubt that this inconsistency is true. Irene lives in the Midlands and has a brilliant community mental health team that she or her husband Gordon can phone at any time, day or night. When she has a bipolar episode, members of the team respond immediately – sometimes within an hour or so of receiving the phone call, there will be at least two CPNs sat on Irene's sofa with her, trying to help her through any difficulties. They'll keep visiting every day until they're happy she's stable, or if she doesn't respond to home treatment, they will support her through the hospitalization process. On the other hand, Rebecca, who lives in Kent, has a key worker who is completely overstretched. If she's on holiday, Rebecca, or her mum Rose, is told to phone in two weeks when the key worker is due back. Rose can spend all day phoning various numbers, desperate for support and she still can't get through to anyone who can help. They've sometimes waited in all day for people to come, and then no one turns up. The contrast between the two standards of care is unbelievable. And others have had similar experiences.

> I couldn't get a CPN for love nor money where I used to live. They only patch people up during a crisis and then they abandon you. It's such a postcode lottery. The mental health services are much better here in the Midlands. I had an assessment with a new consultant and now I see the same CPN every single month. She got me on an anxiety management course. She's like a safety net. I know I can ring – for example, recently I had my antidepressant dosage reduced and I started feeling anxious. I phoned my CPN and because she knows me, she suggested I go back to my GP and get the dose increased again. If I hadn't had that support I might have delayed going to my GP. It definitely helped that I could call her. And there's been a marked difference in my well-being. I'm less anxious and more confident. My CPN's really pleased with me.
>
> (Rachel)

> My CPN is good. She helps me 'manage' the condition and gives me tips on relaxing and how to deal with negative thoughts.
>
> (Jude)

I've got the number of my son Neil's CPN that I can ring if I see any danger signals. I haven't had to do it yet, but I could do. And I've got the CPN's email address too, but I've got to put it past Neil. I promised him I would speak to him first.

(Gill)

I get bugger all support. The community mental health team? Who? My CPN didn't actually contact me after I'd taken an overdose. She's so busy she's never available. I can understand why there's no help. It's the system not the people.

(Sharron)

If it's impossible to get hold of a CPN, the only alternative is to get help from other sources, such as a GP or psychiatrist. But even if a CPN is available, this doesn't guarantee optimum support. 'It's true that even if you can get access to a CPN, some CPNs aren't as good as others. The industry definitely still has issues of training and supervision,' says Tim McDougall. The only answer in this case is to ask a GP for a change of CPN – although as yet this isn't an automatic right. Unfortunately, it's a case of pot-luck. The only consolation is that as the holistic approach outlined by Tim becomes more widespread, the odds increase favourably year on year.

The crisis resolution team

Most areas in the UK have a mental health crisis resolution team (CRT) which is part of the wider CMHT. These teams are made up of psychiatric nurses, social workers and support workers, and are meant to:

- be available 24 hours a day, seven days a week
- respond to a crisis within four hours (wherever possible)
- carry out assessments under the Mental Health Act
- provide support and short-term help until another team is available or the help is no longer needed.

The theory behind a crisis team is that instead of someone who's acutely ill going straight to hospital, they're given medication and supported at home until the crisis has passed. The NICE bipolar guideline recommends crisis resolution and home treatment instead of hospital based care, because:

- hospital admissions are reduced
- the average length of stay in hospital, if needed, is shorter
- home care is more acceptable than hospital based care
- service users tend to stay in contact with health professionals
- clinical outcomes are marginally improved.

When a crisis strikes, someone who's being supported by a community mental health team should have a crisis number they can phone for immediate help – even during long weekends and holidays. When the system works, it's brilliant:

When my partner went high and eventually ended up in hospital I don't know what I'd have done without the help of a crisis team. Tom had been drinking all day and, after an argument with his son where I thought he might become physically violent so I'd stepped in between them, he locked himself in the living room, which faced on to a main road. He was playing music very loudly and wouldn't come out. He was shouting. I couldn't communicate with him. I was frightened that he was going to hurt himself. He'd been cutting himself previously and punching things. I didn't know what he was going to do next. He felt dangerous, out of control. He was really aggressive. I felt like he really hated me. He had the phone and was ringing ex-girlfriends, shouting at me to leave him alone. At this point I knew I was out of my depth. I phoned the doctor, who said a member of the crisis team would come round in 40 minutes. I sat outside. But then I tried the door and the room was empty. I went outside. Some people on the street told me that he'd jumped out of the window – we're a storey up. They pointed towards the tube station. I ran up to the tube station in a blind panic. Tom was sitting there. He had pierced his nose and upper lip with a safety pin. He's also tried to cut off a tattoo of an ex-girlfriend on his arm with a penknife. I said, 'I've called the crisis team, please come with me.' He wanted to get another drink from the off-licence so we had to go there first, but then he came back with me. They turned up in time. I've got nothing but praise for them ... they were my salvation. When they arrived, Tom decided to put some pornography on. It was mortifying and embarrassing, but to be honest, it was pure relief that somebody was there to help me and they could see what he was really like, that this wasn't stable behaviour. He agreed to go into hospital.

(Jo)

For Tom and Jo, and many others, support from the crisis team is there when they need it. But yet again, the level of service is inconsistent across the country. Part of the reason for this was highlighted in research carried out by the Healthcare Commission (*No voice, no choice*, July 2007) which found that provision of out-of-hours CRT services varies widely across the UK – a small but significant percentage (12%) of areas had no crisis resolution teams providing an out-of-hours service at all, and 59% had no crisis accommodation available on a 24 hour basis.

This is illustrated by Sarah's sister Rebecca's experience:

 Rebecca had been stable for about 18 months, but then started arguing a lot with her boyfriend, drinking more than usual. Mum and I knew she was heading for a high, and we tried to persuade her to go for help, but she wouldn't listen. One night, after a row with her boyfriend and drinking a lot, she phoned the crisis team saying that she was suicidal and asking for help. No one could come out to her and so eventually she took an overdose. The help just wasn't there when she needed it.

So what can be done if a crisis team isn't available when needed? Frustratingly, not a lot! In a crisis situation, the only alternatives are to go straight to A&E or to phone for an ambulance. After an experience of receiving inadequate crisis support, it's worth writing a letter of complaint (see question 82, p. 232 for more information). Surely if enough people highlight the lack of resources, eventually the message will get through and positive changes may happen.

Even when there is a crisis service, there's clearly a problem in getting the information to those who really need it. According to the same Healthcare Commission research, only 49% of people who use mental health services actually had the phone number of someone they could call out of hours in a crisis. That's a shocking statistic. It sounds so obvious – but mental health professionals must ensure that everyone who might need crisis support knows how to get it. Just providing the services is not enough.

Anyone with a bipolar diagnosis (who may need to call the CRT urgently if they experience a fast-moving mood swing) should ask a member of the CMHT for a crisis phone number to pin up next to the phone. They need to give it to their close friends and family members too.

In the US, most municipalities – often at a county or district level – have crisis teams available to assess someone with a mental health condition quickly.

Q41. What is an advocate?

The UK charity Mind describes an advocate as, 'someone who supports us to communicate our needs, explore options and get things done'. Most advocates are employed by a voluntary organization and work with people in and out of the hospital environment. They're trained to 'listen respectfully' to the needs and wishes of those with a mental health condition and to help get those needs and wishes listened to and taken seriously by other mental healthcare professionals. This can be achieved through helping someone access information, or write letters, if they have a complaint about their care, for example.

There are two types of advocacy – group advocacy (where users of mental health and social services come together in groups to discuss the services) and formal advocacy (where one-to-one advice is given).

To find an advocate, contact the United Kingdom Advocacy Network (UKAN), a service-user-run network of advocacy groups in the UK. The charities Mind and Rethink also run advocacy services.

In the US, NAMI (National Alliance for the Mentally Ill) offers an advocacy service through its legal centre.

Contact details for all of these organisations can be found in Extra resources, p. 248.

Q42. What role do family and friends play in the recovery of someone with a diagnosis of bipolar disorder?

It's reassuring to know that the professionals are finally acknowledging what family and friends have known for decades – that loved ones can be key when it comes to supporting someone with a psychiatric disorder. One study, for instance, shows that those with bipolar disorder who return to high-conflict families have more manic and depressive episodes nine months after hospitalization than those who return to low-conflict families. Research also shows that individuals with bipolar disorder are much more likely to suffer a relapse if they live with families with high levels of expressed negative emotion, such as criticism, blame, sarcasm and emotional over-involvement with the person with bipolar. In other words, the more emotionally healthy and supportive the family environment, the better.

The NICE guideline for the treatment of bipolar states that families and friends have a very significant role to play in the management of the patient's condition. They can:

- help the person to recognize the onset of symptoms
- support their loved one through crises
- provide healthcare professionals with information about symptoms and behaviour that might help to reduce hospital admission in the long term.

Clinical psychologist Sara Tai says that if there's a basic foundation of trust, a family member or friend is in a much better position to monitor signs of relapse than healthcare professionals. 'Loved ones can help the person seek help before it's too late,' she says.

It does seem that some people with bipolar disorder find the support of their friends and family invaluable:

Neil sometimes says to me, 'What would people that haven't got the support do, Mum?' My daughter and I watch him for warning signals if he's getting ill. If he says anything out of character, alarm bells start ringing, and I ask him when he's going to see his CPN. To someone whose adult child is going through bipolar, I'd say, 'Be there for them when they need you, but give them their independence. Help them, but also help them to lead a separate life.'

(Gill)

I've been with my partner for five years and he's very supportive. He accepts me for who I am.

(Sharron)

I was told by a CPN that my husband David wasn't getting more help because I lived at home with him and looked after him. The doctors have always said that David's family is his anchor. He worships the kids. We deal with his condition together.

(Jackie)

My partner Jane has been so supportive through it all. She's my rock. She's there and rationalizes it out for me. It must be so hard for her, my swinging up and down. She can deal with it really well.

(Dave)

My family has been very supportive. If I hadn't had that support from my family, I dread to think where I'd have ended up.

(Lesley)

I have a great support system. There's my daughter's father who helps out. And I've got my mum and my cousin.

(Reka)

Being only 15, Vicki relies on me for pretty much everything. I'm very involved in her care. She asks things like, have I eaten enough? Is this right? Is that right? I want her to try and learn to manage herself as well as having my guidance. I'm trying to give her some independence so she can recognize things that might trigger her mood changes.

(Alison)

On the other hand, support from family and friends isn't always forthcoming:

My parents didn't have a clue what was going on and how to deal with me as a teenager. My mum just thought teenage boys were different from girls as my older sister is fairly stable. My dad's very quiet. He didn't deal with it at all.

(Paul)

My family mostly just ignore my illness. When I told my parents when I was first diagnosed, my mother said, 'I'm sure they've got tablets for that.' They're all in denial.

(Debbie)

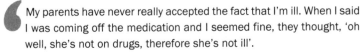

> ‛My mum would come over and help out with the children when I wasn't well, but she only ever once came to visit me in hospital – it was just 'don't talk about it, it isn't happening'. So she'd come over and do housework and look after the children, but not talk about it.'
>
> (Sue)

> ‛My parents have never really accepted the fact that I'm ill. When I said I was coming off the medication and I seemed fine, they thought, 'oh well, she's not on drugs, therefore she's not ill'.'
>
> (Tamara)

In *The Bipolar Disorder Survival Guide*, David J Miklowitz says that family and friends are able to offer more support when they're better informed about the condition. 'The first step in dealing effectively with family members after an episode is to educate them about your disorder. It is important that they understand that at least a portion of your behaviour is biologically and chemically determined. Family members who know the basic facts will also be more supportive of your efforts to maintain consistency in your treatment.'

In an ideal world, family members would read up on the subject in books and on the internet. If that's not likely to happen, Miklowitz suggests giving out a short, absolute beginners' fact sheet on bipolar disorder – photocopy the one on p. 121.

In the USA, The National Alliance for the Mentally Ill (NAMI) offers a ten-week course called 'Family to Family', which educates friends and loved ones about major mental illnesses and the available treatments. The course also works as a support group, encouraging friends and family to share how they feel about the illness. See www.nami.org for details.

What is bipolar disorder?

Bipolar disorder causes extreme mood swings that go from high and energized (manic) to low and lethargic (depressed). These swings can last from a few days to a few months. The illness occurs in phases, but it is possible to remain well for long periods in between.

What are the symptoms?

Someone who's high may feel overly happy and excited or overly irritable and angry. They may also feel like they can do things that no one else can do (grandiosity). They may sleep less than usual, talk faster, spend lots of money and be easily distracted and impulsive.

Someone who's depressed may feel very sad, unmotivated, irritable and anxious. They may sleep too much, have little or no appetite, have trouble concentrating and making decisions, have low self-esteem and contemplate suicide.

What causes bipolar disorder?

Bipolar disorder is probably caused by an imbalance in the brain's neuro-chemistry involving the ways that cells communicate with each other. There is sometimes a genetic link. Mood swings can also be affected by other factors, such as stress, hormones, sleep patterns, alcohol and recreational drugs.

How is bipolar disorder treated?

Most people with bipolar are on mood-stabilizing medication; some also take antidepressants to control anxiety and antipsychotic drugs to prevent losing touch with reality. Some have therapy or attend support group meetings. Lifestyle factors, such as sleep, stress and diet, also play an important part in managing the symptoms.

How does bipolar disorder affect the family?

Having bipolar disorder can affect someone's ability to relate to others, often causing conflict and misunderstandings. Family counselling or a family support group can help.

Q43. On a practical level, how can family and friends help someone with a diagnosis of bipolar disorder?

There's no end to the practical ways someone can support a loved one with bipolar disorder. Sarah's mum Rose supports Rebecca in many ways:

Rebecca doesn't drive so Mum is always taking her to appointments, picking up prescriptions and medication, driving her to the supermarket and to social events. Mum also does all her washing and cooks her dinners two or three times a week. They go swimming together in the evenings and clothes shopping at weekends. I honestly don't know what Rebecca would do without Mum.

Much of the practical help revolves around helping them to stick to regular eating and sleeping patterns, which tend to be disrupted during periods of depression and mania. Also, household tasks tend to be put on hold during periods of instability. A family member or friend can offer practical support by, for example:

- picking up prescriptions and/or medication
- driving them to appointments
- updating a diary or calendar so important appointments aren't forgotten
- encouraging them to see their GP
- accompanying them to support group meetings
- going supermarket shopping with or for them
- making a hot drink
- cooking their favourite meal
- making meals for the freezer
- bringing them some fruit

- encouraging them to drink plenty of water
- running them a bath
- taking them for a drive in the country
- hiring a favourite DVD for them
- offering them a foot massage
- accompanying them for a walk
- helping them with housework
- washing and ironing their bed sheets
- sorting out bills and household admin.

Another important practical way a family member or friend can support someone with a bipolar diagnosis is by planning ahead for a possible relapse. They can do this by:

1. Making a list of warning signs that indicate help is required.
2. Keeping a list of useful numbers for use in an emergency (such as the community mental health team, GP and psychiatrist).
3. Discussing what action they need to take when different scenarios unfold.

Q44. On an emotional level, how can family and friends help someone with a diagnosis of bipolar disorder?

Perhaps even more important than the practical details, someone with bipolar often needs extra support on an emotional level. Clinical psychologist Dr Sara Tai says there are several ways you can support someone emotionally:

- Be non-judgemental and unconditional (remember that a person's behaviour can be understood as their attempt to control their perception of what is going on around them; many people have traumatic experiences and in this context, their behaviour is usually understandable).

- Be consistent.
- Try to help them establish some routine and to feel safe.
- Provide them with the space and opportunity to be heard and understood.
- Don't always give answers; sometimes listening is just as important.

Julie A. Fast, the author of *Loving Someone with Bipolar Disorder*, recommends devising a holistic treatment plan. She says: 'The most effective way to treat bipolar disorder is to have a holistic treatment plan ready and waiting when bipolar disorder symptoms start appearing. Medications are the backbone of treatment, but a treatment plan will teach you and your loved one to *respond* to what the illness says and does instead of *reacting* to the symptoms as though they come out of thin air. When you learn to memorize the specific symptoms individually, you will no longer have to wonder constantly, what is wrong? Instead you can look at your symptoms list and determine the exact problem your partner (or loved one) is facing and what you both need to do to stop it. It's often difficult to know how to help when they are ill. The solution is to write down what works and what doesn't, so that you can read the list as soon as you see the first signs of bipolar disorder. The symptom list becomes a tool you can both use to separate bipolar disorder from your relationship.'

Different things work for different people:

 My partner Jane walks in and can see that I've gone low and she'll say, 'Well, I'm not feeling low so I'm off to the gym.' That's great because when I'm feeling down I don't want to be pestered. Then when I'm ready, I'll come round. I definitely believe that reflective listening is one of the best tools a partner can have. It's a skill my partner has. It requires her to be silent even when the silence is uncomfortably long.

She rephrases what I've said to show she understands and that she's been listening. It's a technique that works so well for us. If Jane uses that on me when I'm down, it works. All she needs to do is to be there and listen; she doesn't need to say much. In fact, it only works if she doesn't say much. That allows me to get right down to the problem, and I get to the trigger thought. At the end of the day, I need to work out that the way I'm feeling is probably me being irrational. But she can't tell me that, I have to work it out for myself. I always end up thinking, 'Yeah, she's right, I'm feeling better now'.

(Dave)

 Dave and I have been together for five and a half years and we talk a lot. The thing is, there's no textbook, and there aren't any hard and fast rules telling you how to deal with someone who's bipolar. Everyone's so different. I just think it's common sense to give people a little bit of space and let them work things through without feeling isolated. I try not to be too judgemental or to try to change him.

(Jane)

I have a really good friend, Elaine, who's on call to me 24/7. If I need her she's here. Four weeks ago when I was very depressed, I self-harmed and got quite upset. I had to have stitches. As soon as I'd done it, I phoned her. She took me to A&E and sat with me for six hours until my sister came home from work. She's done a lot of research on the internet. She's also got some books and watched the Stephen Fry documentaries. I feel like she really accepts me. Although she doesn't understand, she just accepts the way I am. She doesn't try to get her head around the way I'm behaving; she just goes along with it. When she's here I can talk absolute rubbish until I'm all talked out. She just sits and drinks tea. She knows when to listen and when not to listen – I'm just getting things out of my system. Once it's all come out we just move on. She doesn't usually ask questions.

(Amy)

Q45. If someone with a bipolar diagnosis feels suicidal, what is the best course of action?

There are no two ways about it – the statistics linking suicide, mental illness and bipolar disorder are alarming:

- 90% of suicide victims have been reported to have a psychiatric disorder at the time of their death.
- The suicide rate for bipolar disorder averages at 1% annually, which is around 60 times higher than the international population rate of 0.015% annually.
- Up to 15–20% of people with bipolar disorder who are unresponsive to treatment kill themselves.
- Approximately 17% of patients with Bipolar I and 24% of patients with Bipolar II attempt suicide during the course of their illness.
- WHO estimates that for each death by suicide that occurs, 20 more non-fatal self-inflicted injuries are carried out.

Amanda's mum Irene's suicide attempt in 1998 marked a new low in her struggle with bipolar:

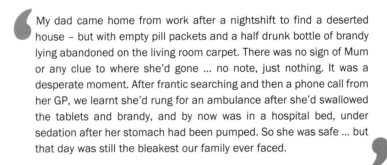

My dad came home from work after a nightshift to find a deserted house – but with empty pill packets and a half drunk bottle of brandy lying abandoned on the living room carpet. There was no sign of Mum or any clue to where she'd gone ... no note, just nothing. It was a desperate moment. After frantic searching and then a phone call from her GP, we learnt she'd rung for an ambulance after she'd swallowed the tablets and brandy, and by now was in a hospital bed, under sedation after her stomach had been pumped. So she was safe ... but that day was still the bleakest our family ever faced.

And the fear of Rebecca committing suicide never lifts for her sister Sarah or their mum, Rose:

'Rebecca has taken several overdoses – usually a combination of paracetamol and her prescription drugs ... whatever medication is around. She also escaped out of hospital and deliberately threw herself in front of a car. It was a miracle that only her ankle was broken. These attempts have all taken place during times of extreme instability. Nothing can describe the fear and frustration my mum and I feel in the period leading up to an attempt. It's like you can see what's around the corner but you're powerless to stop it. Perhaps the worst time for us was during Rebecca's darkest depression when Mum found several towropes with a noose tied in them in the loft. Mum would throw one away and the next week she'd find another one. It got to the point where Mum dreaded going home for fear of what she might find. The worst thing was that there was absolutely nothing we could do to help because we couldn't connect with Rebecca at all. The shutters were down. If I saw Rebecca or spoke to her on the phone I'd wonder if it was the last time I was ever going to see or speak to her. Mum and I would talk on the phone every day about how anxious we felt. Our conversations never deviated from that one subject – who else could we share this extreme fear with? We did phone the psychiatrist and went to see her GP. They'd offer words of sympathy and change her medication, but nothing helped. Mum lost weight and looked terrible. We were literally worried sick, but all we could do was stand by helplessly, watching, waiting and hoping the fog of depression would lift ...

After a suicide attempt, Rebecca always looks so fragile, vulnerable and pale lying in a hospital bed. She says she's sorry and tells us how much she loves us, that she would never want to hurt us. We try to understand that she must be experiencing unimaginable emotional pain, but all we want to scream is, Why? Why?

Then you find yourselves questioning why you couldn't have helped to prevent her getting so low, why you couldn't have stopped it happening. That's when the guilt kicks in – like a physical wrenching pain in the stomach. How could this have happened – again? Why couldn't we have rescued somebody we love so very much?

Yet even during times of stability, when the risk of Rebecca attempting suicide is practically non-existent because she's feeling so well, Mum and I can't let go of the fear completely. It's like a constant companion, a feeling of dread gnawing away in the back of your mind. '

Many people with bipolar disorder have suicidal tendencies during periods of instability:

> At the worst point of my illness I tried to throw myself out of a top floor window and had six people trying to hang onto me ...
>
> (Richard)

> In my late twenties and early thirties, I attempted suicide around 20 times, although it's true what they say – you want to switch off the pain rather than want to die. I currently get a mood stabilizer injected once a fortnight because I don't trust myself with the medication.
>
> (Sharron)

> Vicki was first admitted to hospital because she took an aspirin overdose. Her medication wasn't working at all so her moods were changing really really fast. And she just didn't want to live. She also had a mixed state episode where she was trying to slit her wrists and also tried to throw herself out of the window. She won't say it to me, but she'll say it to the doctor, 'I do want to die'. I worry whether she's going to have a future. You have to be very strong. Nothing shocks me anymore.
>
> (Alison)

> My daughter moved the cutlery because she was afraid of her dad killing himself. She took every knife and fork and spoon out of the drawer, put them in a plastic bag and hid them in her room. I don't quite know what she thought he was going to do with the spoons!
>
> (Jackie)

> We suspect my mum's sister, my aunt, was Bipolar II. She committed suicide in hospital. She was very depressed and hanged herself. It's impossible to describe how absolutely devastated we were.
>
> (Jayne)

So what can a family member or friend do to help avoid the worst possible case scenario?

1. Let go of guilt

The first important thing to remember is that loving someone – however much – is not enough to rescue or save them. However hard it is to accept, if someone is determined to take their own life, they will. Nobody can be responsible for somebody else's life.

2. Know the risk factors

As well as mental illness, other factors are known to be associated with an increased risk of suicide, such as drug and alcohol misuse, unemployment, social isolation and family breakdown. Previous suicide attempts are also an indication of greater risk. Up to 20% of survivors try again within a year, and as a group they are 100 times more likely to go on to kill themselves than those who have never tried before. Many suicides take place during a depressive phase and/or after a recent negative life event.

Other factors can increase the risk of suicide:

- The risk of suicide is much higher during depressive and mixed episodes.
- In almost all cultures, the suicide rate rises with age, with the highest rates in the UK for men over the age of 75.
- Overall, more than three times as many men as women kill themselves.
- For men, being single, divorced or widowed is a risk factor.
- The number of suicides by young people has increased and is now one of the main causes of death for this age group, with young men particularly at risk.
- Nearly 63% of people who kill themselves had a history of self-harm (most commonly by cutting, burning, scratching or bruising).
- Anyone with physical pain or illness is at greater risk of suicide.

3. Recognize the warning signs

The signs that depression might be leading to suicidal thoughts or intentions vary from person to person, but they may include some of the following:

- experiencing or expecting a personal loss or bereavement
- feelings of failure, hopelessness or worthlessness
- feeling and becoming withdrawn and isolated
- lack of self-care, such as poor personal hygiene or not eating properly
- building up supplies of medication or equipment which could be used in a suicide attempt
- suddenly making changes to wills, taking out life insurance or giving things away
- stopping medical routines, such as medications or special diets
- talking about suicide
- risk-taking behaviour.

4. Get help

Never ignore threats of suicide – on average, more than half of those who commit suicide tell their next of kin or a medical professional what they're planning to do before carrying it out.

So what's the best course of action in a crisis situation?

First, try to have an open discussion and encourage them to talk about their feelings. A loving gesture, such as a hug, can sometimes help. Next, try to persuade them to seek help or get help immediately on their behalf. And though the support available varies depending on the situation, whether or not a person is known to psychiatric services, and the area of the country they live in, help is always available in some form or other – a community mental health team, a psychiatrist, a GP, A&E, or emergency services.

Whichever professional they see, encouraging the person to be open and honest about their feelings is useful. If they allow it, go with them to the appointment and, if they find it difficult to be honest, share as much information as possible.

Family and friends of those with bipolar disorder have had various experiences of support during suicidal crisis situations.

 For two weeks until a couple of days ago, Laura was having mixed states and constantly talking about killing herself. She stopped taking her medication altogether. I didn't know whether she was really going to do it or not. When I went home, I honestly didn't know what I was going to find. She had plugged the hairdryer into a socket in the kitchen and filled the kitchen sink with water. But then I found her asleep in bed. I phoned the mental health team and her GP for help, but they just said there's nothing they could do because she had to make the contact.

(June)

I was feeling suicidal, so I rang a doctor who could fit me in. He spoke to the crisis team who were waiting for me when I got home and I've been under them for two weeks. I'm back on medication and for the last 48 hours I've been feeling myself again.

(Debbie)

The Samaritans

If other professional help isn't available or hasn't improved the situation, The Samaritans is a UK charity that provides confidential emotional support 24 hours a day to any person who is suicidal or despairing. They won't judge or offer advice, but simply listen with an open mind and provide the time and space for someone to talk, think and find a way through their difficulties. Calls are charged at local rate and are anonymous.

UK Helpline:	08457 90 90 90
Rep of Ireland:	1850 60 90 90
Email:	jo@samaritans.org

	Expect a reply within 24 hours from a human volunteer (not an automated service).
Website:	www.samaritans.org.uk
	For information about the service, useful fact sheets about depression, self-harm, suicide and other mental health problems and a local branch index (there are over 200 in the UK).

There are also a number of other organizations set up to support those who feel suicidal:

Lifelink

Free support and advice to those in crisis and at risk of self-harm or suicide.

| Tel: | 0808 80 11 315 |
| Website: | www.lifelink.org.uk |

Be ... foundation

Aims to offer help and information on youth suicide and self-harm.

| Email: | info@be-foundation.org |
| Website: | www.be-foundation.org |

CALM – Campaign Against Living Miserably

A UK based organization, their aim is to reach young men before they become depressed and suicidal.

| Tel: | 0800 585 858 |
| Website: | www.thecalmzone.net |

Suicide and Mental Health Association International

Dedicated to suicide and mental health related issues in the USA.

Tel:	1 75101 0702
Email:	smhai@suicideandmentalhealthassociationinternational.org
Website:	www.suicideandmentalhealthassociationinternational.org

National Suicide Hotlines

Toll-free crisis lines in the USA.

(800) SUICIDE

(800) 273-TALK

Q46. What is the best way for a loved one to cope during the really tough times?

It is an understatement to say that bipolar disorder can take a terrible toll on those who love and care for people with the condition. Someone who's in the grip of a mood swing is often unable to think rationally which can mean it's impossible to persuade or reason with them. The unpredictability is inevitable. It's as though the loved one is temporarily gone and bipolar disorder has moved in. Partners and other family members can feel lonely, frustrated, guilty, stressed, exhausted, fearful, ashamed and confused, in equal measure. Both the highs and lows of the illness can be devastating, as can the transition from a depressive to a manic phase.

Mania, excessive spending, infidelity, offensive/abusive/domineering behaviour, and talking incoherently, can cause distress to other family members and friends. It can be particularly upsetting when a person becomes manic for the first time, because their behaviour can seem out-of-character and inexplicable.

Depression takes a toll in a different way. The patient can seem 'cut-off' from their loved ones, isolated in their own misery. Their loss of interest and any enthusiasm in life makes it hard to get on with the daily routine as normal. Partners who responded to a survey by MDF The BiPolar Organisation reported that they found the depressive phase of the illness more difficult to cope with than mania. Depressive episodes were felt to be more time-consuming, upsetting and disruptive to family life, and caused partners more feelings of guilt and worry. They may also live with the fear that their relative or friend will attempt suicide. During depressive episodes, partners said they felt less able to talk to their loved one about how they were being affected by the illness. This difficulty in sharing their worries and concerns with their partners, when the partners were depressed, affected their ability to cope with the situation.

Due to the episodic nature of the condition, family and friends need ongoing support, but an MDF survey reported that they felt their needs were largely overlooked. Sarah's mum Rose gets physically exhausted when Rebecca is unstable:

> I'm always on edge when Rebecca is going through a bad patch. Either I'm with her – which is inevitably stressful – or I'm worrying about her, waiting for her to call so that I know she's OK. I don't sleep well. I can't relax. I get more and more exhausted until I wonder if I'll end up in a bed next to hers in the psychiatric ward. The trouble is, it's always about Rebecca, never about me. As much as I feel sorry for Rebecca because she's been through so much, I can't help wondering sometimes, 'What about me? What about me?' As a carer you give all the time. Most of the time I can cope with getting very little in return. But when I get exhausted and low, I can't. I think the trouble with bipolar thinking is that it makes the person very inward looking and very focused on their own needs. I suppose that must be a coping mechanism, but it's hard on the carers because their needs go completely unnoticed. I suppose I get some kind of relief when Rebecca goes into hospital because then somebody else is looking after her, but then I feel so guilty that I can't cope. Visiting Rebecca in hospital is emotionally exhausting. As you park the car, you just feel so apprehensive. What mood will Rebecca be in today? Also, we never know what staff will be on duty. Will it be the friendly, relaxed nurses today or the less friendly ones who can't make eye contact? And what mood will the other patients be in? A couple of times, I've witnessed extremely aggressive behaviour. And though it's rare (most visits pass without incident) and I have compassion for anyone experiencing such extreme emotions, it can still be pretty frightening. Even though it's a relief to come home, I then always feel so desperately guilty leaving Rebecca behind.

And Amanda's dad Gordon has suffered ill-effects on his health:

Dad has always managed to keep reasonably well, even during the worst times of Mum's illness when he felt more emotionally exhausted than physically ill. But the last couple of years, as she moved towards more rapid mood cycling, really took their toll on his health. He started having panic attacks – his chest would suddenly feel very tight and painful, as if he had heavy weights pressing down on him, he couldn't breathe properly, his heart would pound, and he would feel too weak and dizzy to even stand up. Within the space of a few weeks, he suffered about a dozen panic attacks – one was so extreme he was rushed by ambulance to A&E. Thankfully the attacks have ceased, but then his blood pressure shot up and has remained high, so he has to take tablets for that now. Dad and his GP are both certain that the stress of looking after my mum is the major reason behind all this.

Many other loved ones have similar stories:

I can't say it hasn't been a strain caring for David. In fact, the stress has brought on lupus. I've also got angina. The doctors say that both conditions are stress-related.

(Jackie)

It's been incredibly stressful. I feel exhausted. I've always been a good problem solver and feel frustrated that I can't solve our family crisis. I feel like I'm cracking up and that I can't actually take care of myself. I'm not even going to be able to pay the mortgage next month because I'm in a constant state of stress. I can't look for work, but even if I did get a job, I'm just too stressed to work. I also feel incredibly guilty that I can't manage Laura's behaviour better. I can't imagine a future for us. I can only think half a day ahead at a time. Thinking further ahead than that is too overwhelming.

(June)

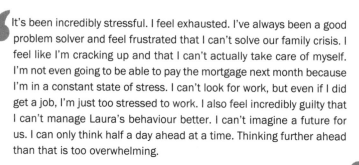

> The worry of my mum's bipolar has made me physically ill. I start off being sick. I get blinding headaches. I'm a civil servant and have to take a lot of time off work.
>
> (Jayne)

It's also common for relationships to suffer. What can seem like the relentless pattern of the illness can put relationships under considerable strain. Perhaps not surprisingly, divorce rates are around two to three times higher for individuals with bipolar than in the general population. This is a reflection of the emotional damage the illness can have on long-term relationships.

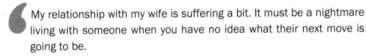

> My relationship with my wife is suffering a bit. It must be a nightmare living with someone when you have no idea what their next move is going to be.
>
> (Paul)

> Bipolar has impacted terribly on personal relationships. I change moods. I get angry really quickly. I get bored. I need to have excitement by causing trouble or having an argument, or causing friction. I like friction, because then I feel alive. I haven't held down a proper relationship for a long time.
>
> (Reka)

> My soul-mate turned into a monster when he was high. When he went into hospital, I felt like I'd failed and that I should have done more to help him. I also felt really sad and lonely and emotional and traumatized by what had happened. Bipolar disorder can be frustrating and confusing. But I knew I had to stay strong for the kids. I got valium from the doctor because I did feel as if I couldn't really cope.
>
> (Jo)

> My diagnosis of bipolar has definitely affected my partner. She finds it hard to understand that some days I am very low. She found the manic side very distressing and until she understood it more, we were on the verge of splitting up.
>
> (Jude)

> Bipolar has had a huge impact on my personal relationships. Up until I was 30, I was in four long-term relationships. I was classically either massively up or massively down, and it's very difficult for the person on the other side of it. And then in my thirties when I got clean, I just avoided relationships the best I could – for about eight years I didn't go near them. And then for the last year I've been in a stable relationship. It's not been without its troubles, but she has an understanding of depression and bipolar from her family, which helps.
>
> (Ashley)

It's not just partners who are affected, but mothers, fathers, brothers, sisters, sons, daughters and friends, too:

> My relationship with my mum has been affected by her bipolar disorder. We probably drifted apart emotionally during my teens, and when she was high she just embarrassed me. In my twenties I used to get quite angry at her for getting so low and so high. She almost didn't seem like my mum, but some imposter. I wasn't sure who my mum really was. Now, when she is low my relationship with her is less tense and I feel close to her because she is so down. I feel sorry for her and I'm more patient. Alternatively, when she is high, I am never good enough. I can't do enough, I can't do anything quick enough or well enough and this disturbs me greatly. My mum's relationship with my children is also affected. She lets them get away with more when she is low. And when she is high she reprimands them for everything.
>
> (Ingrid)

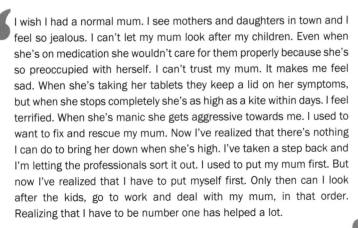

I wish I had a normal mum. I see mothers and daughters in town and I feel so jealous. I can't let my mum look after my children. Even when she's on medication she wouldn't care for them properly because she's so preoccupied with herself. I can't trust my mum. It makes me feel sad. When she's taking her tablets they keep a lid on her symptoms, but when she stops completely she's as high as a kite within days. I feel terrified. When she's manic she gets aggressive towards me. I used to want to fix and rescue my mum. Now I've realized that there's nothing I can do to bring her down when she's high. I've taken a step back and I'm letting the professionals sort it out. I used to put my mum first. But now I've realized that I have to put myself first. Only then can I look after the kids, go to work and deal with my mum, in that order. Realizing that I have to be number one has helped a lot.

(Jayne)

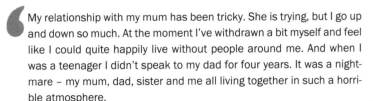

My relationship with my mum has been tricky. She is trying, but I go up and down so much. At the moment I've withdrawn a bit myself and feel like I could quite happily live without people around me. And when I was a teenager I didn't speak to my dad for four years. It was a nightmare – my mum, dad, sister and me all living together in such a horrible atmosphere.

(Paul)

Julie A. Fast acknowledges that it's extremely difficult to have a healthy relationship when one partner is a caretaker and the other is a patient. Her advice? 'Answer this question honestly: What is my role in this relationship and how do I feel about it? If balance is to be found, you need to be happy with your caretaking role. If you're not happy with the role, you need to change it. Everyone gets tired eventually. You don't want to lose yourself.'

She recommends the following to create a more balanced relationship:

- Help the partner find independence so that the bipolar disorder doesn't end up defining the relationship.
- Establish clear and firm limits, adopting the view 'I do care and I will help, but I'm not devoting my whole life to rescuing'.

- Focus on prevention, looking to and planning for the future.

For further information, see details of the 'Partners in Care' campaign at www.rcpsych.ac.uk/campaigns/pinc/index.htm

There's also a carers' support group – Carers UK – a national network of support and advice. See Extra resources, p. 250 for regional contact details.

Q47. What support do mental health charities offer?

There are a number of mental health charities all over the world set up to offer information and advice for those with bipolar disorder. Many of these groups offer emotional support too, via group meetings and web chat rooms. MDF The BiPolar Organisation, for instance, runs self-help groups across the UK where people with bipolar and their friends and family meet up monthly to support each other, share information and ideas and learn to cope with the highs and lows. Comments from group members include:

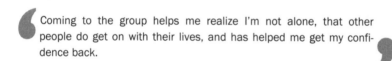

Coming to the group helps me realize I'm not alone, that other people do get on with their lives, and has helped me get my confidence back.

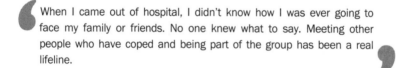

When I came out of hospital, I didn't know how I was ever going to face my family or friends. No one knew what to say. Meeting other people who have coped and being part of the group has been a real lifeline.

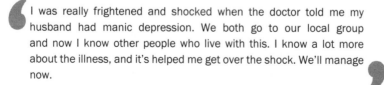

I was really frightened and shocked when the doctor told me my husband had manic depression. We both go to our local group and now I know other people who live with this. I know a lot more about the illness, and it's helped me get over the shock. We'll manage now.

Others also find these organizations invaluable:

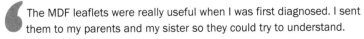

> If I met someone who had just been diagnosed with bipolar, I would recommend groups like MDF The BiPolar Organisation because they offer so much information and support.
>
> (Sue)

> The MDF leaflets were really useful when I was first diagnosed. I sent them to my parents and my sister so they could try to understand.
>
> (Neil)

> I think the website for MDF The BiPolar Organisation is really useful. I spend a lot of time on the message board. It's good to share things with people who can really understand what you're going through. Last week I put a post up on the MDF website asking about the funniest things you've done while you're manic. Loads of people replied with some brilliant stories. Instead of it being such a depressing subject, bipolar can also be a source of fun. People with bipolar really do some funny stuff. It's important to remember that and not only focus on all the negative stuff.
>
> (Paul)

According to an MDF survey, family and friends of those with bipolar can also benefit. Carers, partners and other family members who attend local self-help and support groups say they feel less negative about the illness, have fewer feelings of worry and guilt, and feel more positive about their relationship with the person with bipolar. Partners who attend groups also report a greater understanding of bipolar disorder and are more proactive about seeking out this information. They report less disruption of family relationships as a result of their partner's illness and experience less worry about the future. They also put a high value on meeting other people who have shared the same experience.

I'm a single parent and it's very intense having to cope alone. I often feel very helpless. Chatting on the MDF forum is useful. The people there are so supportive. There's one mother whose teenage son was diagnosed two days before Vicki. It's so helpful talking to her because she knows exactly what I'm going through.

(Alison)

Talking on bipolar forums has helped a lot. I'm not alone anymore. I used to feel so lonely and wouldn't talk to people about it. It was such a taboo subject, and I felt ashamed and embarrassed. Now I can get advice from people who are going through the same thing. And to help other people is really great.

(Jayne)

I find the Bipolar 4 All board really helpful. It's a support network. I can talk about total rubbish with people who really understand what I'm going through. The chat room is just as much for carers as it is for the sufferers. I find it good therapy and have a lot of nice friends in there. Otherwise, how would I know where to find people who are in the same boat as us? After all, David's the only bipolar in the village!

(Jackie)

For a complete round-up of mental health charities (including their contact details) in the UK and beyond, see the Extra resources section, p. 248.

CHAPTER FOUR

HOSPITAL CARE

Q48. What are psychiatric hospitals like?

To the outside world, the reality of life inside psychiatric hospitals remains steeped in stigma and stereotype. The old joke about 'being carted off by the men in white coats' is still in popular use, and in one study, an overwhelming majority of the public admitted that they thought mental health units resemble the 1975 film, *One Flew Over The Cuckoo's Nest*, where treatments were essentially punishments, administered by domineering doctors and nurses more interested in social control than psychiatric recovery.

Yet psychiatric hospitals have changed a great deal since the 1970s, and certainly since the days of the Victorian asylums. The wards are less obviously over-crowded, and the duration of the average stay is much shorter. Patients get dressed in their own clothes, whereas years ago they would spend a hospital stay in pyjamas. But perhaps the biggest difference of all is that a lot more emphasis is now placed on an individual's human rights.

The average mental health in-patient stays in hospital nearly 12 times longer than someone with physical problems. So what are today's psychiatric hospitals actually like?

Types of psychiatric units

There are four main types of psychiatric hospital care in the UK: acute admissions wards, intensive care wards, medium secure units and high security special hospitals.

Acute admission wards have around 15 to 25 beds, with a staff ratio of five patients to one nurse. These wards can be part of a general hospital, or in a separate psychiatric unit, and are usually the first stage of hospital care for a mentally ill person, especially if this is the first time they've been admitted. Assessment and first treatment steps will be carried out here, but these are short-term stay wards – some patients may only remain here for a few days and are able to return home, whereas others will then transfer to intensive care wards or medium secure wards (see below). Other people will be admitted straight to these two types of wards, bypassing the acute admission wards altogether if:

- They have been sectioned before admittance.

- They have been in psychiatric hospital care before and, for example, have on their personal care plan that they should go straight to a medium secure ward.

- They are showing signs of aggressive or potentially harmful behaviour to themselves or others.

Intensive care wards are usually small – the bed numbers vary across the UK (with sometimes as few as seven beds), and often are part of a larger psychiatric unit or hospital. The wards are usually locked and cater for people who need short-term intervention and treatment, with a ratio of seven patients to three or four nurses, or three patients to two nurses.

Medium secure units (also called interim wards or units) are usually much larger wards with high levels of security, catering for patients needing longer-term care. Some of the large general hospitals in the UK have medium secure psychiatric units, and will take patients from a large geographic area. Medium secure units may take someone for whom a bed can't be found in a local psychiatric intensive care ward, and will also cater for people who have been sent from the criminal justice system for assessment. Despite the size of these wards, the staff ratios are almost as high as the intensive care wards, with one nurse for every two patients.

High security special hospitals (such as Broadmoor and Ashworth) cater for people with a mental illness detained under Home Office section as a result of criminal proceedings, as they have specific needs and security issues that are hard to meet in other psychiatric hospitals. On average, the patients are detained for five to seven years, although it can be longer in some cases.

Rules and regulations

Unlike other parts of a general hospital, many psychiatric units are locked to the outside world, so it's often necessary to ring a buzzer to be allowed in through the main door. Inside, psychiatric units have the power to set their own day-to-day rules and operational policies, which patients and visitors are expected to follow. Because it can be a struggle respecting patients' independence, whilst at the same time maintaining a safe environment for everyone, these rules can sometimes seem strict and unnecessary. Patients may have restricted kitchen access, so they're unable to make drinks for themselves or their visiting family, for example, and they may not be allowed to use china cups or sharp cutlery. Patients sometimes aren't allowed out into the garden area without being accompanied by a psychiatric nurse or a relative – and sometimes not even with a family member. Sarah has some painful memories of the impact the rules have had on her sister:

 When Rebecca was in a psychiatric hospital for a year, there was a rule that the staff made tea on the hour. At the time, Rebecca wasn't allowed kitchen access for her own safety. Once, I turned up at five past three and Rebecca's request for a cup of tea for her visitor was denied. I could only stay until four o'clock, so I didn't get a drink. I wasn't particularly bothered, but Rebecca kept on saying 'This is supposed to be my home, but I can't even give you a cup of tea.' Another thing that would frequently happen is that she would be waiting to be taken out on a planned trip at a certain time – either for a walk around the grounds or into town – and then it would turn out that there wasn't a psychiatric nurse available to take her after all. I understand why the rules are in place, but I think that the huge impact they have on someone's day-to-day life, and ultimately their sense of self, is often overlooked.

As with any other type of hospital environment, there are usually set meal times on a psychiatric ward throughout the day, and access to regular drinks. This is especially important as some medications produce a dry mouth side effect. Patients usually receive their medication after meals, as it's often better to take the drugs on a full stomach, and usually before bedtime too, as some patients may be medicated to help them settle at night. Sleep is an essential part of the recovery process, so patients are encouraged to go to bed earlier rather than later, although a ward doesn't usually have a 'set' bedtime or 'lights out'. Visiting hours are generally confined to afternoons and evenings, with a time between the two sessions when the ward is usually closed to visitors while patients eat their evening meal. But family members can usually come to a ward at other times, by prior arrangement with the staff, for example to meet with a psychiatrist.

Ian Hulatt, Mental Health Advisor to the Royal College of Nursing, says that establishing stability and security through rules and routines is particularly important in a psychiatric ward, because the patients can be a potentially volatile mix of different conditions. And, he says, the situation is getting worse because of the shrinking number of beds. (There were around 154,000 NHS psychiatric beds in England and Wales in 1954, reduced to about 30,000 by 2002.) 'The number of psychiatric beds in the UK has fallen, which means the nature of in-patient work has radically changed over the last ten, 15 years because the concentration of very ill people is greater,' he says. 'For people with bipolar, they may be hypomanic, very uninhibited, very irritable, full of energy and feeling on top of the world, and we're trying to medicate them and keep them on a locked ward, with other people around them who are very unwell too. It can be a very difficult environment.'

The hospital environment

In the UK, two Mental Health Acts (1983 and 2007) govern the care and treatment of patients with mental disorders, and contain a Code of Practice, which was put in place to protect their rights. The full version of the code can be found on the Department of Health website www.dh.gov.uk in the publications section. Amongst other things, the Code of Practice recommends:

- giving each patient a defined personal space and a secure locker for the safe keeping of possessions
- ensuring access to open space
- organizing hospital wards to provide quiet rooms, recreation rooms, single sex areas and visitors' rooms
- providing all necessary help for patients with any type of disability.

Despite these guidelines, staying in a psychiatric hospital isn't always a good experience. As well as a lack of beds, a report published by the Mental Health Act Commission 2006 identified other problems, saying, 'some acute services are unable to provide a quality of care that patients will welcome ... with staffing shortages and unpleasant ward environments undermining the therapeutic purpose of inpatient admission'. In the same report, 56% of mental health in-patients rated their ward as 'unpleasant'. Lack of privacy means that treatment is sometimes carried out in full view of other patients:

My experience in hospital nine years ago was very short and very bad. The first morning I work up, another patient in the bed opposite started getting a bit animated. He wasn't really doing much other than rocking backwards and forwards and making a bit of noise. The medical staff ran in, held him down, and forcibly injected him. I was shocked to see that.

(Dave)

Amanda recalls some of her mum Irene's early stays at a hospital in Birmingham where the wards used to be divided into curtained cubicles:

Mum's peace and privacy were so easily disrupted. She would sometimes return to her cubicle to find another patient asleep on her bed, and this made her feel even more vulnerable – she felt that she had nowhere safe to go. During another stay, one woman became obsessed with Mum's shoes and kept sneaking into her cubicle to steal them. At night the ward was often very noisy, with other patients shouting or being disruptive, and even with medication Mum would still have disturbed sleep. None of this was very helpful to her recovery.

Since then, some of the wards at the hospital have been refurbished with single rooms and Irene's recent stays there have been more comfortable and peaceful. Nationally, however, ward refurbishment (like many aspects of UK healthcare) is a postcode lottery, and some units are still badly in need of modernization. And a ward is still more likely to be mixed gender than single sex, despite the fact that the UK's Labour government pledged to scrap mixed-sex wards in all hospitals when it came to power in 1997. In fact, the *Count Me In* report by the Healthcare Commission in March 2007, which gave the results of the 2006 national census of mental health inpatients, found that 55% of psychiatric patients had to share sleeping accommodation or bathroom facilities with members of the opposite sex.

Saying all that, there are small, but positive signs of change in the UK. In April 2006, a £130 million investment into mental health services was announced by the Department of Health, which in its press release declared that the money should primarily be used for:

- 'Development of women-only facilities, such as wards or crisis houses, and women-only areas of wards. Ideally, women and men should be segregated so that there are clear areas of the ward that are exclusively for women. These areas should contain all the bedrooms for women, their bathrooms and toilets and a day/

activities/facility room so that there is no need for women to enter areas of the ward which are mixed or men-only if they do not want to. This sort of development might include environmental security developments to control entry and exit from women's areas or entry and exit from the ward more generally, such as swipe card systems.

- Development of outside gardens/space that is single-sex.
- Development of private space within wards such as provision of single rooms, en-suite facilities or lockable bedrooms.'

Slowly and steadily, it seems that improvements to psychiatric hospital environments are being made, which can make a huge difference to the general atmosphere and recovery process:

> I do volunteer work in a new psychiatric ward, with facilities that are absolutely state of the art. Every room is fully fitted and kitted like a hotel room. It's made a hell of a difference. A consultant said to me that he couldn't believe we actually worked in those disgusting old wards, environments where it's impossible for anyone to get well. What you need is a nice fresh environment, with plenty of light – clean, tidy, modern surroundings. Everybody should have a private room, preferably with en-suite facilities. In the twenty-first century, why should you spend weeks or months in that ward system? Sharing a bathroom down corridors is medieval. It's also important to have easy access to the outside – a courtyard or garden – so you can get sunshine and fresh air outside. It makes a tremendous difference. I can see it's really working.
>
> (George)

> In 1999 I was in an older-style ward that was part of the hospital, for 11 weeks. I just had a curtain pulled across a cubicle, so there was very little privacy and I was totally bored out of my brain. But my last stay in hospital, which happened in 2005, was very different. They've built a new unit separate to the hospital where you get your own room.
>
> (Rachel)

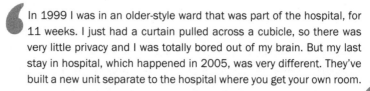

Private healthcare

For those who can afford it, paying for treatment in a private psychiatric hospital is another option. If medical insurance is being used, a referral will still be needed from a GP, who may know a suitable psychiatrist at a local private psychiatric unit (often because the psychiatrist works in local NHS hospitals too). Alternatively, a private hospital can be selected by the person with bipolar (or their family) but this needs careful thought – look beyond the smart décor and swimming pools. Ideally an independent hospital should be able to demonstrate that they have experience of treating bipolar disorder specifically – bipolar shouldn't just be lumped into their general treatment category of depression. Go by personal recommendation if possible and make sure that the hospital is a member of a recognized professional body such as the Independent Healthcare Advisory Service.

> The NHS hospital eventually referred me to this voluntary counselling organization – and they wouldn't take me on. They said I was too complicated!! So in the end, my social worker said the best option I had was to go private and pay for my healthcare, which is what I did in the end, and I went to the Priory. It really helped – it was a very supportive environment, although I had to have two more stays there last year. The nursing staff were brilliant. I still see the psychiatrist from there every two weeks, and I see their psychologist in the week in between, for CBT (cognitive behavioural therapy). In terms of aftercare, there are different options you can take ... you can continue some of the group therapy, which I chose not to do because it was incredibly expensive. But I needed more individual therapy anyway. The only time I have anything to do with the NHS now is when my GP does my prescriptions and sick notes.
>
> (Lesley)

But be warned – the private hospital route may cut someone off from NHS post-hospital support:

'Because my healthcare is now in the private sector, the NHS won't give me a CPN or social worker.

(Lesley)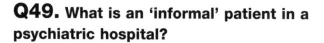

Q49. What is an 'informal' patient in a psychiatric hospital?

Anyone who agrees to admit themselves to a psychiatric hospital voluntarily is known as an 'informal' patient:

'I was relieved to be in hospital, to be honest, because I was really struggling to get the help that I needed. It was such a relief, and I think it was a relief for my family as well, that I was taken out of harm's way. I recognized that I needed to be there.

(Lesley)

Many psychiatric patients are admitted informally and, in theory, are free to walk out of hospital at any time. But, if the hospital believes they need to start applying for legal processes to detain an informal patient, the patient can be stopped from leaving hospital for a further 72 hours. This is known as a 'holding power', and is in place to allow a doctor to assess someone and decide if the application should be made. If a doctor isn't available, a psychiatric nurse can also exercise a holding power for up to six hours until a doctor can begin the assessment. So, although an informal patient is free to leave in theory, this isn't always the case in practice:

'They treated me as a voluntary patient because I didn't try to escape, but I think I would have been sectioned if I had twigged what was going on and had wanted to leave. If I'd tried to leave, they would have stopped me. It's happened like that a couple of times ... staff say, 'You can't leave' and I'll say, 'Yes I can' and they'll say, 'Well, if you do, we'll section you'.

(Keith)

Q50. What does it mean if somebody is sectioned?

In the UK, 'being sectioned' is an unofficial phrase which means compulsory admittance to a psychiatric hospital or ward. In other words, someone with a mental illness can be kept in hospital for assessment and treatment without their consent, if doctors feel their condition is serious enough and/or if they might pose a threat to themselves or other people. This is done through a legal process using different sections from the Mental Health Act (1983), which is where the term 'sectioning' comes from. And it's an extremely complicated process.

The decision to section someone has to be agreed by three people, usually two doctors and an approved mental health practitioner (AMHP) – this is a new title introduced by the Mental Health Act of 2007 and replaces the previous title of approved social worker or ASW. If both doctors agree that a person should be admitted into psychiatric care, the AMHP will then decide if a section application should be made – he or she has up to 14 days to consider if this is the right course of action or if there's any alternative to compulsory hospital detention.

Sectioning can seem like an alien, upsetting process to patients and their families, particularly if it's the first time it has happened.

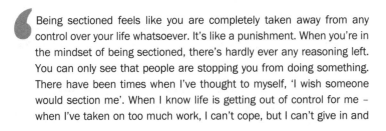

Being sectioned feels like you are completely taken away from any control over your life whatsoever. It's like a punishment. When you're in the mindset of being sectioned, there's hardly ever any reasoning left. You can only see that people are stopping you from doing something. There have been times when I've thought to myself, 'I wish someone would section me'. When I know life is getting out of control for me – when I've taken on too much work, I can't cope, but I can't give in and say no, I sometimes think, 'this is the time when I need to be sectioned to stop it getting any worse'. By the time you are sectioned, you've lost that power to reason. You can no longer look after yourself.

(Sharron)

And on top of this, if someone is forcibly resisting admittance and treatment – especially if they're as high as a kite with mania and can't see why they should go to hospital – the section order allows for physical intervention to be used. Sometimes, if the psychiatric professionals can't physically manage to admit a patient on their own, the police have to become involved in taking the patient to hospital. Sarah's mum Rose cites the first time her daughter Rebecca was sectioned as one of the worst moments of her life.

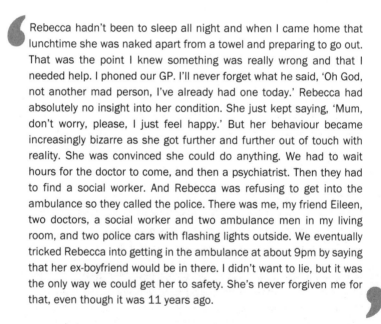

Rebecca hadn't been to sleep all night and when I came home that lunchtime she was naked apart from a towel and preparing to go out. That was the point I knew something was really wrong and that I needed help. I phoned our GP. I'll never forget what he said, 'Oh God, not another mad person, I've already had one today.' Rebecca had absolutely no insight into her condition. She just kept saying, 'Mum, don't worry, please, I just feel happy.' But her behaviour became increasingly bizarre as she got further and further out of touch with reality. She was convinced she could do anything. We had to wait hours for the doctor to come, and then a psychiatrist. Then they had to find a social worker. And Rebecca was refusing to get into the ambulance so they called the police. There was me, my friend Eileen, two doctors, a social worker and two ambulance men in my living room, and two police cars with flashing lights outside. We eventually tricked Rebecca into getting in the ambulance at about 9pm by saying that her ex-boyfriend would be in there. I didn't want to lie, but it was the only way we could get her to safety. She's never forgiven me for that, even though it was 11 years ago.

For the families of someone who's been sectioned, the feelings are mixed – relief that they are safe after maybe days, weeks or even months of instability, coupled with fear, anger, despair, helplessness and uncertainty about the future. Guilt is also a common reaction after a relative is sectioned – guilt at feeling relieved, guilt that they're the healthy one left at home (survivors' guilt) and guilt that they weren't able to 'save' their loved one and stop them going into hospital in the first place.

Overwhelming guilt is the overriding feeling Sarah (and her mum) feel each time Rebecca is sectioned:

> Your instinct is to protect the ones you love; you feel responsible for their well-being. Handing them over to complete strangers because you can't cope makes you feel like such a failure. You feel guilty that you couldn't make them better and that you couldn't ride the storm without turning for help. You feel guilty that your life is carrying on while the one you love is locked up like a prisoner.

Accepting that someone can be detained for hospital treatment against their will, in a supposedly 'free' society, can be difficult ... the process appears more custodial than caring. But it may help to view the psychiatric ward as a 'safe' environment, rather than a 'locked' one.

And if it's any small comfort during this difficult time, although it may feel as if a loved one must be the only person in the world going through this experience, Department of Health (DoH) figures from 2005–6 show that 47,400 section orders (also known as 'involuntary detentions') were issued in the UK. This breaks down into two distinct groups – 27,400 formal admissions (when people are detained in psychiatric hospital at the start of their treatment), and a further 20,000 section orders for detaining people already in hospital as informal patients. The figures cover detentions in both NHS and independent hospitals.

In the US, involuntary hospitalization is the process of admitting someone to a psychiatric hospital against his or her will. It can only happen for three reasons:

1. If the person poses a danger to him- or herself.

2. If the person is a danger to others.

3. If the person can't care for him- or herself.

This is a simpler process in some states than in others, but all states require at least one (more often two) physician to evaluate the person first. The initial hospitalization lasts only for a few days; after that period, a court hearing is necessary to detain someone in hospital against their will. When it comes to involuntary medication, states vary widely in their procedures, but action typically requires at least one court hearing.

Q51. Are there different types of sectioning procedures?

The Mental Health Act (1983) contains different sections that can be used to admit someone to psychiatric care, depending on the circumstances – sections 2, 3 and 4 are the three most frequently used ones, and are explained briefly below:

Section 2

This is for detaining a person with a mental disorder for up to 28 days. During this time, the patient will be assessed so that appropriate treatment can be recommended. At the end of this period, the section can't be renewed but doctors can make an application for further detention under section 3.

Section 3

Doctors will apply for section 3 to detain a patient if they believe that effective and appropriate treatment is only available in hospital and/or that the patient could be a danger to themselves or others if released. This detention can last for up to six months, and can be renewed (initially after another six months, then annually).

Section 4

In an urgent case, if there are enough reasons to apply for section 2 but there isn't enough time to get more than one medical opinion, a person can be detained and assessed in hospital under section 4. This allows for a detention of only 72 hours, during which time the second medical opinion must be obtained in order to make a section 2 detention.

The type of section order used can influence where someone might be treated – in either an acute or an intensive care psychiatric ward, for example.

Mental Health Acts

In July 2007 the Mental Health Bill (which contained amendments to the 1983 Mental Health Act) was finally passed by the UK government and became the Mental Health Act 2007. Amongst other measures, the new Act included:

- the scrapping of the definitions 'mental illness, mental impairment, severe mental impairment and psychopathic disorder' from the 1983 Mental Health Act and switching to a more generic definition of mental disorder as 'any disorder of mind or brain'

- changes to the criteria for ECT treatment (see question 34, p. 95)

- changes to nearest relative definitions (see question 55, p. 162)

- new advocacy rights for detained patients (see questions 41 and 53, pp. 116 and 156)

- the so-called 'treatability test' (where people should only be detained if treatment appropriate for their mental disorder is available)

- the creation of Community Treatment Orders for some post-discharge patients (see question 59, p. 169)

- new safeguards for children and young adults under 18 who are treated in hospital (see question 37, p. 99).

Q52. Can someone refuse to be sectioned?

No. Detention under the Mental Health Act (1983) is lawful, and once the correct section papers have been prepared, there are no legal grounds for resisting the section process. The best course of action for someone being sectioned is to keep communicating with the psychiatric professionals working on their case. This could mean asking questions about what's likely to happen next, or voicing any concerns about treatment. It might help to have a family member (see question 55, p. 162 on nearest relative) or an advocate (see question 41, p. 116) present, although the professionals don't have to wait until an advocate is found before going ahead with the section process.

A patient can also ask to speak to a solicitor, although this won't prevent the section order being applied for, and won't stop a detention from taking place.

Q53. What are a person's rights if they have been sectioned?

The rights of people who have been sectioned are protected by the 1983 and 2007 Mental Health Acts:

- Patients have the right to be told what's happening to them, to have their questions answered, and to have their views listened to, although the mental health professionals don't have to act on those views.

- The 2007 Mental Health Act states that all patients detained under section orders 2 and 3 should be told that advocacy services are available – an advocate can help a patient, for example, by going with them to meetings with a psychiatrist or asking for more information on their behalf. An advocate also has the right to meet with a patient in private, and see the patient's medical records if the patient is capable of giving consent for this. See question 41, p. 116 for sources of independent advocacy, or a hospital may have its own advocacy service – ask at reception.

- With the help of a solicitor, a detained patient can seek discharge by applying to the Mental Health Review Tribunal, an independent panel that decides if a patient should continue to be detained. (See Extra resources, p. 252 for contact details.)

- It's a popular belief that someone who's been sectioned loses their right to vote in local or general elections, but this isn't necessarily true. A detained patient can still use their vote, as long as their name is on the electoral roll of their home address or of the hospital (for long-term admissions). Their doctors can give them permission to leave the ward in order to vote, or if this isn't possible, a postal vote can be arranged. But a patient can be prevented from voting if doctors believe that they don't have the mental capacity to make a rational choice.

Although this isn't specifically covered by the Mental Health Act, psychiatric patients should also be protected from sexual abuse and exploitation, and the associated risks of sexually transmitted diseases and unwanted pregnancies. A small research study conducted in 2004 by Dr James Warner of Imperial College London, looking at 11 wards across three psychiatric units in London, found that ten out of 100 patients had engaged in sexual activity, and there were instances of unwanted sexual advances. The report throws up a difficult question – if a person is unable to consent to treatment, how can they consent to sexual activity? Sexual harassment of patients by other patients (or staff) should not be tolerated, and the hospital must be told if someone on a ward is making unwanted sexual advances towards another person, so that the rights of vulnerable patients can be protected.

Q54. Who looks after patients in a psychiatric hospital?

Anyone diagnosed with bipolar disorder is assigned a named consultant psychiatrist (see question 40, p. 105) who is responsible for their treatment regardless of whether they are in or out of hospital. During a hospital stay, they are likely to see their consultant once a week for review meetings (sometimes called ward rounds). On a day-to-day basis, they're more likely to see a junior psychiatrist, known as a SHO (senior house officer) or registrar, who is still in training, and who usually refers to the consultant before making any major decisions. Further members of the hospital team include psychologists (again, see question 40, p. 105 for more information) who also work with a patient in and out of hospital, and other professionals who tend to be more hospital-based – psychiatric nurses, psychiatric pharmacists and occupational therapists.

Psychiatric nurses

The front line staff in a psychiatric ward, with whom patients have the most daily contact, are the psychiatric nurses.

Every ward has a ward manager in charge, plus a deputy ward manager, and each patient has a 'named' nurse (also called a key worker) who is responsible for their care during their stay, with at least one other nurse who can step in when the named nurse is off-duty, so that there's a continuity of care. This role is particularly important, so that a patient feels there is a connection of trust between them and their named nurse – the Mental Health Act's Code of Practice reinforces this by asserting that all psychiatric hospitals should assist in 'developing a therapeutic relationship between each patient and key/nurse worker'.

All UK nurses train through a 12-month common foundation programme, followed by two years in the student's area of specialization, such as mental healthcare. After qualifying, a mental health nurse may specialize even further, possibly training in drug and alcohol work, or cognitive behavioural therapy. Degree courses in mental health nursing are also becoming available. But there's much more to working in a psychiatric hospital than qualifications, as Julie King, the ward manager of a psychiatric unit in Essex explains: 'You can only teach someone skills and knowledge, but experience and attitude can't be taught ... It's so important to respect a patient's dignity and remember that they're much more than just a walking illness, that they're a human being. A kind word or gesture from one of us can make all the difference to their recovery. They need to feel safe. All of our clients have their stories, often heart-breaking stories and it's our compassion and non-judgement that will assist their recovery as much as the drugs and time. A good nurse gives so much more than their time, they give themselves. It's not an easy job, but it can be extremely rewarding. I like to think that the people in my team are here because they love helping people. This is much more than just a job. It's not something you do just for the money.'

Sarah has witnessed both insensitivity and kindness in her sister Rebecca's care, and says that the difference it makes to the recovery process can't be underestimated:

> I've seen Rebecca laughed at, ignored and shouted at by hospital staff in the past. Yet during her last stay in hospital, a psychiatric nurse put her arm around Rebecca's shoulder and said, 'Rebecca is such a lovely girl. It's a pleasure having her in here.' It's no coincidence that Rebecca's recovery under such a lovely team was much quicker. And not only is it so much better for the person who's staying in the unit, but it's so reassuring for us, the family, to know she's liked and well cared for on an emotional level.

One of the most important roles carried out by psychiatric nurses is observation. Close one-to-one observation isn't unusual when a patient is first admitted, for a variety of reasons ... a patient might be aggressive, agitated, elated, trying to take their clothes off, too depressed to eat, intent on doing themselves harm or even suicidal. Any psychiatric patient in any type of ward can be put under close observation – the decision to do this is usually made by a psychiatrist, and the patient (or their family) should be told if this is happening, as well as the reasons for it. But psychiatric nurses are, in a sense, always observing the patients in their care – the Code of Practice directs them to look at the patients' 'general behaviour, movement, speech, expression of ideas, appearance, orientation, mood and attitude, interaction with others, and reaction to medication'.

Pharmacists

Psychiatric pharmacists work with psychiatrists to prescribe the right combination of medications. Qualifying as a pharmacist takes five years, which includes a master's degree and a one-year pre-registration course; on top of this, training as a psychiatric pharmacist takes at least two extra years. Psychiatric pharmacists may be accredited members of the College of Mental Health Pharmacy, or hold a further qualification in Psychiatric Pharmacy. Psychiatric pharmacists and technicians are represented by the UK Psychiatric Pharmacy Group, whose website can be found at www.ukppg.org.uk.

Ian Maidment, Senior Pharmacist, Kent & Medway Partnership NHS Trust, and Senior Lecturer, Kent Institute of Medicine and Health Studies, Kent University, describes the role of a psychiatric pharmacist in more detail: 'As a pharmacist based in two admission wards, I would go to every ward round, advise the doctors and all the nursing staff on prescribing, speak about medication to any patient who wanted to see me, on a one-to-one basis, also speak to families and carers if the patient was happy with that. I would also run a patient education group twice a week, where patients could ask me questions. This would involve educating the patients about their drugs, how to take them, and what side effects to look out for. I would really try to encourage patients to self manage their own illness ... I also do a lot of education and training, not just of patients but also of nursing staff, doctors, social workers, support workers, etc., because they will all get asked about medication. We're also involved in developing drug protocols and providing written information on drugs.'

Sounds great, doesn't it? But, as with many aspects of mental health care, this service is not always available. A report carried out by the UK's Healthcare Commission found that 24% of psychiatric wards received no visits from pharmacy staff at all, and 86% received less than five hours of pharmacy staff time in a week. The same report found that a shocking 36% of people in psychiatric hospitals were prescribed more than the maximum recommended dose of antipsychotic medicines. It's not hard to make a link between these facts, especially when the Commission also reveals that when mental health pharmacists are involved in medication reviews, 70% of the reviews lead to change in a patient's medicine.

If a patient and/or their relative have concerns over medication, it's worth asking a hospital staff member if the local health organization has a psychiatric pharmacy service, as well as speaking to their psychiatrist.

Occupational therapists

The Mental Health Act's Code of Practice also states that hospitals should 'provide structured activities by professional staff', and many psychiatric units, particularly medium secure units where patients are more likely to stay for longer periods of time, employ occupational therapists as part of the psychiatric care team. The NHS Careers website defines occupational therapy (OT) as 'the assessment and treatment of physical and psychiatric conditions using specific, purposeful activity to prevent disability and promote independent function in all aspects of daily life'. In simple terms, participating in OT activities, as well as helping to pass the time on a ward, can help a patient's recovery by giving them confidence and satisfaction in developing new life skills. Sarah noticed that during Rebecca's most recent hospital visit, an aerobics instructor came in and held classes a couple of times a week and that there's definitely more emphasis on creative pursuits, such as art therapy. And others describe how facilities are improving:

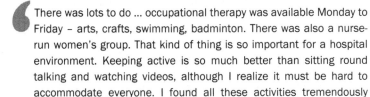

There was lots to do ... occupational therapy was available Monday to Friday – arts, crafts, swimming, badminton. There was also a nurse-run women's group. That kind of thing is so important for a hospital environment. Keeping active is so much better than sitting round talking and watching videos, although I realize it must be hard to accommodate everyone. I found all these activities tremendously useful.

(Rachel)

Q55. What is a 'nearest relative'?

The Mental Health Act 1983 also gives rights to the patient's 'nearest relative', who can then act in the patient's interests. Section 26 of the Act lists the people who can be considered a patient's nearest relative in descending order – so, for example, if the patient has no spouse or partner, the Act will view an adult child as the next most likely candidate. The official order is:

- husband, wife or civil partner (now including, since the Mental Health Act 2007, same sex partners)
- son or daughter
- father or mother
- brother or sister
- grandparent
- grandchild
- uncle or aunt
- nephew or niece.

If more than one person from a category qualifies – for example, if there are two adult children of a patient – then the oldest will be considered as the nearest relative. If a nearest relative can't be found according to the hierarchy described above, the courts can nominate a suitable alternative.

A patient can object to the nearest relative selected by making a court application that declares them as 'not a suitable person' – although the patient can't object on the grounds of simply wanting to choose someone else.

The nearest relative has a number of rights:

- They can apply for their loved one to be sectioned under Sections 2 and 3 of the Mental Health Act 1983.
- The nearest relative can't stop a Section 2 order application being made by an AMHP – although the AMHP should try to keep them informed and listen to their views – but they can object to a Section 3 application. The AMHP can overrule this objection by

applying to the courts to have the nearest relative removed from their position and for the role to be given to someone else.

• The nearest relative should be kept informed about the patient's care – if someone has been detained in hospital, they should be told why. They can't intervene or prevent treatment for a patient who has been sectioned, although they can discuss the treatment with staff or make a complaint. It's worth remembering, though, that under the Mental Health Act, the patient can object to the nearest relative being told any of this information.

• The nearest relative also has the right to be told if and why a patient is being discharged and to be involved in planning the patient's post-discharge after care. Again, the patient can object to their involvement.

• Technically, the nearest relative has the right to discharge the patient from a psychiatric hospital, even if they're detained under Section 2 or Section 3 of the Mental Health Act. They must give the hospital 72 hours' notice of their intention. The patient's consultant psychiatrist can stop this process by issuing a barring certificate within the 72 hour notice period – and the nearest relative can be removed from their role if they try to discharge a patient 'without regard to patient or public welfare'.

Q56. How can friends and family support a loved one in a psychiatric hospital?

There are three main ways a friend or family member can help someone who's in a psychiatric unit – give them time, offer them practical help, and provide staff with useful information.

Time

Put simply, the most valuable way to support someone is by giving them time, as psychiatric ward manager Julie King explains: 'People often feel abandoned when they come to us, as if they've been forgotten by the outside world. Phone calls, letters and visits can all help make that person stay connected and feel loved. It's the little things that make such a big difference.'

Sarah is convinced that the visits Rebecca receives from friends and family when she's in hospital make a world of difference to her recovery:

> Mum and I contact Rebecca every day when she's in hospital, as do her many friends. We phone a lot – just to connect and to see how she's feeling. And we visit as much as possible. I know Rebecca really looks forward to those visits. She's such a sociable person and even when she's really ill she misses friends and family so much. Her face lights up whenever I turn up – even if she knows I can only stay for half an hour because I've got to get back for the children. I think she needs that contact with the outside world.

It's also helpful to the patient if a family member (who may also be their legal nearest relative – see question 55, p. 162) can be there at review meetings, when a patient's case is being discussed. Sarah's mum, Rose, goes to as many of Rebecca's review meetings as possible to keep up-to-date with the treatment changes and to support Rebecca emotionally. And Amanda's dad, Gordon, always goes to her mum Irene's review meetings, giving her invaluable support:

> My mum can become intimidated and tongue tied when faced with a room of people, and not feel able to say what she wants. There have been times when she has been quite animated before a review meeting, discussing with my dad what she wants to say, but as soon as she walks in, she clams up, especially if there are faces around the table she doesn't recognize. So it's always really helpful for my dad to be there with her, as he communicates my mum's viewpoint on her behalf. For someone who's mentally ill, a meeting like this, even though it's being held in the patient's best interests, can be very stressful, and

a family member can be a real support at these times – for example, voicing concerns about treatment if there have been side effects.

Family members can ensure a patient gets the best out of hospital care by helping make their feelings and wishes known, taking an active part in planning their future treatment and asking questions – for example, in a review meeting, a relative can ask all health professionals present to identify themselves and state clearly what they do.

Practical help

Practical help is also important for someone in a psychiatric unit, as ward manager Julie King explains: 'On a practical level, people who come to us often need things like toiletries, cigarettes, sweets, change for the phone, clean clothes etc. That kind of help is invaluable. Also, remember that people in hospital often find the days are incredibly long and they get bored staring at the same four walls. It's always useful when a relative or friend brings in some magazines or a jigsaw or an appropriate game – just to help relieve the boredom.'

Here's a list of what someone who's just been admitted into hospital might need:

- comfortable clothing
- nightwear
- personal toiletries
- family photos
- a pillow or blanket
- books/magazines
- card games/puzzle books/jigsaw
- change for the phone/a phonecard/important phone numbers
- mobile phone (if allowed on the ward)
- sweets/chewing gum

- cigarettes and lighter
- notepad and pen.

Before handing anything over (especially anything potentially dangerous, such as a lighter, nail polish remover, nail scissors or a pen knife), it's best to ask for permission from a member of staff.

Information

One thing to remember is that the psychiatric staff may not have met the patient before they walk through the door, whereas their friends and family know them and their habits, their preferences, their behaviour and their personal story better than anyone else. Make sure that all the staff are aware of any special requirements, like dietary or religious needs, or if there are any language difficulties which might need the help of an interpreter. Any information can help staff to support the patient more effectively – Amanda's mum Irene, for example, used to cause concern about her eating habits:

 My mum doesn't have a large appetite, and usually only eats breakfast and dinner, with just fruit for lunch – but in the early days, when she was first admitted to the psychiatric unit, the staff weren't aware of this, and Mum didn't explain. So they kept insisting that she should eat lunch and pestering her to come to the dining room. Then they would write on her notes that she was 'refusing' to eat, as if this was unnatural behaviour ... when of course it was perfectly normal for her! Once my dad had explained, they became more relaxed and stopped viewing it as a symptom of her illness or anything to be alarmed about.

It can be difficult for a relative to know who to speak to, but it's best to communicate with the nurse in charge, or the patient's named nurse. If this isn't possible, writing down anything they think the team needs to know, with as much detail as possible, is useful. Most psychiatric teams usually then brief each other at the changeover of each shift.

Q57. How can friends and family forge a good relationship with those who care for their loved one in a psychiatric hospital?

For friends and family, it can be hard to come to terms with seeing their loved one in a psychiatric hospital and this can put a huge strain on the relationship between the professionals and the family. Mental Health Advisor to the Royal College of Nursing, Ian Hulatt puts it like this: 'Psychiatric staff engage in processes that people don't necessarily value or want, but we do so because we believe it's in the patients' best interests and we have the legal powers to do so. That brings with it some very real challenges because people want to leave, people don't want to take their medication, people don't think they are ill. Relatives might find that the work we do looks custodial ... and society is very confused about what mental health problems are about.'

He says that to establish a good relationship with psychiatric staff, it's important for relatives to try to understand why their loved one is being admitted to hospital, and what the reasons are for their treatment: 'For families, what they need to do is see that nurses and psychiatrists are not there to spoil life for the individual, but they are there to support the individual and work with the family to keep the individual well. We need to have good lines of communication between family members and people caring for patients. We have to all work together.'

In an ideal world, there should be a two-way process, with hospital staff viewing family members as part of the healing process. Family members can be particularly helpful in spotting warning signs for mood swings, as they know the patient so much better than the staff, who according to Ian Hulatt, increasingly recognize that the family is essential in maintaining the health of the patient: 'There's research that shows it's the family who notice signs of relapse long before medical staff or nursing staff. It's the family who know when someone is becoming unwell. We have to consider family members as partners in someone's care and all work together.'

Another way of forging a good family/staff relationship is if a relative asks a nurse: 'Is there anything I can do to help?' It might be persuading the patient to take their medication willingly, or even something as simple as brushing their hair or helping them to take a bath. Psychiatric staff will usually appreciate that kind of support – sometimes a family member can communicate better with a patient and get through to them when a nurse can't.

Q58. Do psychiatric hospitals allow smoking?

Research by the King's Fund (an independent charitable foundation) estimates that 70% of patients in UK psychiatric hospitals smoke, of whom 50% are heavy smokers, compared with 25% and 9%, respectively, of non-psychiatric patients. Until recently, most psychiatric units have allowed patients to smoke, usually in designated smoking rooms.

 The smoking room is the only place of comfort in a psychiatric unit. Smoking is a great stress reliever and a comfort for people with mental health problems.

(George)

But this has changed. New UK legislation banned smoking in all indoor public places from July 2007. Although psychiatric hospitals were given a temporary exemption, at the time of writing there were plans to scrap the exemption in July 2008 and all units in England, Wales and Northern Ireland would have to comply with the law. The exemption was set to continue in Scotland, however, so Scottish psychiatric patients would be free to light up indefinitely.

But how would staff and patients react to the smoking ban? The King's Fund research said that 90% of the psychiatric nurses it surveyed were worried about the effect the ban could have on patients. They feared a ban on cigarettes could lead to agitation and even aggression in some patients, and were concerned that the ban was unworkable.

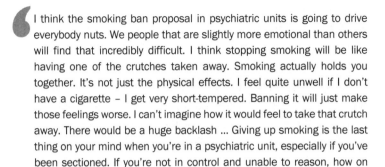 I think the smoking ban proposal in psychiatric units is going to drive everybody nuts. We people that are slightly more emotional than others will find that incredibly difficult. I think stopping smoking will be like having one of the crutches taken away. Smoking actually holds you together. It's not just the physical effects. I feel quite unwell if I don't have a cigarette – I get very short-tempered. Banning it will just make those feelings worse. I can't imagine how it would feel to take that crutch away. There would be a huge backlash ... Giving up smoking is the last thing on your mind when you're in a psychiatric unit, especially if you've been sectioned. If you're not in control and unable to reason, how on earth could you give up smoking? Reason goes out of the window.

(Sharron)

The UK mental health charity Mind acknowledged the rights of non-smoking patients to live in a smoke free zone, but added: 'Whilst it is desirable that people are supported to reduce or stop smoking if they would like to do so, it is unrealistic and unfair to require people to stop at the time of admission to hospital. This is likely to cause distress and to be seen as an additional deprivation of liberty and coercion at a time when they already have many aspects of their liberty restricted.'

The charity called for a number of measures to help psychiatric patients adapt to the new anti-smoking legislation, including designated sheltered smoking areas in hospital grounds, a wider range of activities on in-patient wards to combat boredom (often cited as a reason to smoke), and offering patients smoking reduction/cessation aids (nicotine patches, gum, etc.) which could be prescribed as part of their medication in hospital – a patient and their family can discuss this with the consultant psychiatrist or pharmacist.

Q59. What happens when a psychiatric patient is well enough to leave hospital?

Before a patient leaves hospital, they are encouraged to think about how to recognize early warning signs of relapse and what the best course of action would be – i.e. which medication to use, who to call, and how to enlist the support of family and friends.

A discharge planning meeting should also be held between the hospital, the patient, local health and social services and a care co-ordinator – usually this is a CPN or support worker. The purpose of this is to work out a post-discharge care plan for the patient, using the Care Programme Approach (CPA) which is a national framework for the assessment and planning of care. The aim of the care plan is to help someone readjust back into their normal life, so that they are at less risk of relapse and being readmitted to hospital (sometimes called 'revolving door' patients.) Other areas can be included in the care plan, for example housing issues, employment advice, or support for vulnerable patients with a history of drug and alcohol abuse.

However, research by the Healthcare Commission (*No voice, no choice,* July 2007) has shown wide variation in how the Care Programme Approach is used across the country:

- Many people are not fully involved in decisions about their own care.

- Too few people are being offered or are receiving a written copy of their care plan – the study showed that almost half had not received one.

- People are not always aware of who their care co-ordinator/key worker is. In some areas, the figure is as low as 39%.

- Not enough care reviews are carried out – only half of the people surveyed in the Healthcare Commission study had received a care review in the previous 12 months.

- Not enough people have a say in decisions about their medication – only 42% of the people surveyed reported that they 'definitely' were involved in decisions about their drugs.

- People need more help with their physical health as part of their care plan – someone with a diagnosis of mental illness is more likely to suffer health problems due to self-neglect, poor diet, lifestyle, drug and alcohol misuse, etc.

- Employment assessments are supposed to be carried out as part of the Care Programme Approach, but only half of people who said they wanted help in finding employment had received any.

It seems so obvious that people leaving psychiatric hospital need support. Bearing in mind the Healthcare Commission's report, a discharged patient and their family can make the Care Programme Approach work harder for them by:

- asking for a written copy of the patient's care plan
- making sure they know their care co-ordinator's name, contact details and hours of availability, who to contact in their care co-ordinator's absence, and how to request a change of care co-ordinator if necessary
- asking for a care plan review at least every 12 months
- asking for written copies of any changes to the care plan after a review
- insisting that their views on medication are listened to during care plan meetings
- asking for help on other issues such as housing, employment, physical health and drugs/alcohol abuse.

Returning home after a section order

If a patient has been detained in hospital under a section order, they are likely to have 'staggered' home leave before the section order is lifted. So for example, after a month's treatment, the psychiatric team might agree that a patient can have a day's leave, returning to hospital in the evening. If this goes well, then the patient might be allowed home leave for a weekend, then a week's leave. If all goes well and the patient is still making good progress outside the hospital environment, the section order will be formally lifted. This is typically what has happened with both Amanda's mum Irene and Sarah's sister Rebecca, each time they have been sectioned into hospital.

Community Treatment Orders

Controversially, the Mental Health Act 2007 introduced a new form of supervised discharge for some patients when they leave hospital, known as Community Treatment Orders (CTOs). These orders have the power to force people (usually patients who were originally sectioned) to comply with treatment regimes after they've been discharged. Initially a CTO is issued for a six month period, and can be renewed for another six months – after this the CTO is renewed annually. The new legislation only affected England and Wales, although a form of the CTO was already used in Scotland (and in other countries including the United States, Australia and New Zealand).

Concerns were raised by a number of sources, including UK mental health charities such as Mind, SANE and the Mental Health Alliance, that this legislation undermined a patient's rights – CTOs give mental health professionals the power to recall people to hospital if it's judged that they're not following the treatment that has been prescribed for them, and to submit to medical examination if required. At the time the legislation was issued, the UK government claimed that CTOs would only be used for a small number of patients, mostly with complex mental health issues who were likely to relapse and potentially cause harm to themselves and other people – in March 2007, a spokesperson for the Department of Health said that: 'Community Treatment Orders (CTOs) are a key part of helping solve the problem of "revolving door" patients. We know many tragedies in mental health are preceded by non-compliance with treatment and CTOs will address this.'

However, Rowena Daw from the Mental Health Alliance said: 'We call on the government to listen to the professionals, patients and families who have expressed such strong concerns about CTOs. We agree with the government that compulsory treatment in the community can help a small number of people in very specific situations, but the current plans go too far. They will not limit the use of CTOs to this small group of people and they will place unnecessary restrictions on people's daily lives.'

Q60. What are the pros and cons of being treated in a psychiatric hospital?

It's an understatement to say that conditions in psychiatric hospitals can be far from perfect. Changes are being made, it's true, but not fast enough. Patients in NHS psychiatric hospitals still report not enough beds, over-stretched staff, even a very small minority of staff who are (intentionally or not) less caring to a patient than they should be:

To get so low, psychotic or manic that you need to go into hospital, to get so unwell that you need to be detained ... it's always going to be an unpleasant experience.

(Rachel)

Add to this the strain of being surrounded by other mentally ill people with their own challenging behaviour to deal with, feelings of grief, anger or even despair at being away from home, a loss of independence and a fear of being stigmatized in the future for having been a psychiatric patient. For many people, psychiatric hospital treatment is seen as the last resort, to be avoided at all costs, as Amanda recalls from the early days of her mum Irene's illness:

In the beginning, for my parents and all our family, the thought of Mum being admitted to a psychiatric hospital was the worst possible thing that could happen to her. We didn't regard it as a place of healing but as a frightening unknown ... We'd heard all the outdated 'mental asylum' stereotypes, so the hospital was a symbol of mentally being at absolute rock bottom. Yet in recent years, these feelings have become more complex. Understandably, Mum never wants to leave home. And none of us – least of all my parents – are happy that she and Dad are apart from each other. Usually she's admitted to hospital when she's in a mixed state, and is paranoid, depressed and agitated and refusing all treatment ... so it's a distressing experience all round. But because she has stayed at the same psychiatric unit so many times, it has become familiar to her, just as she has become familiar to the psychiatrists, nurses and other staff, who now understand her better, and who usually care for her with great kindness and compassion. Within a few days of treatment, they are able to interrupt the circle of despair she's trapped in. Hospital treatment is not perfect by any means, but for Mum, her psychiatric unit has become a place of safety and healing – not the end of the line, but the beginning of her road back towards stability.

Admittance to hospital can give someone the breathing space to break a cycle of destructive behaviour (for example, if someone is self-harming) in a safe, low-stimulation environment, where they can be observed and cared for, where a normal daily routine can be re-established and where healing can take place without having to cope with the pressures of the outside world. Sarah's sister Rebecca doesn't sleep or eat properly for days when she's on a manic high, and can begin her recovery process only once she's safely cared for in the structured hospital environment. Or someone may have attempted suicide – they could still be dangerously depressed and require constant vigilance for their own safety, something their own (possibly exhausted) family may not be able to give.

A stay in a psychiatric hospital ward is a chance for someone with bipolar disorder who's become seriously unwell to find out what's happening to them, and why. They can begin to understand more about their condition, learn to recognize warning signs and develop ways of dealing with them. It's also an opportunity for their treatment and medication to be reviewed and stabilized, and for their future treatment to be planned – ideally with input from everyone involved in their care (them, their family and the appropriate team of mental health professionals).

CHAPTER FIVE

LIFESTYLE CHOICES

Q61. Can a healthy lifestyle lower the chance of relapse for someone with bipolar disorder and reduce the risk of developing it in the first place?

It's not rocket science ... All the healthy-living rules apply. Research proves without a shadow of a doubt that making sensible lifestyle choices reduces both the chance of someone with a high genetic risk of bipolar developing full-blown symptoms and the risk of relapse for someone who already has a diagnosis. The ultimate health-promoting choices include:

- Eating a balanced, nutrient-packed diet
- Taking nutritional supplements
- Not smoking
- Drinking no more than two caffeine-loaded drinks in a day
- Drinking only one or two alcoholic drinks in a day
- Not taking recreational drugs
- Exercising regularly

- Avoiding too much stress
- Getting plenty of relaxation
- Getting seven to eight hours' sleep a night.

Q62. What is the link between stress and mood swings?

High Blood Pressure and Health Policy, a document unveiled at the European Parliament in Brussels, shows that high blood pressure now affects 25% of the world's adults – about one billion people. And the report warns the figure will grow to 60% by 2025 unless action is taken.

When stressed, the body produces more of the so-called 'fight or flight' chemicals, adrenaline and noradrenaline, which prepare the body for an emergency. Blood pressure increases, the heart beats faster and stomach activity increases (often referred to as 'butterflies').

Because the body doesn't actually need these chemicals to fight or run away, they remain in the system and, over time, damage health and well-being. Short term, stress can cause headaches, indigestion, nausea, aches and pains and palpitations. In the longer term, the risk of heart attack and stroke rockets through the roof. On an emotional level, chronic stress increases anxiety, fear, anger, frustration and depression. Stressed people can also become withdrawn, indecisive, inflexible, irritable, tearful or aggressive.

Many bipolar people cite stress as one of their main triggers for a mood swing into mania or depression:

Stress and elation are huge triggers for me. For instance, when I pranged the car – I reversed out of parking space and didn't see a concrete pillar – I was in an acute psychiatric unit within two weeks. The smallest things can tip me over the edge.

(Sharron)

The stress of a car accident at 70mph on the motorway definitely tipped the balance. David was on his way home and I got a phone call. 'The car's smashed up, a wreck,' he said. When he got home he went to bed and pulled the covers over his head. After the accident his whole way changed. He was so depressed and bad-tempered. Before that he had never raised his voice. But then he started punching doors. Every door in the flat had a hole in it.

(Jackie)

Yet it's not only negative stressful events that can set off a mood swing. Positive stressful events can be a trigger too. Sarah says that her wedding in 1996 was the event that sparked Rebecca's first real manic episode.

With hindsight, of course, we look back and recognize all the warning signs. At my hen party, Rebecca was full of non-stop energy – talking and laughing and dancing. At the wedding rehearsal, we were all quietly going through the order of service in the church when the main doors burst open and Rebecca actually cycled in. It was funny, and a bit embarrassing, although Rebecca wasn't in the slightest bit embarrassed. She just parked her bike in the back of the church and ran up the aisle, apologizing to the vicar for being late. On the morning of my wedding she was up first – probably at around 5am – and had done several jobs around the house, including setting up the breakfast table. I remember that all the cup handles and spoons were pointing in the same direction. Yet, at the time, we didn't pick up that anything was wrong. We were all excited and on a kind of wedding 'high'. It was only the next day when she got higher and higher that my mum realized anything was wrong.

Amanda also believes that her fortieth birthday party was a trigger for one of her mum's hospitalizations:

I threw a big party to celebrate my fortieth birthday, and invited hordes of friends and family, including Mum and Dad. The party was fantastic, and Mum seemed to be enjoying herself – laughing, chatting, dancing. It was such a great night. She was still in a positive mood when they drove home the next day, if a little tired and I breathed a sigh of relief that the party hadn't affected her. How wrong I was. Her mood began to change almost as soon as they got back, and within hours she was lost in her usual mixed state of depression and agitation. Her CPN and psychiatric team initially tried to treat her at home, but a few days later she was back in hospital. Her psychiatrist said she may have experienced a mood swing anyway, but that the high emotion of the evening probably contributed to it. There's a lovely photo of her from the night of the party ... she's arm in arm with me and my Dad, and she looks so happy – we all do. It's hard to believe that, less than a week after the picture was taken, she would be sectioned again.

Of course, it's virtually impossible to eliminate stress completely (from being caught in an unexpected rain shower to losing a loved one), but lifestyle choices play a huge role in nipping the stress reactions to those events in the bud. Here's how to tip the scales in favour of a less stressful life:

- Whenever possible, avoid people and situations which create problems.
- Include a form of relaxation, such as deep breathing or meditation, into your daily routine.
- Exercise every day.
- Eat a healthy diet.
- Restrict or stop smoking, drinking and recreational drug use.
- Take part in enjoyable activities.

Q63. How can regular sleep patterns help to control symptoms of bipolar disorder?

It's been said that sleep and mood are joined at the hip. That's true for anyone, but even more so for anyone with a diagnosis of mental illness.

According to one study, 80% of psychiatric patients have sleep disorders, the severity of the insomnia matching up with the intensity of symptoms.

Sleep is a powerful regulator of brain chemistry and people with bipolar commonly sleep too much, not enough, not at all or not deeply enough.

Sleep and depression

There's a huge overlap between the symptoms of depression and sleepiness – social withdrawal, fatigue and difficulty concentrating. Research has linked persistent insomnia with the onset of a major depressive episode within one year.

Sleep and mania

According to the British Association of Psychopharmacology, sleep disturbance is perhaps the most common final pathway to mania. Even the loss of a single night's sleep can place someone at severe risk of tipping into full-blown mania.

For many people with a bipolar diagnosis, good sleep plays a huge part in their mood and behaviour.

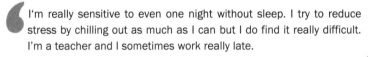

I'm really sensitive to even one night without sleep. I try to reduce stress by chilling out as much as I can but I do find it really difficult. I'm a teacher and I sometimes work really late.

(Jude)

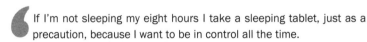

If I'm not sleeping my eight hours I take a sleeping tablet, just as a precaution, because I want to be in control all the time.

(Neil)

Sarah notes that one of the most telling clues to Rebecca's moods is her sleep pattern:

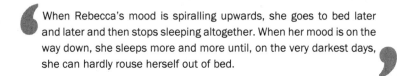

When Rebecca's mood is spiralling upwards, she goes to bed later and later and then stops sleeping altogether. When her mood is on the way down, she sleeps more and more until, on the very darkest days, she can hardly rouse herself out of bed.

And when Amanda's mum Irene is on the verge of a mixed state, Irene's sleep pattern is always disrupted – at first she will start to wake up for periods during the night, but as the mood swing starts to escalate into agitation and paranoia, she becomes unable to sleep or rest at all.

A night of uninterrupted sleep tops up the body's energy tank enough to cope with the following day and helps ensure that hormones and neurotransmitters in the brain can work efficiently. And though sleep problems are one of the main symptoms of bipolar disorder, it is possible to practice good habits to maximize the chances of a good night's rest.

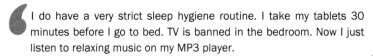

I do have a very strict sleep hygiene routine. I take my tablets 30 minutes before I go to bed. TV is banned in the bedroom. Now I just listen to relaxing music on my MP3 player.

(Debbie)

I have a relaxation CD that bores me to sleep.

(Carl)

Good sleep rules

- Try to go to bed at the same time every night and wake up at the same time every morning. This will 'train' the body to stick to a good routine.

- Get between seven and eight hours' sleep a night – that's the optimum amount, according to the world-renowned Sleep Research Centre in Loughborough, England.

- Avoid shift-work as it prevents establishing a regular sleep pattern.

- Don't nap. In the same way as a snack blunts the appetite for food, a nap takes away the appetite for sleep.

- Avoid sleep-preventing caffeine and other stimulants, particularly after 4pm. See question 71, p. 205 for caffeine-free alternatives.

- Turn off the TV. Watching television stimulates the brain instead of switching it off.

- Do a soothing activity during the hour before bedtime. For instance, have a warm bath laced with calm-inducing lavender essential oil or listen to a relaxing classical music CD.

- Turn on an electric fan. Studies show that background 'white noise' can help induce sleep.

- Don't exercise in the evening. Research shows that, due to the production of the hormone adrenaline, physical activity increases mental alertness for four hours afterwards, which can lead to insomnia.

- Check medication. These usually help stabilize and normalize sleep, but they can also cause side effects such as insomnia or excessive sleeping so it's worth speaking to a doctor about their sleep-disrupting potential.

- Take medication. As a last resort during periods of poor sleep, a doctor can prescribe sleeping tablets or other medication to help re-establish a good routine.

- Have sex. The body releases a cocktail of hormones during sex, many of which trigger sleep.

- Be aware that long haul airplane journeys across different time zones can disrupt the body clock and sleep patterns – there's some evidence that jetlag can be a trigger for mania.

Q64. How does exercise affect bipolar symptoms?

When it's a struggle to get out of bed to make a cup of tea or when the mind's racing so fast the body has a job keeping up, it's unlikely that exercise is high up on the agenda. However, there's no getting away from the fact that physical activity is one of the best ways to keep the body strong and the mind calm. There's a whole catalogue of scientific studies to support the value of exercise for those with mental health problems. One even found that regular exercise is as effective as antidepressants for those with major depression. And a report by the Mental Health Foundation found that antidepressant use could be significantly reduced if GPs offered exercise on prescription to all patients with depression – that's because exercise triggers the release of endorphins (natural opiates that create a sense of well-being).

One fantastic scheme based in the UK tangibly proves that exercise can help boost mental health. The Positive Mental Attitude League (PMAL), affiliated to the Football Association, boasts 14 teams from six mental health trusts around London. All the players have been diagnosed with a mental illness, yet since they started training two hours a week with their team and playing in the league, the average rate of relapse has been significantly reduced. The pre- and post-season questionnaire each team member playing with Hackney FC for a season filled out also shows that three-quarters were able to cut down their medication, reported a better social and family life, and found a job or a college course. They cut down on tobacco and street drugs, took up more exercise, lost weight and ate more healthily. In fact, the results have been so positive, a similar scheme has been set up in the Manchester area. Inspirational league-founder Janette Hynes (winner of the award for Social Entrepreneur of the Year 2007) eventually plans to set up local leagues in cities across Europe. Visit www.leaguewebsite.co.uk for more details.

Yet exercise doesn't have to be sport-based to lift the spirits. Research at the University of Essex, UK found that, after a country stroll, 71% of the participants reported reduced levels of depression and tension, and 90%

reported a boost in self-esteem. In contrast, only 45% said they felt reduced levels of depression after walking in a shopping centre, and 22% said they actually felt more depressed.

On the other side of the bipolar coin, exercise can also help release excess energy:

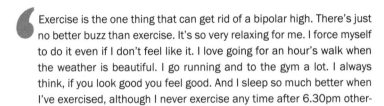

> Exercise is the one thing that can get rid of a bipolar high. There's just no better buzz than exercise. It's so very relaxing for me. I force myself to do it even if I don't feel like it. I love going for an hour's walk when the weather is beautiful. I go running and to the gym a lot. I always think, if you look good you feel good. And I sleep so much better when I've exercised, although I never exercise any time after 6.30pm otherwise I can't get to sleep.
>
> (Dave)

And on a physical level, exercise helps to eliminate toxins, oxygenate every cell in the body and burn off calories, helping to shift any excess weight. Whenever possible, aim to get 30 minutes' worth of exercise a day plus three hour-long sessions a week. The best heart-pumpers? Walking, swimming, cycling, dancing, skating, running and aerobics (class or DVD).

Q65. Can complementary therapies help control bipolar symptoms?

Complementary medicine is just that: a treatment that *complements* mainstream medicine. It isn't intended to replace it, but to work alongside it. An estimated 5.75 million people in the UK see a complementary practitioner each year and an increasing number of treatments are available on the NHS.

Although some experts dismiss complementary therapies, saying that not enough evidence exists to prove they work, research carried out by the Mental Health Foundation shows that mental health service users want greater access to complementary therapies and that where these are provided, they are found to be well received and helpful. Many people with bipolar disorder find that including holistic therapy in a treatment plan can help to control symptoms and prolong periods of stability. Just make sure that any practitioner is registered with a professional association or regulatory body. So which therapies can help?

Acupuncture

A branch of Chinese medicine, acupuncture involves placing very fine needles into the skin at different points (called acupoints) in order to stimulate the flow of Qi (pronounced 'chee'), the body's energy. One study in America found that a group of seriously depressed women experienced a 43% reduction in their symptoms after a 16-week course of acupuncture, compared with a 22% reduction in symptoms for the placebo group.

Cost: £30 to £40 a session

Contact: British Acupuncture Council on 0208 735 0400, www.acupuncture.org.uk

Aromatherapy

A form of treatment using botanical essential oils, aromatherapy is now widely used in clinics and hospitals to reduce anxiety and promote relaxation. When inhaled, the scents work on the brain and nervous system through the stimulation of the olfactory nerves. In fact, work carried out at Yale University in America found that the scent of spice apple reduced blood pressure by an average of three to five points in healthy volunteers. Other essential oils known for their calming properties include bergamot, chamomile, clary sage, frankincense, geranium, grapefruit, jasmine, juniper, linden blossom, lavender, mandarin, marjoram, Melissa, neroli, orange, palmarosa, rose, sandalwood, vetiver and ylang ylang. Simply add a few drops of one or more essential oils to a bath or burn in an aromatherapy burner. Only buy products with the words 'pure essential oil' on the label as this means they contain active botanical ingredients with healing properties. Cheaper imitations probably contain very little, if any, of the active ingredients.

Cost: Essential oils vary enormously in price, but expect to pay at least £6 or £7 for 20ml. An hour-long consultation with a medical aromatherapist costs around £30 to £40.

Contact: Association of Medical Aromatherapists on 0141 332 4924.

Homeopathy

From the Greek word 'homoios' – meaning same – and 'pathos' – meaning suffering – homeopathy works on the idea that like will cure like. The remedies are taken in extremely dilute forms and no matter how many symptoms are experienced, only one remedy is taken, which is aimed at all of the symptoms. Although there haven't been any published clinical trials yet, several studies have reported positive results in the treatment of depressive disorders using homeopathy alongside conventional medication, including high levels of patient satisfaction.

Cost: Around £30 to £40 for a consultation, plus sometimes there's also a small charge for the prescribed remedy.

Contact: UK Homeopathy Medical Association on 01474 560336, www.the-hma.org or the Alliance of Registered Homeopaths on 08700 739339, www.a-r-h.org

Massage

One of the oldest healing techniques, massage can be relaxing or stimulating, depending on which techniques are used and can relieve tension and stress as well as combat general aches and pains. A study at the Touch Research Institute at Miami University's School of Medicine, Florida, USA shows that massage therapy plays an important role in the alleviation of stress and stress-induced illnesses.

Cost: Around £30 to £40 for an hour-long treatment.

Contact: Massage Therapy UK, www.massagetherapy.co.uk

Meditation

A discipline, rather than a therapy, meditation aims to achieve total relaxation of body and mind. Although there are many different forms, the underlying goal is to clear your mind. Once learnt, it can be practised anywhere – in the bath, in bed, on the bus – for an instant feeling of well-being and calm. The most common form of meditation in the West is Transcendental Meditation (TM) which involves sitting still with eyes closed, clearing the mind and repeating a word or mantra for 20 minutes twice a day. Instruction takes place in four sessions on consecutive days; each is approximately 90 minutes long. There is considerable medical evidence to show that regular practice helps to relieve anxiety and alleviate many stress-related symptoms, such as insomnia and fatigue.

Cost: Variable

Contact: www.transcendental-meditation.org.uk, 0870 514 3733.

Reflexology

Based on the principle that certain points on the feet and hands (called reflex points) correspond to different parts of the body, reflexology is a treatment given by a trained practitioner who applies pressure to these specific points, helping to release tension and boost the body's own natural healing process. In a report on reflexology research published at www.reflexology-research.com, a Chinese study demonstrated how reflexology alleviated the effects of extreme stress. Twenty patients being treated for 'neurasthenia' – a condition of extreme emotional stress – were given daily reflexology for a week at the hospital's department of physiotherapy. 40% of the patients experienced a complete cure, 35% were greatly improved, 15% were mildly improved and 10% reported no change.

Cost: Around £20 to £40 for an hour-long treatment.

Contact: Association of Reflexologists on 0870 567 3320, www.aor.org.uk or British Reflexology Association on 01866 821207, www.britreflex.co.uk

Reiki

Reiki is a Japanese word meaning 'universal life force energy'. It is a non-invasive, hands-on therapy, which works to rebalance mind, body and spirit that was rediscovered just over 100 years ago in Japan. Reiki practitioners are 'attuned' to open their own healing channels to allow the Reiki energy to pass through them so they can heal themselves and others. In one study published in the journal *Alternative Therapies in Health and Medicine*, participants who received weekly Reiki treatments for six weeks reported significant reduction in depression, hopelessness and stress.

Sarah, who learnt Reiki in 1998 and who became a Reiki Master (which means she can teach Reiki) in 2006, has given Rebecca several healing treatments over the years.

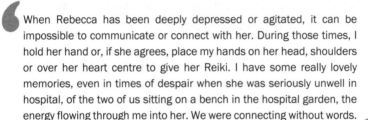

When Rebecca has been deeply depressed or agitated, it can be impossible to communicate or connect with her. During those times, I hold her hand or, if she agrees, place my hands on her head, shoulders or over her heart centre to give her Reiki. I have some really lovely memories, even in times of despair when she was seriously unwell in hospital, of the two of us sitting on a bench in the hospital garden, the energy flowing through me into her. We were connecting without words.

Cost: an hour-long treatment costs between £10 and £50, although many Reiki practitioners are open to 'pay-what-you-can' donations. Contact: The Reiki Alliance on 01449 673 449, www.reikialliance.org.uk, or the Reiki Association on www.reikiassociation.org.uk or UK Reiki Federation on 0870 850 2209, www.reikifed.co.uk

Yoga

Yoga dates back to at least 3000 BC and fans say that practising the different poses – some simple, some complicated – helps keep the body stretched and supple and the mind calm and clear. There are many different forms of yoga – hatha and Iyengar are the most common forms taught in the West. A study published in the *Evidence-Based Complementary and*

Alternative Medicine journal showed that after 20 classes of Iyengar yoga, patients with clinical depression had significant reductions of depression, anger, anxiety and neurotic symptoms.

Cost: Classes usually last 60 to 90 minutes and cost £5 to £15.

Contact: The British Wheel of Yoga on 01529 306 851, www.bwy.org.uk

In the UK, the Institute for Complementary Medicine provides information on various therapies – call them on 020 7237 5165 or visit their website: www.i-c-m.org.uk

In the US, find a list of qualified practitioners for a range of complementary therapies at: therapists.psychologytoday.com

Q66. What dietary changes can help control the symptoms of bipolar disorder?

More and more evidence shows that diet has a huge impact on mood and behaviour and a lasting effect on mental health, as Dr Andrew McCulloch, Chief Executive of the Mental Health Foundation, explains: 'We are only just beginning to understand how the brain, as an organ, is influenced by the nutrients it derives from the foods we eat, and how our diets have an impact on our mental health. We know that the brain is made up in large part of essential fatty acids, water and other nutrients. We know that food affects how we feel, think and behave. In fact, we know that dietary interventions may hold the key to a number of the mental health challenges our society is facing.'

In 2006, the Mental Health Foundation commissioned a report and ran a 'Feeding Minds' campaign with another charity, Sustain Alliance (For Better Food and Farming), to raise awareness of the links between diet and mental health. The report recommended that healthy diet advice should be given to everyone with a mental illness as an important cornerstone of treatment. Maybe one day soon it will be ... In the meantime, more people than ever are coming round to the same conclusion – that food really does have a noticeable impact on mood.

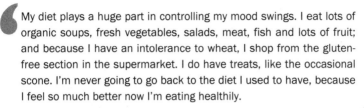

My diet plays a huge part in controlling my mood swings. I eat lots of organic soups, fresh vegetables, salads, meat, fish and lots of fruit; and because I have an intolerance to wheat, I shop from the gluten-free section in the supermarket. I do have treats, like the occasional scone. I'm never going to go back to the diet I used to have, because I feel so much better now I'm eating healthily.

(Dave)

Caffeine is bad for me at any time. And sugar's not good either. There have been times when I have been on a low sugar diet and felt loads better.

(Ashley)

Thinking about making dietary changes may sound daunting, but it's actually possible to tweak just a few simple things that can make a world of difference to mood and mental health.

Top 10 bipolar-busting diet changes

1. Eat more fish
2. Eat more fruit and vegetables
3. Eat lots of low-fat protein
4. Eat less processed food
5. Eat less sugar
6. Eat breakfast
7. Snack on nuts and seeds
8. Drink lots of water
9. Drink less coffee and tea
10. Cut down alcohol intake.

Here's why these changes will help:

Eat more fish

Worldwide research clearly shows that the lower a country's overall fish intake, the higher the rates of depression, post-natal depression, seasonal affective disorder and bipolar disorder in its citizens. The reverse is also true – the more fish eaten, the fewer cases of mental health disorders.

Sadly the proof is all too obvious – people in the UK eat 59% less fish than they did in the 1940s, while the number of mental health disorders in the UK population continues to soar by the decade.

Why fish? 20% of the fat in our brain is made from the essential fatty acids omega-3 and omega-6. They are termed 'essential' as they can't be made within the body, and must come from the diet. Each fatty acid performs vital functions in the structuring of brain cells (or neurons), ensuring that good communication is possible within the brain. Unequal intakes of omega-3 and omega-6 fats are linked to various problems, including depression, and concentration and memory problems. Yet most people consuming Western diets eat far too much omega-6 (found in a lot of processed foods) and not enough omega-3. Fish is loaded with omega-3, so getting three portions a week will help restore this important balance.

The best fishy dishes (in order of omega-3 content from most to least) are kippers, anchovies, mackerel, herrings, sprats, pilchards, salmon, sardines, tuna, trout, shrimps, crab, halibut, mussels, oysters, cod, scallops and lobster.

Eat more fruit and vegetables

A number of studies show that people with low intakes of certain vitamins and minerals are far more likely to be depressed than those with higher intakes. Nutrients in the research spotlight include folic acid (or folate), calcium, magnesium, iron, zinc and vitamins B1, B2, B6, B12 and C. Yet since the 1940s there has been a 34% decline in UK vegetable consumption, with the latest figures suggesting that only 13% of men and 15% of women eat at least five portions of fruit and vegetables a day.

Why fruit and vegetables? When there's a lack of nutrients, the body can't make neurotransmitters (chemicals that relay nerve impulses between brain and body), which can result in mood swings, depression and a range of psychiatric problems. Getting five portions of fresh (or frozen) fruit or vegetables a day will ensure good nutrient intake. Though *all* fruit and vegetables are loaded with vitamins and minerals, a team of researchers in the US has rated their brain-protective potency with the ORAC (short for Oxygen Radical Absorbance Capacity) scale. These are the most protective foods (in order of highest potency to the least): prunes, raisins, blueberries, blackberries, kale, spinach, raspberries, strawberries, Brussels sprouts, plums, alfalfa sprouts, broccoli, beetroot, oranges, red grapes, pepper, cherries, kiwi fruit, pink grapefruit, onion, corn on the cob and aubergine (eggplant).

Eat lots of low-fat protein

Research shows that a deficiency in certain amino acids, found in protein, can lead to feelings of depression, apathy, a lack of motivation and an inability to relax. Protein is rich in amino acids, the brain's messengers, which the body needs to make neurotransmitters (as mentioned above, these are the chemicals that relay nerve impulses between brain and body). Different amino acids make different neurotransmitters. For example, the neurotransmitter serotonin, known as the 'happy chemical', is made from the amino acid tryptophan. Adrenalin and dopamine, the 'motivation chemicals', are made from phenylalanine. For a brain-healthy intake of amino acids, experts recommend getting at least one portion of meat, dairy, fish, eggs or tofu and two servings of beans, lentils, quinoa, seeds, nuts and wholegrains daily. Getting more protein can also help stop the carbohydrate cravings that many people with bipolar describe:

The trouble is, I eat too much when I'm down. I crave carbohydrates. I go through boxes and boxes of cornflakes and other cereals. I'm also trying to cut down on bread. I'm a couple of stone overweight.

(Paul)

Eat less processed foods

Processed foods damage the brain by releasing toxins or oxidants that harm healthy brain cells. They have been linked to an increased risk of mood disorders by interfering with the way the body processes nutrients, weakening the immune system and triggering hormonal imbalance. In general, a poor diet puts a huge strain on the liver, so it becomes sluggish and unable to detoxify the body effectively. This means more toxins find their way into the bloodstream, affecting the function of the brain, causing erratic mood changes, a general feeling of depression, a 'foggy' brain and the inability to concentrate or remember things. Common brain-drainers and mood-shifters include:

- 'Trans' fats – found in deep-fried food and food containing hydrogenated vegetable oils, these block absorption of mood-friendly essential omega fats.

- Chemicals, additives and preservatives – research shows that high levels are linked to mood disturbance.

- Simple carbohydrates (such as white bread and pastries) cause blood sugar imbalance which is linked to problems, such as fatigue, irritability, dizziness, insomnia, excessive sweating and/or thirst, poor concentration and forgetfulness, depression and crying spells, digestive disturbances and blurred vision.

- The manmade sweetener aspartame (found in diet drinks and foods) may contribute to depression as well as other psychiatric problems, though more research is needed.

Eat less sugar

Sugar (often labelled glucose, fructose, dextrose, maltrose, lactose or sucrose) and sugary foods, including honey, deplete the body of vitamins and minerals, and cause blood sugar levels to rise and fall rather than remain stable (an important factor in mood swings).

Eat breakfast

Research consistently shows that skipping breakfast leads to a noticeable effect on mood, memory and energy level. And a number of studies report that providing children with breakfast improves their daily and long-term academic performance. Experts recommend eating no later than one hour after waking up. Good breakfast options include porridge and berries, wholegrain cereal, or beans or egg on wholegrain toast.

Snack on nuts and seeds

Nuts and seeds are a great source of brain-protecting omega-3 essential oil and there are a number of other vegetarian sources (listed in order of decreasing omega-3 content): flax seeds oil, walnuts, pumpkin seeds, flax seeds, walnut oil, rapeseed oil (canola), soya beans, green leafy vegetables (although they contain relatively less omega-3 than fish).

Drink lots of water

There is good research to show that dehydration seriously affects mood. Aim to drink 1.5 litres of water every day. Filtered or bottled is best.

Drink less coffee and tea

Caffeine, found in coffee, tea and cola drinks, can affect mood. See question 71, p. 205 for more about the effect of caffeine on bipolar symptoms.

Cut down alcohol intake

Alcohol is one of the brain's worst enemies. See question 72, p. 208 for more about the effect of alcohol on bipolar symptoms.

For more useful information on how food can affect mood, visit www.foodandmood.org

Q67. What is the 'Mind Meal'?

Launched by the UK mental health charity Mind, the Mind Meal is a simple-to-cook, three-course meal made up of the best mood-balancing foods around. It's bursting with vitamins and essential fats crucial for good mental health, yet doesn't contain any artificial added sugars or stimulants like coffee, which have all been linked to depression. There's also no wheat or milk, which can trigger food allergies and imbalances in the brain.

1. Avocado salad and seeds

Ingredients

250g/8oz bag of mixed lettuce or 80g/4oz bag of watercress
One avocado
Handful of sunflower seeds
Handful of pumpkin seeds

Method

- Place the mixed salad in a serving dish.
- Remove the skin and stone from the avocado. Cut into small pieces and add to the mixed salad.
- Sprinkle on the seeds.
- Serve plain or with olive oil or salad dressing.

2. Wheat-free pasta with pesto and oil-rich fish

Ingredients

250g/9oz wheat-free pasta, such as corn and vegetable pasta shells
100g/4oz pesto sauce
170g/6oz tin of salmon (or herring, sardines or pilchards)

Method

- Cook the pasta in boiling water following the instructions on the packet.
- When the pasta is ready, add one tablespoon of pesto sauce per person and mix.
- Drain off the liquid from the fish, remove or crush any large bones, and flake with a fork. Add to the pasta and pesto and mix gently together.

3. Fruit and oatcakes

Ingredients

2 bananas

2 apples

8 dried apricots

8 to 12 oatcakes

40g/2 oz /½ cup (broken) walnuts

Method

- Peel the bananas and rinse the apples and dried apricots.

- Cut the fruit into small pieces, removing the apple core, and place together in a small saucepan.

- Add three tablespoons of water and simmer gently for ten minutes, or until the fruit is soft, adding more water if needed to prevent the mixture becoming too dry and sticking to the pan.

- Break and arrange the oatcakes in the bottom of individual bowls.

- When the fruit is soft, pour into individual bowls to cover the oatcakes. If the fruit mixture contains enough liquid, the juices will soak into and soften the oatcakes.

- Serve with a sprinkling of broken walnuts.

Q68. Can nutritional supplements minimize the symptoms of bipolar disorder?

Nutritionist Patrick Holford, author of the best-selling book *Optimum Nutrition For The Mind*, is convinced that taking supplements can dramatically reduce symptoms for people with depression and bipolar disorder. 'In one study at the University of Calgary in Canada, 11 bipolar adults were given 36 vitamins and trace minerals in addition to their prescribed medication,' he says. 'Over the next six months, on average, they halved their need for the medications and every patient experienced between a 55–66% reduction in symptoms.'

And the greatest news of all is that it only takes three simple changes to achieve all these fantastic benefits:

Top 3 bipolar-busting supplements

1. Take a good-quality multivitamin daily and/or supplements to ensure intake of the following: calcium, folic acid, iron, magnesium, manganese, vitamins B1, B3, B5, B6, B12 and C and zinc.
2. Take a good-quality omega-3 supplement daily.
3. Sprinkle a tablespoon of lecithin granules over breakfast cereal every day.

Here's why making these changes and loading up on the extra nutrients can help:

Calcium

A lack of calcium affects the central nervous system, and causes nervousness, apprehension, irritability and numbness.

Food sources: low-fat dairy produce, leafy green vegetables, almonds, brazil nuts, sesame seeds, tofu, dried fruit, wholegrain cereal.

Ideal daily intake: 800mg

Folic acid (or folate)

Research consistently shows that a lack of folic acid increases the risk of depression, and in one study at Kings College Hospital Psychiatry Department in London, a third of 123 patients were found to have low levels of folic acid.

Food sources: leafy green vegetables, broccoli, melon, asparagus, beetroot, brewer's yeast (Marmite/Vegemite), wholegrains.

Ideal daily intake: 100mcg.

Iron

Low levels of iron have been linked to fatigue, poor concentration, depression, weakness, lack of appetite and headaches.

Food sources: red meat, wholegrain cereals, leafy green vegetables, pulses such as kidney beans and lentils, dried fruits.

Ideal daily intake: 14mg

Magnesium

A deficiency in magnesium can cause anxiety, irritability and hypersensitivity to noise and has been linked to an increased risk of depression and confusion, anxiety, agitation and hallucinations. One study of nine people with rapid cycling bipolar symptoms found that half of them were stabilized by magnesium supplementation, and intravenous magnesium sulphate has been used with some success for calming manic patients.

Food sources: leafy green vegetables, soya products such as tofu and soya milk, seeds, nuts, wholegrains, bananas, dried apricots, avocados.

Ideal daily intake: 200mg

Manganese

This metal plays a role in amino-acid formation, so a deficiency may contribute to depression that stems from low levels of certain neurotransmitters.

Food sources: nuts, wholegrains, dried fruit, pineapple, green leafy vegetables, oats, brown rice.

Ideal daily intake: 3mg

Vitamin B1 (Thiamine)

The brain uses this vitamin to help convert glucose, or blood sugar, into fuel, and without it, the brain quickly runs out of energy, leading to fatigue, depression, irritability, anxiety and even thoughts of suicide.

Food sources: red meat, peas, spinach, wholemeal bread, nuts, bran flakes, soya beans.

Ideal daily intake: 25mg as part of a B vitamin complex to ensure maximum absorption.

Vitamin B3 (Niacin)

A lack of vitamin B3 is linked to agitation, anxiety and mental 'fog'. Pellegra, a condition that leads to psychosis and dementia among other symptoms, is caused by vitamin B3 deficiency.

Food sources: red meat, poultry, fish, peas, peanuts, soya beans, kidney beans, wholegrains.

Ideal daily intake: 25mg as part of a B vitamin complex to ensure maximum absorption.

Vitamin B5 (Pantothenic acid)

Symptoms of deficiency are fatigue, chronic stress and depression. Vitamin B5 is also needed for good hormone function.

Food sources: sweet potatoes, avocado, mushrooms, yoghurt, red meat, fish, lentils, broad beans, haricot beans.

Ideal daily intake: 25mg as part of a B vitamin complex to ensure maximum absorption.

Vitamin B6

A lack of B6 means the body is unable to make serotonin (the happy chemical) so efficiently, which could potentially lead to depression.

Food sources: wholegrains, brown rice, soya products, bananas, strawberries, oats, broccoli, asparagus, fish, chicken, watermelon.

Ideal daily intake: 25mg as part of a B vitamin complex to ensure maximum absorption.

Vitamin B12

Without vitamin B12, neither the senses nor the brain can work properly and it has been shown to be vital for a healthy nervous system.

Food sources: brewer's yeast (Marmite/Vegemite), fish, meat, poultry, eggs, low-fat dairy products.

Ideal daily intake: 10mcg

Vitamin C

Low levels of vitamin C are associated with an increased risk of depression and one study found that about a third of psychiatric patients had blood vitamin C levels that were below the threshold that has been associated with behavioural problems.

Ideal daily intake: 1,000mg

Zinc

Someone with bipolar disorder has a high probability of lacking in the mineral zinc, which has been linked to apathy, lack of appetite and lethargy. When zinc is low, copper levels in the body can increase to toxic levels, resulting in paranoia and fearfulness.

Food sources: chicken, fish, shellfish, low-fat dairy products, peanuts and legumes.

Ideal daily intake: 10mg

Essential fatty acids

Two papers published in the *British Journal of Psychiatry* show that, put simply, taking 2g of omega-3 essential fatty acids daily can help decrease depression, suicidal behaviour and stress. Dr Andrew Stoll and his team at Harvard Medical School also found that patients with a bipolar diagnosis who took omega-3 fats had much longer periods without any symptoms than another group who were taking an olive oil placebo. 'The mode of action appears to slow down the electrical activity in the brain,' explains pharmacist Shabir Daya.

Food sources: oily fish, nuts, seeds, nut and seed oils, soya beans, leafy green vegetables.

Ideal daily intake: a fish oil concentrate that contains between 1.5 and 4g of the active ingredient EPA (eicosapentaenoic acid).

 What have really helped to control the lows are the fish oil supplements I take. From my research on the Internet, I found out that there are a lot of grades of fish oil, starting from the old fashioned cod liver oil right up to Rolls Royce fish oil – high grade EPA concentrates. I've been taking PuraEPA capsules for five years. They didn't seem to make much of a difference at first, but then I read somewhere that it's not a miracle cure. It takes a minimum of three months for the oil to be fully absorbed. You have to be patient. Also, trans fats in the diet can put the brakes on the absorption process so I tried to cut them out. Now I take six capsules a day; two in the morning and four at lunch-time. The body can't absorb a large amount of oil in one go, so I split them up.

(Dave)

Choline (in the form of lecithin)

A nutrient similar to the B vitamins, choline has shown some promise in small trials in the US with people who have rapid cycling bipolar disorder. It's thought that choline accelerates the synthesis and release of the neurotransmitter acetylcholine, which is involved in many nerve and brain functions.

Food sources: eggs, beef, cauliflower, tofu, almonds, peanuts.

Ideal daily intake: 500–800mg daily. Nutritionist Patrick Holford recommends adding a tablespoon of lecithin granules (the body absorbs choline more easily in the form of lecithin) to breakfast cereal every morning.

The best way to ensure a good intake of these nutrients is by eating a healthy diet. It's also perfectly safe to take a good-quality multi-vitamin and minerals supplement and a good-quality omega-3 supplement (in the doses recommended above) without consulting a professional, even when taking prescribed medication. Both are widely available from health food stores.

The future

Although more clinical trials are needed to back up current knowledge, it's thought that taking extra amino acids in supplement form can help bump up the supplies of neurotransmitters in the brain (a lack of which is linked to depression). It's claimed that taking various doses of some nutrients, such as amino acids L-tyrosine, L-phenylalanine, L-tryptophan, L-theanine, TMG,

GABA or SAMe can improve symptoms of mental health conditions, but these should only be supplemented under the guidance of a professional. To find a qualified nutritionist in the UK, contact The British Association for Nutritional Therapy (BANT) on 08706 061284 or at www.bant.org.uk In the US, visit www.findanutritionist.com

Q69. Can herbal remedies help control bipolar symptoms?

It's important to stress that unlike the nutritional supplements mentioned above, herbal remedies are not necessarily safe to take alongside prescription medication. 'The interactions between herbs and medicines may not have been fully recognized yet because not enough research has been done,' says pharmacist Shabir Daya. 'And some herbs may not be suitable to treat bipolar regardless of whether you're taking medication or not.'

For example, St John's wort (Hypericum perforatum) – perhaps the best-known and best-researched herbal remedy to help lift low mood – is licensed in Germany and other European countries as a treatment for mild to moderate depression, anxiety and sleep disorders, and has been shown in clinical trials to boost the production of serotonin (the brain's 'happy' chemical). A daily dose of 900mg of the standardized extract (which means the amount of active ingredient is guaranteed) is as effective in counteracting mild depression as some prescription antidepressants. Reported side effects include stomach complaints, oversensitivity to sunlight and fatigue. And, because of potential adverse interactions, St John's wort should not be taken at the same time as other antidepressants or with some medications, including indinivir (used to treat HIV), the contraceptive Pill, theophylline, warfarin, digoxin, reserpine, cyclosporine and loperamide. Perhaps more importantly for those with a diagnosis of bipolar disorder, in spite of its great antidepressant effect, there have been a few cases of St John's wort inducing mania.

There's a small (yet growing) body of research and lots of anecdotal evidence to show that other herbal remedies – including kava kava (which is currently banned in the UK), valerian, magnolia rhodiola, ginkgo biloba and black cohosh – can help control bipolar symptoms. But Shabir Daya's advice for anyone with anything more serious than mild depression or the slightest indication of a family history of mania: 'Always seek professional help before taking any new herbal supplement.'

To find a qualified herbal practitioner in the UK, contact the National Institute of Medical Herbalists on 01392 426022, www.nimh.org.uk or The Association of Master Herbalists at www.associationofmasterherbalists.co.uk

In the US, a list of qualified herbalists is available via The American Herbalists Guild (AHG) – see www.americanherbalistsguild.com

Q70. How does nicotine affect bipolar symptoms?

In the grand scheme of things, giving up smoking is hardly likely to be high up on the list of priorities when someone's experiencing a manic episode or down in the depths of depression.

I started smoking when I was 13 – the year after I can pinpoint when my behaviour started to change and when my bipolar symptoms kicked in. I've had lots of periods when I've not smoked. In fact, I don't smoke at all when I'm manic. I'm too busy doing everything and anything to find time to smoke. When I'm stable, I don't really smoke at lot – probably five or six a day, usually in the afternoon with a cup of tea. But when I'm low, I smoke constantly. I've always got a cigarette on the go. That's because when I'm depressed I become a thinker. I don't smoke in the house. I go in the garden and sit on the doorstep. It's amazing how long I can make a cigarette last when I'm depressed. I use it as time for thinking and dwelling. Smoking is a comfort thing when I'm depressed.

(Amy)

However hard it is, quitting during a period of stability is definitely worth thinking about. As well as the huge expense, a single puff of a cigarette

contains a trillion cell-damaging oxidants, which immediately travel into the brain. The chance of getting cancer goes up and the risk of fetal abnormalities in pregnancy increases. Smokers also take in high levels of the heavy metal cadmium, the gradual accumulation of which depletes the depression-fighting nutrients zinc and vitamin C. Cadmium has also been linked to disturbed mental performance and increased aggression. One study by Dr Corvin of St James' Hospital in Dublin found that smoking doubled the incidence of psychotic symptoms among patients with manic depression.

Passive smoking also has significant risks. According to research in the *Journal of the American Medical Association*, just 30 minutes in a smoky environment can damage your heart by reducing its ability to pump blood.

So what's the best way to give up?

Studies show that using Nicotine Replacement Therapy (NRT) – patches, gum, lozenges or tabs – doubles the likelihood of success. And in the UK, the NICE guideline for smoking cessation states that NRT can be prescribed if a smoker makes a commitment to stop on a particular date. The guideline recommends the following timetable for collecting the prescriptions:

- Quit date or before – two weeks supply
- At two weeks after quit – a further two week supply
- At four weeks after quit – four weeks supply
- At eight weeks after quit – final four weeks supply

The guideline also states that if a smoker's attempt to quit is unsuccessful, the NHS should normally fund no further attempts within six months (unless external factors such as an unexpected stressful life event interfere with the attempt to stop smoking, in which case it may be reasonable to try again sooner).

- Attending a local NHS-run smoking cessation group or another support group increases the chance of quitting long term by 13–19%. Call the NHS Smoking Helpline on 0800 169 0 169 or Quitline on 0800 00 22 00.

- Allen Carr, the late give-up guru and celeb favourite with the likes of Richard Branson and Ruby Wax, has clinics in 18 countries and claims a 90% success rate. It's also possible to learn about his techniques via his book or CD (*Allen Carr's Easy Way to Stop Smoking*). See www.allencarr.com or call 0800 389 2115 for more information.

- In an article published in *New Scientist* magazine, it was reported that 'hypnosis is the most effective way of giving up smoking, according to the largest-ever scientific comparison of ways of breaking the habit'. And in a study conducted at the Scott and White Memorial Hospital in Texas, smokers were given eight sessions of hypnotherapy over two months and told to quit smoking one week after beginning the course of treatment. By the end of treatment 40% had given up. At a follow-up 12 weeks later, 60% had quit. Find a practitioner at www.hypnotherapistregister.com

- Research published in the international medical journal *Addiction* shows that moderate exercise, such as walking, greatly reduces nicotine withdrawal symptoms. The theory is that exercise boosts the body's levels of the hormone dopamine, which enhances mood and reduces the need for nicotine.

- For more information on giving up smoking, see the NHS website www.givingupsmoking.co.uk

- In the US, The Foundation for a Smoke-Free America runs campaigns and offers support and advice to anyone trying to quit. Call 1 310 471–0303 or see www.anti-smoking.org

I started smoking in a mental hospital when I was first ill at the age of 18. I'd used marijuana quite a lot before then, but in hospital there was a bloke who smoked and I thought, well, I'm allowed to smoke in here so I will. I smoked 20 or more Marlboro a day for 20 years and didn't quit until I was 38. The reason I stopped was because my wife nagged me. By that time we had kids, and she was pulling out that card. Quitting smoking was part willpower, part Nicorette gum and part nagging by my wife. It was pretty hard, especially the first time. I would quit and then start again. I'd try and hide it from my wife, but eventually it was easier to stop, especially as I was working in a non-smoking office at the time and I used to have to sneak off to the toilets. I haven't had a cigarette at all for six years now. Health-wise, I feel so much better. I can exercise without running out of breath.

(Carl)

A word of warning ...

Zyban – a nicotine-free quit-smoking prescription drug – contains the same active ingredient as the antidepressant Wellbutrin. It works by boosting the levels of several chemical messengers in the brain, which leads to a reduction in nicotine withdrawal symptoms and a weakening of the urge to smoke. More than a third of the people who take Zyban at the same time as participating in a support programme are able to quit smoking for at least one month. However, Ian Maidment, Senior Pharmacist, Kent & Medway Partnership NHS Trust, and Senior Lecturer, Kent Institute of Medicine and Health Studies, Kent University, says: 'Zyban contains Bupropion (also marketed as an antidepressant). Like all antidepressants, it can cause mania in bipolar, induce seizures and cause problems in children and adolescents. According to the March 2007 British National Formulary (a standard prescribing reference book), Zyban is contra-indicated in bipolar, so yes it should be avoided in a patient with bipolar.'

Q71. How does caffeine affect bipolar symptoms?

Tea, coffee, chocolate and cola drinks contain caffeine, a stimulant that takes over and eventually replaces the natural processes in the brain for increasing alertness and motivation.

> I constantly drink tea. I feel like it kick starts my brain, especially if I've done nothing for a while. I have set times that I drink it – 7:30am, 11am, 2pm, 4pm, 7pm and 9pm. I *have* to have it at those times. The first one of the day is particularly important as I can't move or see properly until I've had it. It's almost an extension of my medication – in fact, I take my meds with it!
>
> (Amy)

Coffee contains between 30 and 150mg of caffeine, depending on its strength. Tea contains between 20 and 100mg. A can of Coke contains 46mg and Red Bull contains 80mg. Chocolate contains small amounts of caffeine. It's also worth mentioning that some over-the-counter medicines (such as pain relief, flu remedies, appetite control pills and fatigue-fighters, such as Pro Plus) can also contain significant amounts of caffeine.

The trouble with caffeine is that it can lead to the over-stimulation of the nervous system, increased anxiety levels and insomnia. And even if it doesn't actually prevent sleep, studies show that an intake of as little as 250mg caffeine per day can reduce the amount of time spent in deep sleep.

But, the irony is that, according to research at Bristol University, drinking coffee doesn't make coffee drinkers feel any more alert and energized than non-coffee drinkers. In other words, drinking coffee simply relieves the symptoms of withdrawal from coffee. And the assumption is that, although they carried out their research on coffee, the caffeine in tea, cola drinks and chocolate will have the same effect in the body, particularly as they contain other chemicals that have also been linked to sleep disturbance. For instance, chocolate contains the stimulant theobromine, whose action is similar to caffeine's. Coffee contains theophylline, a chemical stimulant known to disturb normal sleep patterns. Tea is loaded with tannin that prevents the body from absorbing certain mood-stabilizing nutrients, such as the B vitamins. Soft drinks and chocolate are laden with sugar.

The good news is that it's not necessary to cut out caffeine altogether. Two caffeine-loaded drinks a day can feature in a healthy diet, but any more can significantly affect mood. It's also worth thinking about what time of day caffeine is consumed. Because of its sleep-disturbing potential, caffeine is better as a morning pick-me-up than as an evening drink or snack, particularly during periods of mania and/or insomnia.

 I tend to avoid stimulating food and drink in the evening ... I won't have a coffee after seven o'clock, or anything very sugary.

(Keith)

I've given up caffeine. I no longer drink Diet Coke and only have one cup of tea in the morning. I then drink decaffeinated tea throughout the day. Now I wake up more easily and sleep better, which means I'm less tired for the rest of the day. Sometimes it's hard at college when others are having coffee in between lectures, but I'm never tempted because my concentration levels are so much better and I'm doing better at college.

(Rachel)

Remember that it is best to cut down caffeine intake gradually to avoid headaches and other withdrawal symptoms, such as fatigue and irritability. If problems do occur, increase water intake and they will eventually disappear.

So what are the alternatives to coffee, a cup of tea, a can of Coke or a bar of chocolate?

Caffeine-free hot drinks

- herbal teas – chamomile is good for inducing calm and sleep, peppermint is good for indigestion, lemon grass is refreshing
- roasted herbal roots, such as barley, chicory and dandelion
- grain coffee – Rombouts and Wilson's Heritage are popular choices.

Caffeine-free cold drinks

- water
- fresh fruit juices (not those made from sugar-laden concentrate or dilute-with-water squashes that are loaded with additives and sugar or saccharine)
- milk.

Caffeine-free chocolate

- carob is a plant extract available from health food stores
- have small chunks of 70% cocoa dark chocolate, as it's lower in saturated fat, additives and sugar than its milk chocolate counterpart.

Q72. How does alcohol affect bipolar symptoms?

So-called dual diagnosis (where a condition, such as bipolar disorder, is accompanied by another clinical condition, such as alcoholism) is common and the World Health Organization says that sufficient evidence now exists to assume that alcohol plays a contributing role in the development of depression. In fact, substance abuse is seen in one third to half of people with bipolar disorder, and alcohol is top of the abused substances list.

 It's really hard to avoid alcohol, but it is a trigger. If I have one drink, well, I'll probably have six or seven. But it doesn't seem to make me drunk; it just makes me more hyper.

(Tamara)

Drinking may be habit and/or a way to shut out the world, but there's no getting away from the fact that alcohol is the brain's worst enemy. It's thought that alcohol uses up and depletes the neurotransmitters that the brain needs to ward off anxiety and depression naturally. It also dissolves brain-friendly omega-3 fatty acids within brain cells and prevents the brain from being able to use them. Too much alcohol can interfere with the liver's normal functioning (the liver is the organ that metabolizes alcohol), trigger blood sugar imbalances (alcoholic drinks contain a lot of sugar) and cause deficiencies in a number of vitamins linked to good mental health.

Alcohol is especially harmful for those with bipolar because it depresses the central nervous system, which leads to less inhibited behaviour and impulse control. It reveals or magnifies underlying feelings, which is why many drinkers become angry, aggressive, anxious or low (worsening the symptoms of depression). Research also shows it interferes with good quality sleep by significantly reducing the time spent in slow-wave (deep) sleep. This can lead to a constant feeling of fatigue, demotivation and depression.

Even more worryingly, alcohol can prevent antidepressants from working properly, interact in dangerous ways with certain medication, including lithium and tranquillizers, and increase the likelihood of suicidal thoughts. The statistics are sobering: 60% of suicides in Britain are alcohol related and alcohol-related deaths have almost doubled since the 1990s.

Tom was worrying he was starting to get high again, but the medication wasn't working. He started drinking a lot of alcohol – eight cans of cider in one go. And as he gradually got worse, he didn't ever seem to get drunk. He started ringing old girlfriends. He started self-harming, cutting himself. He would also bring random people home he'd met drinking on the streets. The day he eventually ended up in hospital he had been drinking all day.

(Jo)

Government guidelines define high-risk use as having more than five drinks daily, moderate risk as three to four drinks daily and low risk as one or two drinks daily (up to seven drinks in a week).

If alcohol dependence isn't an issue, cut down to one or two drinks daily (and ideally have two booze-free days a week) or stop drinking altogether. If alcohol dependence is a problem, talk to your doctor who may prescribe a certain type of medication (benzodiazepines) to help minimize withdrawal symptoms from alcohol, which include the 'shakes', sweating, headaches, nausea, stomach pains, poor appetite, insomnia, anxiety, low mood, mood swings and, in some rare cases, even hallucinations, paranoia, disorientation, psychosis, severe memory problems and epileptic fits. For this reason, anyone with a bipolar diagnosis and an alcohol dependency should never go 'cold turkey' – give up alcohol suddenly – but seek medical help first. See www.drinkaware.co.uk

Contacting Alcoholics Anonymous (AA) is also highly recommended. Founded in 1935, AA has more than two million members in 150 countries and is well known for the high success rate of its Twelve Step Programme and the support provided at weekly meetings. The basic premise of AA is to get well and sober. Don't pick up the first drink; acknowledge and accept one's powerlessness over alcohol; try to live a day at a time; accept that there is a greater power, whatever or whoever that power might be. AA suggests a codeword for new members to remain sober – HALT: try to be never Hungry, Angry, Lonely or Tired.

For information about AA in the UK, call 0845 769 7555 or see www.alcoholics-anonymous.org.uk To find a local AA group anywhere in the world, see www.alcoholics-anonymous.org

> My bipolar was masked by self-medicating with alcohol over the years. I am an alcoholic. From the age of 21, I probably drank daily. I drank lager, bitter and whisky, and sometimes would drink all day. On a Sunday, I would make a fry-up with a can at my side. Then I'd take a nap at lunchtime. I kidded myself that alcohol was keeping me on an even keel and that it prevented me from getting too high and helped me to sleep. I never got really drunk. In my mind, the drinking was justified because I was using it to make me a better person and feel better. But it got to be too much. When I left my job as a motorcycle mechanic and became a house-husband, I would drink all day and was lying to my wife about my drinking and hiding it. I would promise

to stop, but couldn't. I began to withdraw into myself rather than communicate with my wife. I was really short-tempered and not a very nice person. Our marriage was falling apart. She was so fed up with me that she was sleeping in a different room and we were talking about separate living arrangements. That made me really sad, and suddenly I realized how serious the situation had become and that I was going to lose everything.

AA was the only way I found I could stop. The reason I went was to try to save my marriage. It was my last chance, basically. They say you have to go to any lengths to stop the drinking and I was willing to do what they said. It's hard to describe the compulsion. Even though you tell yourself you're not going to do it, you do. I started by going to three meetings a week and I still do now. I haven't had a drink for two years and seven months. My life is much better for having left that vice behind me. I'm more clear-headed. I feel much more on top of my whole personality and find it much easier to let go of things. I'm no longer so compulsive, obsessive or perfectionist. My marriage has never been better. I'm able to talk to her and I have the empathy to know when she needs to talk about things.

(Carl)

Q73. Can over-the-counter medications be harmful for someone with bipolar disorder?

Some everyday medicines bought from the pharmacy without a prescription (over-the-counter, or OTC medicines) aren't necessarily safe for somebody with a bipolar diagnosis. It's always worth checking with the shop pharmacist or a psychiatrist that prescription and OTC medication can be taken together. Potentially harmful OTC medicines include:

Ibuprofen pain relief, such as Nurofen

'You should avoid taking ibuprofen at the same time as lithium because it can affect the way lithium is passed out of the kidneys and increase lithium levels in the blood by about 20%, potentially causing toxicity. Aspirin should also be avoided, although paracetamol is thought to be safe,' says Ian Maidment, Senior Pharmacist, Kent & Medway Partnership NHS Trust, and Senior Lecturer, Kent Institute of Medicine and Health Studies, Kent University.

Decongestants

'Decongestants you take for blocked sinuses or a cold, found in medicines like Sudafed, can potentially cause mania and make a person with bipolar a bit speedy, although I don't think it's a major risk,' Ian says. 'Ideally someone with bipolar would avoid taking too many decongestants.'

Cough medicine

'The problem is that cough suppressants, such as pholcodine, could induce euphoria, although again this is not a major risk,' says Ian.

Q74. Can prescription drugs taken for conditions other than bipolar disorder influence recovery?

'Numerous prescription drugs can affect symptoms of depression or mania,' says Ian Maidment. Although a GP or psychiatrist writing out a new prescription should advise about any possible interactions between different medications, it can't harm to know the following facts:

- Antidepressants and corticosteroids (usually prescribed to treat inflammatory skin disorders), such as prednisolone, can trigger mania.

- Research by the University of Bath in 2007 reported that the drug Roaccutane, prescribed for severe acne, may disrupt the production of serotonin in the brain, leading to depression and even suicide – at least 26 deaths in the UK and more than 200 in the US have been linked to the drug.

- Beta-blockers (usually prescribed to lower blood pressure) and some anti-convulsants (for epilepsy), such as topiramate, can cause depression.

- Larium (mefloquine) – the prophylactic anti-malarial medication – can trigger psychiatric disorders in some people.

- People who have been prescribed the appetite suppressant drug Rimonabant (marketed as Acomplia) are 40% more likely to become depressed than those who take a placebo drug, according to Danish research published in *The Lancet* in November 2007.

Q75. How do recreational drugs affect those with a bipolar diagnosis?

Regardless of mental health, the misuse, abuse or dependence on any recreational (or 'street') drug can seriously damage well-being and lead to a number of problems, including psychotic symptoms, relapse of psychotic illness or a need for the dosage of medication to be adjusted. Whatever the reason for taking drugs – to numb painful memories, pump up mood or hide feelings of shyness or inadequacy – the 'benefits' are short-lived, while the negatives are huge.

In short, the use of recreational drugs can only delay diagnosis of the real problem or make an existing problem a hundred times worse. So what effects do the most common recreational drugs have?

Cannabis (pot, skunk, weed)

Some people claim that cannabis can ease pain associated with various conditions, such as cancer, multiple sclerosis and AIDS. Usually mixed with tobacco and smoked in a joint or inhaled through hand-held apparatus commonly known as a 'bong', occasionally it is baked into cakes or brownies and eaten. Cannabis has a disorienting effect that can be pleasurable (users can feel relaxed and giggly) or horrible (symptoms of depression, psychosis, paranoia and anxiety are common). Some experts – including Professor Robin Murray at the Maudsley Hospital in London – believe cannabis may tip an individual susceptible to psychosis into full-blown schizophrenia. Even more worryingly, there are new strains of cannabis and marijuana now available, known as skunk, that are much more powerful and likely to cause symptoms and addiction – worryingly, mental health hospital admissions in England due to cannabis have risen by 85% since the late 1990s. An increasing body of research suggests long-term use of cannabis can contribute to various mental health problems and the inability to live a happy life.

> My youngest son developed bipolar symptoms in his late teens. We didn't recognize the symptoms as bipolar at first as his presented themselves differently to mine ... he started doing a lot of cannabis which we didn't know about at first and started self-harming which is not something that I've ever done. So the symptoms kind of appeared in a different guise for him – it was only later that we realized it was all part of a grand picture. I do think the cannabis could have been a trigger ... we found out too late that he was going out every night and getting stoned with his mates. And it's much stronger stuff now.
>
> (Keith)

> I put a lot of energy into just trying to get to a level where I felt how I imagined everybody else would feel. But I didn't feel right – my moods were all over the place. I had to devote my time just to feeling OK. Alcohol and drugs gave me temporary relief, and I experimented until I found the right sort of level ... it was mainly weed and I did a fair amount of acid. But weed was mainly the drug. I wanted something to bring me down – I hated drugs that took me up. I had so much hyper energy, so I did anything to bring me down. For a while it was alcohol, but that sort of faded out and I basically became a classic stoned pothead, just chain smoked dope all day long. If I didn't have it, I was hyper agitated and anxious ... it was like living in an electric shock. That's one of the sadnesses and regrets about my teenage years and my twenties. I put a hell of a lot of energy into going nowhere, and I think a lot of people with bipolar probably feel the same.
>
> (Ashley)

Cocaine (charlie, coke)

Extracted from the leaves of the coca plant in South America, cocaine usually comes in powder form that a user snorts up the nose through a rolled up bank note. The effects – increased confidence and energy, a higher body temperature, pulse rate and blood pressure – last around 30 minutes. Crack cocaine (a powder blend of cocaine, baking soda and water) is usually smoked and has a similar but more concentrated and shorter effect to cocaine. Both are highly addictive and can lead to serious mental health problems ranging from mild depression to the extremes of cocaine psychosis, in which the user has symptoms similar to schizophrenia. Heavy regular use can cause restlessness, confusion, paranoia and feelings of desperation.

Ecstasy (E)

This is a man-made drug sold as a tiny pill, often taken in dance clubs. Its effects last for anywhere between an hour and six hours, with an initial adrenaline rush followed by calm energy. The user will find colours, music and emotions more intense and an increased feeling of empathy for others. It also affects body temperature – government statistics show that 20 people a year die from taking ecstasy, usually as a result of hypothermia, dehydration or over-hydration caused by drinking too much water. The next day, low mood, aching bones and fatigue are common. In the long term, there's an increased risk of memory loss, depression and anxiety.

Heroin (smack, gear)

Derived from the poppy plant, a small dose of heroin – usually in liquid form injected into the arm – gives an instant high. A bigger dose can cause drowsiness, unconsciousness or even instant death. It suppresses pain, but also affects concentration and increases feelings of anxiety and fear. It is highly addictive. Long-term use means more is needed for the user to feel normal, and horrendous withdrawal symptoms last for at least three days: hot and cold sweats, aching, vomiting, sneezing and spasms. Long-term use usually causes financial problems and even criminal activity to fund the drug – a heroin habit can cost thousands of pounds a year – and can lead to a total breakdown of normal life.

LSD (acid)

A powerful hallucinogenic drug, LSD comes from a fungus found growing on rye and other wild grasses. A 'trip' lasts for up to 12 hours, altering perception, movement and time. Trips can be enjoyable or disturbing, and there's no way to stop one once it's started. Users often experience fear, paranoia and disorientation. And long after the drug has been taken, flashbacks can occur without warning. LSD can worsen symptoms of depression and anxiety in the long term, and a bad trip can trigger bipolar:

> My first manic episode happened when I was 18 following an LSD trip – it was a flashback sort of thing, and I wound up sectioned for 14 days. I got out and they put the whole thing down to the drug taking. I wasn't diagnosed with manic depression until five years later when I was 23.
>
> (Carl)

Speed (whizz, uppers)

One of the most impure drugs in circulation, speed is often mixed with talcum powder or bicarbonate of soda and sold in the form of a powder that's sniffed up the nose. Its effect is described as 'an adrenaline rush that lasts for several hours' linked to a faster heart rate and quickened breathing. Users feel increased energy and confidence and appetite is suppressed. The next day, the user often wakes up feeling lethargic, hungry and deeply depressed (known as the 'speed blues'). Anyone with a bipolar diagnosis is likely to find that taking speed greatly exaggerates mood swings.

Three ways to get help

- In the UK, many local councils have dedicated drug and alcohol support teams – see www.direct.gov.uk to contact the 'health and well-being' services.

- The National Drugs Helpline is a free and confidential telephone helpline that's open 24/7. Tel: 0800 77 66 00.

- Founded in 1953, Narcotics Anonymous can be found in 90 countries and, like Alcoholics Anonymous, uses the 12 steps as the backbone of its recovery programme. In the UK, call 020 7730 0009 or see www.ukna.org – to find an NA support group anywhere in the world, see www.na.org

CHAPTER SIX

LIVING WITH BIPOLAR

Q76. What is the best way to explain bipolar disorder to other people?

There's no getting away from the fact that mental illness can still be a source of shame and stigma – defined as 'a sign of disgrace or discredit, which sets a person apart from others'. And that's not just from random strangers ... a report by the Mental Health Foundation found that 70% of people with mental health problems have experienced discrimination from family, friends and health professionals. And in a public opinion survey in the UK, 80% of people agreed with the statement that 'most people are embarrassed by mentally ill people', and about 30% admitted, 'I am embarrassed by mentally ill people'.

Graham Thornicroft, a professor at King's College in London and one of the world's leading researchers in psychiatry, says: 'In all my years as a psychiatrist, I've listened to patients tell me that the discrimination is as bad as the mental illness they are experiencing. Discrimination blights the lives of many people with mental illness, making marriage, childcare, work and a normal social life very difficult.' Feelings of shame, blame, secrecy, isolation and social exclusion are common.

Amanda's mum finds it very difficult to talk about her condition:

> When my mum was first diagnosed with bipolar and for years after-
> wards, she was deeply ashamed of her condition. No one could
> mention it in her presence. Even when she'd been in hospital, we
> didn't directly say what was wrong – it was the proverbial 'elephant in
> the room'. Things have changed, and in conversation with her we can
> cautiously refer to her being ill, but even now the phrase we all have
> to use in her presence is that she 'isn't very well' – I've never once
> heard her use the terms 'manic depression', 'bipolar disorder' or
> 'mood swing'. She hates those words, because she feels there is a
> stigma attached to them.

Many others have had similar experiences.

> My dad's illness was kept very secret, and it wasn't actually until I had
> my diagnosis in my late 30s that I found out about his. When we were
> younger, every time he went into hospital we were told he'd had a heart
> attack. He must have had the most heart attacks of anyone I'd ever
> heard of! Even after I was diagnosed, my family would not talk about it.
> It was just, you know, you don't talk about it, it isn't happening.
>
> (Sue)

> Though bipolar is definitely not a big secret in our immediate family, it
> is outside the family. David's mum says, 'He's got nerve trouble'.
> There is still a stigma attached to mental illness. People say 'he's a
> nutter' or 'he's a fruitcake'. Because they can't see it, they don't think
> anything's wrong. That infuriates me. You need to get to know the
> person behind the illness. There are some lovely people with mental
> illness who are just struggling to get through each day. It's upsetting
> to see them blamed for not being perfect. You can't imagine how
> hurtful comments can be.
>
> (Jackie)

> At first my diagnosis was like a big pile of dirty washing in the cupboard ... a big secret. Only my ex-husband knew, but I didn't confide in anyone else. When I met my current partner I didn't tell him the truth about my illness, but I finally told him a few weeks ago. He had thought I just suffer from depression, but since I told him about the bipolar, he's been amazing and so supportive. He says he'll do anything that he can do. He talks to the team. We speak to each other all day long. I'd like to think it is possible to get rid of the stigma.
>
> (Debbie)

> My father is a manic depressive, although I didn't know anything was wrong until I was 25. He was an actor. He was always cheery and putting on a brave face. He would always whistle and sing, but I knew that there was a lot more going on under the surface. His real feelings were always hidden but his children sensed what was really going on even from a young age.
>
> (Carl)

> I have a brother who's three years younger than me, and I think it's been really hard for him ... I suppose it's like anyone having an illness in the family, but there was quite a lot of shame there because I don't think he felt he could talk to anyone about it.
>
> (Tamara)

So is it better to keep a diagnosis quiet or to shout it from the rooftops? One day, telling someone about a bipolar diagnosis will be as easy as saying, 'I've got diabetes'. There will be no shame, no stigma, no blame, no guilt, no ignorance. Yet, for now, it's not that simple. Neil Hunt, a consultant psychiatrist, who's written a book for GPs about how to recognize and deal with bipolar patients in their care (*Bipolar Disorder: Your Questions Answered*), offered this suggestion in 2005: 'When it comes to telling friends and colleagues, you need to judge this according to the person you are talking to.

Many people will have very little understanding of manic depression and so you need to be wary about using the term ... When talking to most people it is reasonable to use the vaguest terms such as stress and depression ... Saying "Yes, I've been having a difficult time, got very stressed but I'm getting back on my feet now", helps both you and your colleague to feel reasonably comfortable.'

We were outraged at that advice, tucked away in an otherwise extremely useful book. We're not saying it's easy to tell somebody that you have bipolar; it's not like telling somebody you've got a blister on your toe; of course it's a big deal. But saying you've been 'stressed' – when people bandy that word around all the time in sentences like 'I'm so stressed because I've just chipped a nail' – is just reinforcing the secrecy and misconceptions that surround mental illness.

The fact is, the stigma of mental illness is shrinking all the time. And thanks to well-known people, such as Stephen Fry, Carrie Fisher, the late Spike Milligan and many others who have 'come out' as manic depressives, more and more people have heard of and are less afraid of the words 'bipolar' and 'manic depression'.

Several surveys indicate that stigma and prejudice against people with mental health problems are reduced when the general public is better informed. The only way shame and stigma can be erased forever is for those with mental illness and their families – one by one – to be honest and open about their condition. That doesn't necessarily mean going into intimate details about the highs, lows and mixed states in between. Saying, 'I have bipolar', or 'He's been diagnosed with bipolar disorder', is enough. Every time those words are spoken it's a nail in the coffin for ignorance, shame and stigma.

And if questions that feel uncomfortable are asked, they can be answered with a simple, 'I don't want to talk about that now, although I might another time'. Someone with bipolar has nothing to feel awkward, embarrassed or ashamed about; just as someone with cancer has nothing to feel awkward, embarrassed or ashamed about.

I've compared bipolar to having diabetes. That's a chemical imbalance in your body; bipolar is just a chemical imbalance in your head.

(Alison)

As a daughter, sister and niece of people with bipolar disorder from two generations, Sarah has completely changed her attitude over the years:

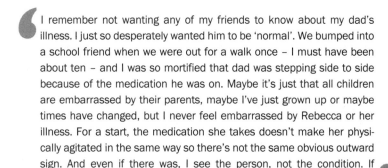 I remember not wanting any of my friends to know about my dad's illness. I just so desperately wanted him to be 'normal'. We bumped into a school friend when we were out for a walk once – I must have been about ten – and I was so mortified that dad was stepping side to side because of the medication he was on. Maybe it's just that all children are embarrassed by their parents, maybe I've just grown up or maybe times have changed, but I never feel embarrassed by Rebecca or her illness. For a start, the medication she takes doesn't make her physically agitated in the same way so there's not the same obvious outward sign. And even if there was, I see the person, not the condition. If anything, I feel proud of her, not ashamed.

Even if people think they're not prejudiced about mental illness, it's astonishing how easily the stereotypes slip out ... Amanda heard an interview on the radio where someone described watching the Positive Mental Attitude football team (made up of young men diagnosed with mental health conditions). At the end of the interview, the person commented how surprised he was that 'none of the players looked like mental patients'. Cue much shouting at the radio from Amanda! Exactly what are 'mental patients' supposed to look like? Are 'they' supposed to look different from the 'rest of us'? Would he have said, 'none of the players looked like they have diabetes'? No! Well, here's a news flash for those who still push these stereotypes, unknowingly or not – guess what, people who are mentally ill look like everybody else, because *anyone* can develop a form of mental illness. Mentally ill people are not a race apart. They don't look any different because they aren't any different. Let's get the world to understand this fact and we'll be a giant leap closer to demolishing such insidious stigma and prejudice.

Q77. What is the best way to explain to a child that their parent has been diagnosed with bipolar disorder?

Telling a child that their mum or dad has been diagnosed with bipolar disorder will never be easy, but Clare Armstrong, a NHS practice development officer in Ayrshire and Arran, Scotland, who's carried out research into the impact of mental illness of a parent on a child, recommends this step-by-step approach:

1. Be honest and open

There is no point in trying to hide the truth from children in order to protect them. Even really young children pick up on moods, behaviour and atmosphere, and seem to have a sixth sense about what's going on. Hiding or diluting the truth will just make them worry more. The best approach is to use age-appropriate language and to be totally honest. So, for an eight-year-old, saying something like, 'Daddy's not feeling very well. He's got bipolar disorder. It's an illness that means he can get too excited or feel very very sad. But he still loves you' is enough. Children don't need complex explanations – it's about the here and now, and how it affects them and their world. An older teenager might need a more detailed explanation, such as, 'Your dad has bipolar disorder which is an imbalance in the brain's neurochemistry involving the ways that cells communicate with each other.' Whatever their age, the next crucial step is to allow them to ask questions in their own time.

2. Listen

When a parent is unwell, they can be hostile, abusive, violent, socially offensive or embarrassing, self-destructive and generally disrupt the daily routine. Once a diagnosis is made, it's important for a child to have the opportunity to be able to share any painful past experiences with someone who will listen. All that some children need is a significant adult in their life to talk to, such as a teacher, grandparent or aunt. If the child's behaviour is worrying for more than a couple of weeks (if they cry excessively, become aggressive or withdrawn, for example) seek help from the GP who can refer them to a specialist CAMHS (child and adolescent mental health) service if necessary. It's also worth keeping the school informed about what's happening so teachers can be supportive.

3. Point out that it's not their fault

Children have a tendency to think that everything's their fault, feel guilty and blame themselves. One of the most important things to say is, 'This is not your fault, it's an illness. Mum still loves you.'

4. Explain what's happening when a parent is in hospital

No matter what their age, most children experience huge separation anxiety when a parent goes into hospital, worrying about their condition, wondering how long they're going to be in for and fearing that they're going to die. Children need to be kept up-to-date with what's happening to prevent them from inventing their own worst-case scenario. Explain that hospital is a place where doctors and nurses can help Mum or Dad get better and that they will come home. And keep lines of communication open with regular phone calls and visits, whenever possible.

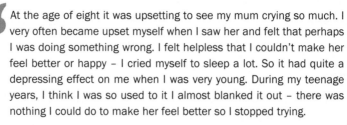

At the age of eight it was upsetting to see my mum crying so much. I very often became upset myself when I saw her and felt that perhaps I was doing something wrong. I felt helpless that I couldn't make her feel better or happy – I cried myself to sleep a lot. So it had quite a depressing effect on me when I was very young. During my teenage years, I think I was so used to it I almost blanked it out – there was nothing I could do to make her feel better so I stopped trying.

(Ingrid)

> I've never hidden it. Because I grew up with it being hidden, I didn't want to do that. We've always talked about it. And my children are quite supportive, although they're a bit embarrassed about some of the things I've done. My youngest son, who's 16, does the cooking and basically takes over when I'm not well. My oldest son, who's 19, is supportive and talks to his friends about my bipolar.
>
> (Sue)

> I only told my children about my bipolar diagnosis recently. It was such a relief to tell them. My 18-year-old son has been amazing – round every day since to see if I'm OK. I suppose my daughter, who is 16, has been a bit flakey. She asked if I'm schizophrenic. I explained to her that I just have wonky neurotransmitters. She'll come round. I'm really proud of them.
>
> (Debbie)

Q78. Is a person with a bipolar diagnosis legally obliged to inform their employer?

The stigma of mental illness has long been an issue in the workplace.

> Years ago you didn't really want to have the word 'depression' on your medical records because there was such a stigma about having depression, and you didn't mention it in jobs or anything like that because you wouldn't get a job if you admitted to having depression.
>
> (Sue)

> When I was first diagnosed with bipolar at the age of 22, 12 years ago, the psychiatrist said, 'We think you've got bipolar disorder, but we don't want to diagnose you as such. You've just got your degree and are at the start of your career, but you'll never get a job if you've got bipolar on your medical records.'
>
> (Lesley)

Has anything changed? Even though the Disability Discrimination Act, made law in the UK in 1995, is supposed to counteract the discrimination disabled people face in employment, a survey by UK charity Mind found that fewer than 40% of employers would consider employing a person with a history of mental health problems. Another survey found that a third of people with mental health problems have been dismissed or forced to resign from jobs; 69% have been put off applying for jobs for fear of unfair treatment; and 38% have been harassed, intimidated or teased at work because of their psychiatric history.

> I work for an insurance company as a recoveries handler. It's not a stressful job, but I can't cope with it at the moment. My colleagues were supportive for the first couple of weeks, but it's a small team, and they have to cover my work. If they don't like it I shall leave and find another job because I have to put my well-being first. I'm sure they'd be more supportive if I told them I had cancer and support me all the way to the end of the treatment. Nobody realizes what a huge impact bipolar has on your life.
>
> (Debbie)

> Last year, around the time I was diagnosed, I had been manic and suspended from work on medical grounds. My work colleagues had seen me high and witnessed some terrible behaviour. Some who were friends are not so close anymore. They just changed with me. This has been the hardest thing for me to deal with, the social side. I no longer get invited out with the gang and people have stopped texting me.
>
> (Jude)

Perhaps not surprisingly, a report by the Mental Health Foundation found that two in three people don't disclose details of their mental health problem on job application forms and 55% hide their diagnosis from colleagues.

When I was originally diagnosed, I did all I could to try to hide my problems from work. In the end I was self managing the symptoms and becoming more and more ill. I thought that if I told work they'd think I was a freak.

(Jude)

While I was manager of a business centre, I took an overdose and told the company I was working for that I had a really bad ear infection. They found out the truth because I had to send in a sick certificate and the name of the hospital was a psychiatric unit and the truth was written on the certificate anyway.

(Sharron)

Legally, this area is extremely complicated. In theory, there's usually no obligation to tell an employer about any medical condition, including a bipolar diagnosis, although there are some instances (defined as 'being in the public interest') where an employer has a right to ask about previous mental health and the employee has an obligation to answer honestly – teaching or working with children for example. Also, there's an argument for being honest with an employer from the outset, because if the illness is later mentioned as, for example, an excuse for poor performance, the employer is less obliged to be supportive than if it were mentioned in the first place.

For more advice, call the Disability Rights Commission Helpline on 08457 622633 or see www.drc-gb.org

MIND also runs a legal advice service – call their helpline on 020 8519 2122.

In the US, the Americans with Disabilities Act has ensured that it's illegal for an employer to sack an employee due to a physical or mental disability. Find out more at www.ada.gov or call 800 514 0301.

Telling employers about a mental illness isn't necessarily a bad thing. A survey shows that within the workplace, over half of those who had been open reported that they 'always' or 'often' had support when they needed it, with a further one in five 'sometimes' getting support.

> Since I got seriously ill, my boss has been amazing.
>
> (Jude)

> I told my employer that I have bipolar disorder after I'd been cleaning for her for two years. Sometimes I clean her house from top to bottom in two hours. Other times I call in sick. Now she's willing to take the rough with the smooth.
>
> (Sharron)

> When I became ill the first time in this job, I knew that I had to be honest, otherwise relapses would keep recurring. I'd been working for my line manager for about a year when I told her what to look out for if I was high and if I was low – for example, a lack of eye contact and not finishing sentences – so I think I've been as upfront as I could be about it. I believe very strongly that honesty is truly the best policy. The relationship between my line manager and me was good, and her reaction was good. Her husband is a trained psychologist and so I know she talked to him. I have always treated having bipolar as if it's the same as a broken leg. I do feel very proud of the way I have handled things and in return I have been treated excellently. Occupational health has been exceptional and done their level best to get me back to work. It was definitely the right thing to do. Even though I am not returning to work in my old position, I have no regrets.
>
> (Neil)

> I'm very open with people about having bipolar. I'll tell anyone who wants to listen to me! If I go back to work now, I would tell my employers. I'm quite proud to be bipolar. It has a special link to being gifted.
>
> (Reka)

> I have absolutely no issue telling people that I have bipolar. I'm really open with my personal training clients. There's no stigma whatsoever as far as I'm concerned.
>
> (Dave)

Q79. What is the most sensible way for a woman with bipolar disorder to approach pregnancy?

Most healthcare professionals are supportive if a woman with bipolar wants to have a baby. 'It's definitely possible for a woman with bipolar to have a baby in a positive way. I would never advise a woman with bipolar disorder not to have children,' says Professor Nick Craddock at Cardiff University.

Pre-conception

As for all women, taking folic acid before and during pregnancy can help reduce the risk of neural tube defects. Zachery Stowe, MD of Emory University in America and a leading expert on mental illness in women, recommends a daily dose of one gram.

Pregnancy

Most women with bipolar disorder will need to take some medication during pregnancy to stay stable, as depressive symptoms and episodes can occur during pregnancy. Certain medications are safer for the fetus than others – this depends on each individual and needs to be discussed with a healthcare professional, ideally before conception.

As well as medication, other options to help pregnant women stay stable include psychotherapy, ECT, light therapy and omega-3 fish oils.

After the birth

For mothers with bipolar disorder, it's been estimated that the risk of relapse (particularly of manic relapse) is perhaps eight times greater during the three months after birth than at any other time. The risk of a condition called puerperal psychosis – where symptoms of confusion, hallucinations and a total loss of reality can come on suddenly – is also greater. At least a third of women with manic depression will relapse at this time, though looking at the statistic in a more positive light means that around two-thirds of women won't. Professor Nick Craddock puts it like this: 'We know that the risk increases immediately following birth. But that means that it's possible to monitor the birth and there are steps you can take to help prevent it. You can never say there wouldn't be an episode of severe illness, you can't make those guarantees, but in my view it's not a reason not to have a baby. The most horrible thing we've seen is women who have been told years ago "You mustn't have a baby because of your illness", but then they have further episodes of the illness anyway – they've experienced the worst of both worlds. We live in a culture these days where everybody's scared about risks. But it's better, I think, to understand about that risk which means people can make an informed decision.'

The key to treating puerperal psychosis following childbirth is an early diagnosis because antipsychotic medication can be prescribed that will nip manic and psychotic symptoms in the bud. This often means a speedy recovery. So the role of midwives, partners, family and friends in observing behaviour and keeping the health team informed is crucial. In other words, if a new mother with a history of bipolar disorder shows even the tiniest sign of a mood swing or losing touch with reality, get help immediately.

Q80. Are those with a bipolar diagnosis entitled to any benefits?

If someone has a mental health problem that has long-term effects on their ability to carry out normal day-to-day activity in the UK, the Disability Discrimination Act (DDA) considers this a disability and sets out certain legal rights – this usually includes financial benefits. 'Long term' is defined as an impairment that has lasted, or is likely to last, at least 12 months. To find out about individual cases in England, Scotland and Wales, call the Benefit Enquiry Line – 0800 882 2200 – a helpline for people with disabilities, their families and representatives. They offer confidential advice and information on benefits and how to claim them. They also send out a range of leaflets and claim packs.

In the USA, the Social Security Administration (SSA) treats mental and physical disabilities equally, although it turns down claims 60–70% of the time, and as there are no definitive medical tests to prove the diagnosis of many mental conditions, it is notoriously difficult to get a claim approved by the SSA. See www.ssa.gov for more details.

Q81. What is a 'lasting power of attorney'?

In the UK, a 'lasting power of attorney' is a document that legally appoints someone to manage someone else's financial affairs if they become unwell and lose 'mental capacity' – the definition of which is defined in detail by the Mental Capacity Act 2005. In October 2007, the law in the UK changed, which meant that a 'Lasting Power of Attorney' (LPA) replaced the existing 'Enduring Power of Attorney' (EPA), although EPAs registered before that date are still valid.

Getting an LPA is a bureaucratic business. A form needs to be filled out at a solicitor's and signed by both parties – the 'power of attorney' and the 'donor' (the person likely to become unwell). The document usually sets out property and financial affairs – these can be enforced before and after the donor becomes unwell. It can include personal welfare matters too, such as health care decisions – these can only be enforced after the donor becomes unwell. The LPA is then sent to the 'Public Guardian' for registration, accompanied by a certificate from the solicitor confirming that the donor understood the purpose and scope of the LPA and that there was no fraud or undue pressure. If all requirements are met, the power will be formally registered. An LPA can be cancelled by completing and signing a 'Deed of Revocation' at any time, as long as the donor has the mental capacity to do so.

For advice, call the Mind*Info*Line on 0845 766 0163 (open from 9.15am to 5.15pm).

Q82. What is the best way to make a complaint about any aspects of care?

In general ...

England

Complaints can be made via the local Patient Advice Liaison Service (PALS), which gives advice, support and information to patients and their families – see www.pals.nhs.uk or call a local hospital, GP surgery, health centre or NHS Direct (0845 4647) for details.

Alternatively, contact the Independent Complaints Advocacy Service (ICAS), which supports patients and their families wishing to pursue a complaint about their NHS treatment or care. See www.cppih.org/icas to find a local ICAS provider or call the Patient and Public Involvement (PPI) Forum – which supports the ICAS providers – on 0845 120 7111.

Wales

Contact the Board of Welsh Community Health Councils at www.patienthelp.wales.nhs.uk or call 0845 644 7814.

Scotland

The Scottish Public Services Ombudsman say they are a 'one-stop-shop' for individuals making complaints about organizations providing public services in Scotland – see www.spso.org.uk or call 0800 377 7330.

In hospital

If a patient, or a member of their family, is unhappy about any aspect of the care and treatment they've received in hospital, Julie King, a psychiatric ward manager, suggests that the first step is to talk to a member of staff: 'It depends on the nature of the complaint. The first port of call would usually be the nurse in charge – in private if that is appropriate. Keeping calm and getting your point across in a calm manner is always helpful, if possible.

Then, if your concerns haven't been addressed, ask to see the ward manager. Next, you can go through official channels. All trusts have a formal complaint system where you can write. Leaflets are available with details on the official procedure. Ideally though, we prefer to deal with situations as they arise on the ward.'

The hospital may have its own advocacy service, which is an independent support and information service. They may be able to help with a complaint – ask the ward manager or at reception for details (see question 41, p. 116).

Alternatively, complain to the Mental Health Act Commission, an independent national organization which describes itself as a 'safeguard for people who are detained in hospital under the powers of the Mental Health Act' – see www.mhac.org.uk or call 0115 943 7100.

Complaints can also be made to a local Member of Parliament (send an email via www.writetothem.com or call the parliamentary information line on 020 7207 2129 for the local MP's name and address).

Complaints about private treatment

Although some private hospitals belong to the Independent Healthcare Advisory Service (which sets Codes of Practice for its members, including the handling of patient complaints – see www.independenthealthcare.org.uk), generally there's no standard complaints procedure in the private healthcare industry. As with making a complaint about NHS hospital treatment, the first step is to raise concerns with staff, and then ask to see a copy of their complaints procedure.

If this route isn't satisfactory, ask for independent advice on pursuing a private complaint from the Patients' Association, an organization which represents the interests of patients – see its website for more information: www.patients-association.org.uk Or contact the Healthcare Commission, which is an independent public body responsible for healthcare standards and can also offer advice on complaining about private treatment. See Extra resources, p. 248 for further contact details of these organizations.

If the treatment has been paid for by private health insurance, contact the insurance company for advice on making a complaint.

Gross professional misconduct

For very serious allegations about a mental healthcare professional working in either the NHS or the private sector, complain to their relevant professional body (see Extra resources, p. 248 for contact details of relevant professional organizations.) It's thankfully a rare occurrence, but someone who commits a very serious offence may need to be struck off their professional register.

Q83. Where can somebody with a bipolar diagnosis get insurance?

Life and travel insurance can be expensive for somebody with a diagnosis of bipolar disorder. For instance, a leading insurer in the UK will cover a 30-year-old person with no existing medical conditions in Spain for a week for around £20. The same cover for the same holiday for someone with bipolar disorder can cost a whopping £300 – from www.medi-cover.co.uk, 0870 735 3600 – 'travel insurance for those who have suffered an illness or accident'. Each quote depends on individual circumstances and questions will be asked such as: 'How recently were you hospitalized or sectioned? Are you currently stable and taking medication? Are you travelling alone?'

For a competitive quote, contact MDF The BiPolar Organisation, who offer a life assurance and travel insurance scheme to members. Contact them on www.mdf.org.uk or 08456 340 540 to find out about membership rates.

Q84. Is it ever unsafe for someone with a bipolar diagnosis to drive?

The Driver and Vehicle Licensing Agency (DVLA) doesn't need to be notified about very minor short-lived illness or about anxiety or depression that doesn't cause significant memory or concentration problems, agitation, behavioural disturbance or suicidal thoughts.

However, the Drivers Medical Group, part of the DVLA, does need to be informed if a medical condition gets worse since a licence was issued or if a new medical condition, including bipolar disorder, is diagnosed. Failure to do so is a criminal offence and is punishable by a fine, currently up to £1000. The driver's licence and car insurance also become invalid. Call the DVLA on 0870 600 0301.

There are three reasons why driving can become unsafe for someone with a bipolar diagnosis:

1. During a manic period, impulsive and reckless behaviour can lead to speeding and dangerous driving decisions, such as overtaking or pulling out when it's not safe. The risk of an accident is far greater and someone who is manic should never drive.

2. Depression can impair concentration and reflexes, slowing response times and resulting in erratic driving. A driver who feels so low he or she doesn't care whether they live or die may make unsafe driving decisions and should never drive.

3. Some bipolar medication can cause side effects that mean it's unwise to drive. For example, benzodiazepines are commonly found in the blood of those involved in accidents. A psychiatrist or GP will explain the potential side effects of each prescription.

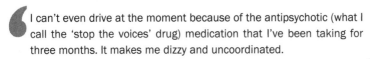

I can't even drive at the moment because of the antipsychotic (what I call the 'stop the voices' drug) medication that I've been taking for three months. It makes me dizzy and uncoordinated.

(Debbie)

But this certainly doesn't mean that a person with a bipolar diagnosis can never drive again. Each individual case is different, but the rule of thumb is that re-licensing will be considered when the person has remained well and stable for at least three months, is compliant with treatment, is free from adverse effects of medication which would impair driving, and is subject to a favourable specialist report.

Q85. What well-known people have/had bipolar disorder?

Although most people who are faced with a diagnosis of bipolar disorder aren't famous of course, more and more people in the public eye are stepping forward to talk about their experiences. And other famous people have been given a posthumous diagnosis based on various aspects of their behaviour. Here's a random round-up:

Paul Abbott (born 1960)

Screenwriter Paul Abbott (best known for the TV dramas *Shameless* and *Clocking Off*) was first admitted to a psychiatric ward at the age of 15 following a suicide attempt. In an interview on Radio 4's *Desert Island Discs* in 2007, he talked openly about his bipolar diagnosis. 'As bipolar, suicide is a constant presence in your life. It's not that you actually feel suicidal, but you don't stop thinking about it. It crosses your mind every day. I was plagued by it for a long time. Except that the love for my family and children is so powerful and so much greater than anything that could make me damage them in that way. They were my immunity [...] I think it forced me to write – the extremity of my mood swings became really rapidly productive. I can't not write. I write every day.'

Sophie Anderton (born 1977)

Model and reality TV star Sophie Anderton was diagnosed with bipolar disorder in 2006 following years of tabloid gossip about cocaine and alcohol addiction.

Adam Ant (born 1954)

Singer Adam Ant (real name Stuart Goddard) made a TV documentary in 2003 entitled *The Madness of Prince Charming* charting his career and his struggle with bipolar disorder. He says, 'When I was sectioned for six months, it was one of the worst experiences of my life, not being able to go out and have freedom. Having experienced it, it's almost inexplicably awful.'

Ludwig von Beethoven (1770–1827)

Beethoven spent most of his life alternating between periods of brilliance (playing the piano, and composing sonatas and concertos) and periods of utter despair and alcoholism. A friend describes what he was like during a busy period: 'He ... tore open the pianoforte ... and began to improvise marvel-lously ... The hours went by, but Beethoven improvised on. Supper, which he had purported to eat with us, was served, but ... he would not permit himself to be disturbed.' Many experts speculate that Beethoven had bipolar disorder.

Frank Bruno (born 1961)

World champion boxer Frank Bruno was sectioned for 28 days in a psychiatric hospital and diagnosed with bipolar disorder in 2003 following his marriage break-up. He describes his behaviour in the run up to his breakdown: 'I got confused and snappy and impatient. I couldn't, couldn't, couldn't function. Losing my wife, seeing my kids less regularly, not eating properly, staying up late, living by myself, getting uptight, wound up, over stupid little things [...] It's like a kettle. I wish I could put a hole in my head and let the steam out.'

Lord Byron (1788–1824)

Known for his eccentric behaviour and charming personality, Lord Byron was one of the most celebrated English poets of the nineteenth century. Fellow poet and friend Shelley wrote that he was, 'an exceedingly interesting person, but as mad as the wind'. Experts who have studied his life say it's almost certain he had bipolar disorder.

Patricia Cornwell (born 1956)

Crime fiction writer Patricia Cornwell has spoken of the depression she experienced during her late teens and describes herself as being wired differently. 'It's not unusual for great artistic people to have bipolar disorder. My wiring's not perfect. The diagnosis goes back and forth, but I'm pretty sure that I am. I take a mood stabilizer.'

Kerry Katona (born 1980)

Pop singer and TV reality star Kerry Katona has spoken openly about her diagnosis: 'I'm an up-and-down person. I can feel lonely, afraid and scared to go out at times. I feel like it's me against the rest of the world. But you'll never see the down person in public. I'm always bright and bubbly. It was a relief when they diagnosed bipolar. I thought I was going insane.'

Kurt Cobain (1967–1994)

Lead singer, guitarist and songwriter of the Seattle-based rock band Nirvana, Cobain was diagnosed with attention deficit disorder (ADD) as a child, then later with bipolar disorder. Troubled by insomnia and an unidentified stomach complaint, Cobaine self-medicated with drugs and committed suicide at the age of 27.

Carrie Fisher (born 1957)

Actress Carrie Fisher, best known for her role as Princess Laia in the Star Wars films, was diagnosed with bipolar disorder at the age of 24 and has often spoken about her experiences: 'I was on drugs for years, and I don't think you can accurately diagnose bipolar disorder when someone is actively drug addicted or alcoholic. I didn't accept the diagnosis fully until I had a psychotic break in 1997. Now I'm fine. I'm on seven medications, and I take medication three times a day. This constantly puts me in touch with the illness I have. I'm never quite allowed to be free of that for a day. It's like being a diabetic.'

Stephen Fry (born 1957)

Actor, comedian and writer Stephen Fry was diagnosed with cyclothymia, a form of bipolar disorder, at the age of 37. In a two-part documentary for the BBC – *The Secret Life of the Manic Depressive*, first broadcast in 2006 – he talks of the downside of the condition: 'I may have looked happy. Inside I was hopelessly depressed. I'm actually kind of sobbing and kind of tearing at the walls inside my own brain while my mouth is, you know, wittering away in some amusing fashion', as well as the upside: 'I love my condition too. It's infuriating, I know, but I do get a huge buzz out of the manic side. I rely on it to give my life a sense of adventure, and I think most of the good about me has developed as a result of my mood swings. It's tormented me all my life with the deepest of depressions while giving me the energy and creativity that perhaps has made my career.'

Vivien Leigh (1913–1967)

Two-times Oscar winning actress Vivien Leigh was affected by bipolar disorder for most of her adult life. According to one of his biographers, her second husband, Laurence Olivier came to recognize the symptoms of an impending episode – 'several days of hyperactivity followed by a period of depression and an explosive breakdown, after which Leigh would have no memory of the event, but would be acutely embarrassed and remorseful'.

Spike Milligan (1918–2002)

Comedian and writer, best known for *The Goon Show* and his wacky sense of humour, Spike Milligan suffered from bipolar disorder for most of his life, having at least ten major mental breakdowns, several lasting over a year. He spoke candidly about his condition and its effect on his life: 'It's like a storm at sea. You don't know how long it's going to last or whether you are going to be able to survive it.' He was patron of the Manic Depression Fellowship (now MDF The BiPolar Organisation).

Sinead O'Connor (born 1966)

Ever since she was 23, Irish singer Sinead O'Connor says she had thoughts of suicide. 'I began to have this quiet little voice every now and then – although "voice" is the wrong way to put it. It's your own thoughts just gone completely skew-whiff: "Look at that tree, you might hang yourself on it". But after my son Shane was born I was really ill, and I was really worried because I was close to actually doing it. So when he was about five months old, I took myself to hospital.' She was diagnosed with bipolar disorder, which O'Connor describes as like having a gaping hole in the centre of her being. She took the drugs she'd been prescribed, and says, 'Within half an hour, it was like cement going over the hole.'

Graeme Obree (born 1965)

Scottish world champion cyclist Graeme Obree candidly describes how he coped with his diagnosis of bipolar disorder and the dark depressions that he's experienced all his life in his autobiography *The Flying Scotsman*. In 2007, the book was turned into a film of the same name, with Jonny Lee Miller playing the lead. Obree says, 'I have suffered depression at various times in my career, and there were times when I wanted to give up riding altogether. But it was only after I retired from international cycling that the illness really took hold. I drank to cope with the effects of depression. I've since been diagnosed as manic depressive, but fortunately doctors have been able to help me with drugs. I used to need cycling to cope with my illness; but with the help of my family, and with counselling, I've begun to overcome the personal issues that caused the depression. Through therapy, I have learned to handle my emotions better, be in touch with what I am and what I feel.'

Sylvia Plath (1932–1963)

American poet and author Sylvia Plath wrote in her journal, 'It is as if my life were magically run by two electric currents: joyous and positive and despairing negative ... ' She committed suicide at the age of 30 by putting her head in an oven and turning on the gas. She has been given a posthumous diagnosis of bipolar disorder.

Tony Slattery (born 1959)

Actor and comedian Tony Slattery suffered what he described as a 'mid-life crisis' in the mid-1990s, which included a period of reclusiveness: 'I rented a huge warehouse by the river Thames. I just stayed in there on my own, didn't open the mail or answer the phone for months and months and months. I was just in a pool of despair and mania,' he says. He was diagnosed with bipolar in 1996.

Vincent van Gogh (1853–1890)

The Dutch artist Vincent van Gogh produced more than 2,000 works, including around 900 paintings and 1,100 drawings and sketches, during the last ten years of his life. Most of his best-known works were produced in the final two years of his life, during which time he cut off part of his left ear following a breakdown in his friendship with fellow artist Paul Gauguin. After this he suffered recurrent bouts of mania and depression (now thought to be symptoms of bipolar disorder), and eventually shot himself, dying in his brother's arms.

Virginia Woolf (1882–1941)

Throughout her life, Woolf experienced drastic mood swings and, though these greatly affected her social functioning, her literary talent remained intact. Before filling her pockets with stones and walking into the river to drown, she wrote: 'I feel certain now that I am going mad again. I feel we can't go through another of those terrible times. And I shan't recover this time ... ' She has been given a posthumous diagnosis of bipolar disorder.

Q86. Can a diagnosis of bipolar disorder ever be a positive thing?

Kay Redfield Jamison is a leading researcher into bipolar disorder and holds the Chair of Psychiatry at Johns Hopkins University in America. In her best-selling book *Touched with Fire: Manic-Depressive Illness and the Artistic Temperament*, she shows how bipolar disorder can run in artistic or high-achieving families. And in her autobiography *An Unquiet Mind*, Jamison writes in a poetic style about her own experiences of the illness, from her darkest days in hospital right through to the benefits she believes having bipolar can bring:

> I honestly believe that as a result of it I have felt more things, more deeply; had more experiences, more intensely; loved more, and been loved more; laughed more often for having cried more; appreciated more the springs, for all the winters; worn death 'as close as dunga-rees', – appreciated it – and life – more; seen the finest and the most terrible in people, and slowly learned the values of caring, loyalty and seeing things through.

Others emphatically agree that a bipolar diagnosis isn't necessarily all doom and gloom:

> When I first met my partner he was on the tail end of being high. He was a really charismatic man – a funny, intelligent, great, exciting person to be around. He was my Mr Fun. After six and a half years together, there's still something quite wonderful about my boyfriend. It's a real shame if people do get put off because of a bipolar diagnosis. I would rather have met him and suffered the highs and low than never have met him.

(Jo)

'My partner David swept me off my feet. He's so loving and adorable. He has more energy than anybody I've ever known. I have a daughter from a previous marriage, Cassie, and she really liked him straight away. He has a very gentle way. Kids love him, mainly because he acts like one himself. In fact, Cassie had to do a 'Who's Your Hero' project at school a few years ago. She talked about her dad. 'No matter how poorly he is (he's got manic depression), my dad still loves me and spends time with me,' she said. It cracked me up. I was in tears. My two children really know how to work him a treat. One great story is that Cassie wanted a kitten. David said, 'No way, we're not having a kitten.' Cassie just said to her brother, Dom, 'Wait till Dad's manic.' Sure enough, they waited and asked again when he was manic. He took them straight to buy one. And now we have a cat!

(Jackie)'

'It's very mixed how I feel about bipolar. Unless you've experienced a hypomanic phase, you can't possibly know how wonderful bipolar can be. That feeling does almost make it worthwhile. It's such a good feeling. No narcotic would give you that kind of feeling.

(Paul)'

'The great thing is that people with bipolar can be so funny when they're on a high. I don't mind having bipolar now it's under control. I like being high. I'm very creative, I get a lot of work done, and me and my partner can have a real laugh – I think she quite likes it. I'm bipolar and Jane's a great listener!

(Dave)'

'My philosophy is that you can learn to live with bipolar. It's a pain in the ass, but it really is possible to turn it into something more positive. All my friends love me to bits.

(Sharron)'

> The positive thing about bipolar is that you tend to look at people differently. People with bipolar are far more sympathetic and compassionate towards others – far more forgiving because we know we're forgiven more easily. We suffer fools gladly. I talk to the stranger on the bus. I always say, but for the grace of God. You never know how far this illness can take you. People with bipolar years ago would have been tied to a chair and left there. That thought frightens me. At least I'm bipolar in the twenty-first century, rather than the nineteenth!
>
> (Debbie)

Q87. What does the future hold for bipolar disorder?

> The future looks good for people with bipolar disorder, or at least significantly better than before. There is now greater positive coverage of the condition in the media. In the UK, the BBC documentary series *The Secret Life of the Manic Depressive* was watched by three million people and there were 100,000 visits to the BBC Health website that featured information on bipolar disorder. In the field of research, there is new and exciting research being undertaken by leading universities such as Cardiff, Lancaster, Birmingham, Manchester and Edinburgh that will lead to more individualized diagnosis and treatment in the coming decades. Comparative work is being undertaken in Canada, Australia and New Zealand. The new concept of mental health recovery linked to self-help means that more and more people are gaining greater control over their lives and futures. People with bipolar dis-order can therefore look forward to less stigma, more effective diagnosis and treatment and greater control over their lives.
>
> (Michel Syrett, editor of MDF The BiPolar Organisation's *Pendulum* magazine and author of *The Secret Life of Manic Depression,* a BBC publication)

'Over the coming years, treatment will improve, prediction will improve, and understanding will improve. Being diagnosed with bipolar will be completely different for people of our children's generation compared to people of our parents' generation.

(Professor Nick Craddock, Cardiff University)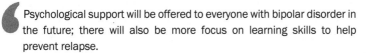

'Psychological support will be offered to everyone with bipolar disorder in the future; there will also be more focus on learning skills to help prevent relapse.

(Dr Sara Tai, Lecturer in Clinical Psychology at Manchester University)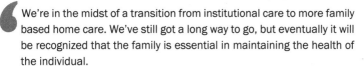

'We're in the midst of a transition from institutional care to more family based home care. We've still got a long way to go, but eventually it will be recognized that the family is essential in maintaining the health of the individual.

(Ian Hulatt, Mental Health Advisor, Royal College of Nursing)

'The current self-help programme by MDF The BiPolar Organisation is extremely useful but people don't always know about it, or they can't always access it in their area. In future, in my view, it would be amazing if the entire care plan could be based on something like that. If people are self-taught, they're much more likely to stay well. It's about people empowering themselves generally. And that could be a reality in ten years' time.

(Professor Richard Morriss, Professor of Psychiatry and Community Mental Health at Nottingham University)

'I hope bipolar disorder will be taken more seriously by policy makers sooner rather than later, as the major personal and public health problem it is. The current neglect is shameful. However, more importantly, I hope the brightest and the best scientists are drawn to study bipolar, so that in a better future we will have ways of preventing its worst manifestations and treating better what remains.

(Professor Guy Goodwin, W A Handley Chair of Psychiatry,
Oxford University)

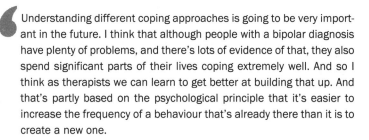

Understanding different coping approaches is going to be very important in the future. I think that although people with a bipolar diagnosis have plenty of problems, and there's lots of evidence of that, they also spend significant parts of their lives coping extremely well. And so I think as therapists we can learn to get better at building that up. And that's partly based on the psychological principle that it's easier to increase the frequency of a behaviour that's already there than it is to create a new one.

(Professor Steven Jones, Professor of Clinical Psychology, Spectrum
Centre for Mental Health Research, Lancaster University)

We fervently hope that in the future:

• No one ever says 'James *is* bipolar', but 'James *has* bipolar' instead. Why should an illness define the person?

• The stigma attached to all mental illness vanishes off the face of the earth – and understanding and compassion replace it.

• Anyone who has a loved one diagnosed with bipolar disorder is given unlimited support, information and understanding from health professionals, friends, other family members and the community in general.

• Everyone diagnosed with bipolar disorder is offered psychological treatments from the outset as this greatly improves likely outcomes.

• Self management programmes are available for everyone with bipolar disorder.

- Holistic care plans – including diet, exercise and complementary therapies – are routinely recommended for those with a mental health condition.

- All GPs and psychiatrists take more care when diagnosing non-bipolar depression because the wrong treatment (i.e. prescribing antidepressants without a mood stabilizer) may worsen the course of bipolar illness.

- A bipolar diagnosis isn't seen as someone's worst nightmare; it's considered a challenge, yes, like a diagnosis of diabetes or asthma might be, but a challenge that doesn't rule out the possibility of living a fulfilling, successful and happy life.

Extra resources

United Kingdom

Alcoholics Anonymous

PO Box 1, 10 Toft Green, York YO1 7NJ

Tel: 01904 644026

Helpline: 0845 769 7555

Web: www.alcoholics-anonymous.org.uk

Helping people with alcohol addiction to become dry and stay dry.

Association of Medical Aromatherapists

11 Park Circus, Glasgow G3 6AX

Tel: 0141 332 4924

Be ... foundation

Web: www.be-foundation.org

Aims to offer help and information on youth suicide and self-harm.

Bipolar4All

Web: www.bipolar4All.co.uk

An online support network specifically for those with a bipolar diagnosis and their loved ones.

The BiPolar Fellowship Scotland

Studio 1016, Mile End Mill, Abbeymill Business Centre,

Seedhill Road, Paisley PA1 1TJ

Tel: 0141 560 2050

Web: www.bipolarscotland.org.uk

British Acupuncture Council

63 Jeddo Road, London, W12 9HQ

Tel: 020 8735 0400

Web: www.acupuncture.org.uk

British Association of Behavioural and Cognitive Psychotherapists

Victoria Buildings, 9–13 Silver Street, Bury BL9 0EU

Tel: 0161 797 4484

Web: www.babcp.com

British Association of Counselling and Psychotherapy

BACP House, 15 St John's Business Park, Lutterworth,
Leicestershire LE17 4HB.

Tel: 0870 443 5252

Web: www.bacp.co.uk

British Psychological Society

St Andrews House, 48 Princess Road East, Leicester LE1 7DR

Tel: 0116 254 9568

Web: www.bps.org.uk

British Reflexology Association

Monks Orchard, Whitbourne, Worcester WR6 5RB

Tel: 01886 821207

Web: www.britrelflex.co.uk

British Wheel of Yoga

25 Jermyn Street, Sleaford, Lincolnshire NG34 7RU

Tel: 01529 306 851

Web: www.bwy.org.uk

CALM – Campaign Against Living Miserably

Tel: 0800 585 858

Web: www.thecalmzone.net

A UK based organization, its aim is to reach young men before they become depressed and suicidal.

Carers Northern Ireland

58 Howard Street, Belfast BT1 6PJ

Tel: 028 9043 9843

Web: www.carersni.org

Carers Scotland

91 Mitchell Street, Glasgow G1 3LN

Tel: 0141 221 9141

Web: www.carerscotland.org

Carers UK

20–25 Glasshouse Yard, London EC1A 4JT

Tel: 0808 808 7777 (Wed and Thurs, 10am–12/2–4pm)

Web: www.carersuk.org

Carers Wales

River House, Ynsbridge Court, Gwaelod-y-Garth, Cardiff CF15 9SS

Tel: 029 2081 1370

Web: www.carerswales.org

The Depression Alliance

212 Spitfire Studios, 63–71 Collier Street, London N1 9BE

Tel: 0845 123 2320 (information pack request line)

Web: www.depressionalliance.org

A UK charity that has a national network of self-help groups for people with depression to share experiences and coping strategies with others in a similar situation. They also publish useful information leaflets and run a pen-friend scheme, putting those with depression in touch with one another.

The Healthcare Commission

Finsbury Tower, 103–105 Bunhill Row, London EC1Y 8TG

Feedback: Freepost, LON15399, London EC1B 1QW

Helpline: 0845 601 3012 (9am to 5pm, Mon to Fri)

Tel: 020 7448 9200 (main switchboard)

Web: www.healthcarecommission.org.uk

A government watchdog, which promotes improvement in the quality of the NHS and independent healthcare.

Independent Healthcare Advisory Services

Centre Point, 103 New Oxford Street, London WC1A 1DU

Tel: 020 7379 8598/020 7379 7721

Website: www.independenthealthcare.org.uk

Advises its members (private hospitals) on operational policies and clinical standards, and develops Codes of Practice, for example on complaints procedures for patients.

Institute for Complementary Medicine

Unit 25, Tavern Quay Business Centre, Sweden Gate, London SE16 7TX

Tel: 020 7237 5165/5855

Web: www.i-c-m.org.uk

Lifelink

Tel: 0808 80 11 315

Web: www.lifelink.org.uk

Free support and advice to those in crisis and at risk of self-harm or suicide.

Massage Therapy UK

Web: www.massagetherapy.co.uk

MDF The BiPolar Organisation

Castle Works, 21 St George's Road, London SE1 6ES

Tel: 08456 340 540 (UK only)

0044 207 793 2600 (rest of world)

Web: www.mdf.org.uk

A user-led charity working to enable people affected by bipolar disorder to take control of their lives. Members of the organization receive their quarterly journal *Pendulum*, can attend one of their 160 self-help groups, have access to a 24-hour advice line, get specialist travel and life insurance and can take their self management training course.

There are also regional offices of the MDF in Scotland and Wales:

MDF The BiPolar Organisation Cymru

22–29 Mill Street, Newport, South Wales NP20 5HA

Tel: 01633 244244

Helpline: 08456 340 080

Web: www.mdfwales.org.uk

The Mental Health Foundation

9th Floor, Sea Containers House, 20 Upper Ground, London SE1 9QB

Tel: 020 7803 1101

Web: www.mentalhealth.org.uk

An independent research organization that helps to develop services, design training, influence policy and raise public awareness about mental health. The website is crammed with the latest information on mental health.

Mental Health Nurses Association

MHNA, Cals Meyn Grove Lane, Hinton, Chippenham, Wilts SN14 8HF

Tel: 07918 630403

Web: www.amicus-mhna.org

The trade union and professional association for UK mental health nurses.

Mental Health Review Tribunal

5th Floor, 11 Belgrave Road, Victoria, London, SW1V 1RS

Tel: 020 7592 1007

Web: www.mhrt.org.uk

An independent panel that decides if a patient should continue to be detained in hospital.

Mind

15-19 Broadway, London E15 4BQ
Helpline: 0845 766 0163 (9.15am to 5.15pm, Mon to Fri)
Tel: 0208 519 2122
Web: www.mind.org.uk

The largest mental health charity in the UK, its mission is to improve life for everyone with experience of mental distress. Mind publishes a wide range of fact sheets about mental health problems and runs a useful helpline.

Mind also has a Welsh office:

Mind Cymru

3rd Floor, Quebec House, 5-19 Cowbridge Road East, Castlebridge, Cardiff CF11 9AB
Tel: 029 2039 5123

Mood Swings Network

23 New Mount Street, Manchester M19 2QN
Tel: 0161 953 4105

Information, advice and support for people whose lives are affected by mood swings, and their families and friends. The Mood Swings Network also runs a weekly drop in, and groups for loved ones and young people.

Narcotics Anonymous

202 City Road, London EC1V 2PH
Tel: 020 7251 4007
Helpline: 020 7730 0009
Web: www.ukna.org

Supports current and past drug addicts in trying to live a drug-free life.

National Institute of Clinical Excellence (NICE)

MidCity Place, 71 High Holborn, London WC1V 6NA
Tel: 0845 003 7780
Web: www.nice.org.uk

The Patients' Association

PO Box 935, Harrow, Middlesex HA1 3YJ

Tel: 020 8423 9111

Helpline: 0845 608 4455

Web: www.patients-association.org.uk

A campaigning charity that represents the interest of patients.

Rethink

5th Floor, Royal London House, 22–25 Finsbury Square, London EC2A 1DX

Tel: 0845 456 0455 (general enquiries)

020 8974 6814 (advice line)

Web: www.rethink.org

Originally registered in England as the National Schizophrenic Fellowship, this charity's mission statement is to 'work together to help everyone affected by severe mental illness recover a better quality of life'. As well as providing a range of information about mental illness and a discussion forum on the website, Rethink is one of 75 organizations who make up the Mental Health Alliance in the UK. The Mental Health Alliance campaigns for better mental health legislation and unites people with mental illness, their families and professionals.

Royal College of Psychiatrists

17 Belgrave Square, London SW1X 8PG

Tel: 020 7235 2351

Web: www.rcpsych.ac.uk

SAD Association

PO Box 989, Steyning, BN44 3HG

Web: www.sada.org.uk

Information and advice for anyone who experiences symptoms of seasonal affective disorder (SAD).

The Samaritans

The Upper Mill, Kingston Road, Ewell, Surrey KT17 2AF

Helpline: 08457 909090 (24 hours)

Tel: 020 8394 8300 (administrative)

Web: www.samaritans.org

The Samaritans provides confidential non-judgemental support, 24 hours a day for people experiencing feelings of distress or despair, including those which could lead to suicide.

SANE

1st Floor, Cityside House, 40 Adler Street, London E1 1EE

Tel: 020 7375 1002

Helpline: 0845 767 8000 (1pm to 11pm, 7 days a week)

Web: www.sane.org.uk

An organization that raises awareness about mental illness, providing information and emotional support. They publish a number of booklets about mental health, undertake research and run a nationwide helpline.

Scottish Intercollegiate Guidelines Network (SIGN)

28 Thistle Street, Edinburgh, EH2 1EN

Tel: 0131 718 5090

Web: www.sign.ac.uk

SIGN publishes regularly updated guidelines and recommendations for the treatment and care of patients in Scotland, using the latest evidence based research.

UK Advocacy Network (UKAN)

Volserve House, 14–18 West Bar Green, Sheffield S1 2DA

Tel: 0114 272 8171

Web: www.u-kan.co.uk

www.zyra.org.uk/ukan.htm

National federation of advocacy projects, patients' councils, user forums and self-help and support groups working in the field of mental health.

UK Homeopathy Medical Association

7 Darnley Road, Gravesend, Kent DA11 0RU

Tel: 01474 560336

Web: www.the-hma.org

UK Mental Health Research Network (MHRN)

PO Box 77, Institute of Psychiatry, Kings College London,

De Crespigny Park, London SE5 8AF.

Tel: 020 7848 0699

Web: www.mhrn.info

The MHRN supports research projects which will help to raise the standard of mental health and social care throughout England, and is managed on behalf of the Department of Health by a partnership between the Institute of Psychiatry and University of Manchester.

UK Reiki Federation

PO Box 71, Andover SP11 9WQ

Tel: 01264 791 441

Web: www.reikifed.co.uk

United Kingdom Psychiatric Pharmacy Group (UKPPG)

Web: www.ukppg.org.uk

The UKPPG aims to ensure the best treatment with medicines for people with mental health needs and their loved ones.

Victoria Health

25a The Broadwalk Shopping Centre, Station Road, Edgware, Middlesex HA8 7BD

Tel: 0800 389 8195

Web: www.victoriahealth.com

A health and natural beauty shop crammed with the very latest holistic healthcare and well-being products; free P&P for online orders.

YoungMinds

102-108 Clerkenwell Road, London EC1M 5SA

Tel: 020 7336 8445

Info line: 0800 018 2138

Web: www.youngminds.org.uk

Mental health charity for children and young people, providing information and advice.

United States of America

American Psychiatric Association

1000 Wilson Boulevard, Suite 1825, Arlington, VA 22209-3901, USA

Tel: 703 907 7300

Web: www.psych.org

American Psychological Association

750 First Street, NE, Washington, DC 20002-4242

Tel: 800 374 2721

Web: www.apa.org

Center for Mental Health Services

PO Box 42557, Washington, DC 20015, USA

Web: www.mentalhealth.samhsa.gov

Child and Adolescent Bipolar Foundation

1000 Skokie Blvd, Suite 570, Wilmette, IL 60091, USA

Tel: 847 256 8525

Web: www.bpkids.org

US based, non-profit making and parent-led organization which offers information and support for young people with bipolar disorder and their families.

Depression and Bipolar Support Alliance

730 N Franklin Street, Suite 501, Chicago, IL 60610-7224, USA

Tel: (Toll free) 800 826 3632

Web: www.ndmda.org

This non-profit making organization has a network of nearly 1,000 patient support groups across the United States, offers information and articles on mental health issues, and supports research into the diagnosis and treatment of bipolar.

Mental Health America (formerly known as the National Mental Health Association)

2000 N. Beauregard Street, 6th Floor Alexandria, VA 22311, USA

Tel: 703 684 7722

Crisis line: 800 273 TALK

Web: www.nmha.org or mentalhealthamerica.net

Non-profit making organization which examines mental health issues in the USA.

National Alliance for the Mentally Ill (NAMI)

Colonial Place Three, 2107 Wilson Boulevard, Suite 300,

Arlington, VA 22201–3042, USA

Tel: 800 950 NAMI

Web: www.nami.org

National Institute of Mental Health (NIMH)

6001 Executive Boulevard, Bethseda, MD 20892–9663, USA

Web: www.nimh.nih.gov

Suicide and Mental Health Association International

PO Box 702, Sioux Falls, SD 57101–0702, USA

Web: www.suicideandmentalhealthassociationinternational.org

Dedicated to suicide and mental health related issues in the USA.

www.bipolar.about.com

International site that contains articles, discussion forums, book reviews and chat rooms.

www.bipolarworld.net

Provides information on bipolar diagnosis, treatment and suicide, an 'ask the doctor' link, personal stories, family support and chat rooms.

www.mcmanweb.com

Founded and run by American John McManamy, who has a bipolar diagnosis, this website offers information and advice on living well with bipolar disorder, research articles and online forums.

www.pendulum.org

An American based non-profit making website established in 1994, it offers information on symptoms, diagnosis and treatment of bipolar disorder, as well as support, research articles and online forums.

Canada

Alliance for the Mentally Ill (Quebec)

5253 Decarie Blvd., Ste. 150, Montreal, Quebec H3W 3C3, Canada

Tel: 514 486 1448

Web: www.amiquebec.org

The Canadian Mental Health Association

Phoenix Professional Building, 595 Montreal Road, Suite 303,

Ottawa ON K1K 4L2

Tel: 613 745 7750

Web: www.cmha.ca

A nationwide charitable organization which aims to support people who experience mental illness, offering information, self-help resources and support groups.

The Canadian Network for Mood & Anxiety Treatments

Email: cmeinfo@canmat.org

Web: www.canmat.org

Runs research and education programmes which seek to increase understanding of mood disorders and their treatment. Members are drawn from major Canadian universities.

Depression & Manic Depression Association of Alberta

Box 6404, Edmonton, Alberta T5K 2J5, Canada

Tel: 888 757 7077

The Mood Disorders Association of British Columbia

202–2250 Commercial Drive, Vancouver, British Columbia V5N 5P9, Canada

Tel: 604 873 0103

Web: www.mdabc.net

The Mood Disorders Association of Manitoba

4 Fort Street, Suite 100, Winnipeg, Manitoba R3C 1C4, Canada

Tel: 204 786 0987

          (Toll free) 1 800 263 1460

Web: www.depression.mb.ca

The Mood Disorders Association of Ontario

36 Eglinton Ave., West, Suite 602, Toronto, ON M4R 1A1, Canada

Tel: 416 486 8046

          (Toll free) 1 888 486 8236

Web: www.mooddisorders.on.ca

Mood Disorders Society of Canada

Suite 736, 3–304 Stone Road West, Guelph, Ontario N1G 4W4

Tel: (519) 824–5565

Web: www.mooddisorderscanada.ca

Non-profit making organization providing information and support for people affected by bipolar disorder, including online forum and self-help resources.

The Organization for Bipolar Affective Disorder

1019 – 7th Ave SW, Calgary, Alberta T2P 1A8, Canada

Tel: 403 263 7408

            (Toll free) 1 866 263 7408

Web: www.obad.ca

Aims to help people understand their mental health and diagnosed disorders, and to live better lives.

Australia and New Zealand

Balance

PO Box 13266, Armagh, Christchurch 8141, New Zealand

Tel: 03 366 3631

Web: www.balance.org.nz

A national network of support groups and online forums, which seeks to provide support, education and advocacy to anyone affected by bipolar disorder.

The Black Dog Institute

Hospital Road, Prince of Wales Hospital, Randwick NSW 2031, Australia

Tel: 029 382 4530

Web: www.blackdoginstitute.org.au

The Black Dog Institute's mission is to advance the understanding, diagnosis and management of mood disorders, including depression and bipolar disorder, by continuously raising clinical, research, education and training standards. The Institute is affiliated with the University of New South Wales in Australia.

Mental Health Foundation of New Zealand

PO Box 10051, Dominion Road, Auckland 1446, New Zealand

Tel: 64 9 300 7010

Web: www.mentalhealth.org.nz

The Mental Health Foundation works to improve the mental health of all people and communities in New Zealand by providing education, training and advocacy, and by lobbying for changes in mental health policy.

The Royal Australian and New Zealand College of Psychiatrists

309 La Trobe Street, Melbourne, Victoria 3000, Australia

Tel: (Toll free) 1800 337 448 (for Australian residents)

          (Toll free) 0800 443 827 (for New Zealand residents)

Web: www.ranzcp.org

SANE Australia

PO Box 226, South Melbourne 3205, Australia

Helpline: 1800 18 SANE (7263) or use their Helpline Online service (via the website) to ask questions about mental illness and related topics.

Web: www.sane.org

A national charity working for a better life for people affected by mental illness, through campaigning, education and research.

South Africa

South African Bipolar Site

Web: www.bipolar.co.za

'Umbrella' website which provides links to local bipolar support groups and other bipolar resources.

Worldwide

Alcoholics Anonymous

To find AA groups outside the UK, visit: www.alcoholics-anonymous.org

Equilibrium – The Bipolar Foundation

1 Rivercourt, 1 Trinity Street, Oxford OX1 1TQ

Web: www.bipolar-foundation.org

An independent, international non-governmental organization dedicated to improving treatment and understanding of the causes and effects of bipolar disorder.

International Society for Bipolar Disorders

Tel: 412 802 6940

Web: www.isbd.org

Aims to promote awareness of bipolar conditions in society, educate mental health professionals and promote international research collaborations.

Narcotics Anonymous

To find NA groups outside the UK, go to: www.na.org

World Federation of Societies of Biological Psychiatry (WFSBP)

Zum Ehrenhain 34, 22885 Barsbüttel, Germany

Tel: 49 40 670882 90

Web: www.wfsbp.org

The World Federation of Societies of Biological Psychiatry is a non-profit, international organization composed of over 50 national societies of biological psychiatry, representing over 4,500 professionals.

Recommended reading

Anglada, Tracy – *Intense Minds: Through the Eyes of Young People with Bipolar Disorder*. Trafford Publishing, 2006.

Carr, Allen – *Allen Carr's Easy Way to Stop Smoking*. Penguin Books, 2006.

Duncan, Alice – *Photographs*. White Bridge Press, 2006.

Fast, Julie A and Preston, John – *Take Charge of Bipolar Disorder*. Warner Wellness, 2006.

Fast, Julie A and Preston, John – *Loving Someone with Bipolar Disorder*. New Harbinger Publications, 2004.

Fink, Candida and Kraynak, Joe – *Bipolar Disorder For Dummies*. Wiley Publishing, 2005.

Holford, Patrick – *Optimum Nutrition for the Mind*. Piatkus, 2007.

Hunt, Neil – *Bipolar Disorder: Your Questions Answered*. Elsevier 2005.

Jamison, Kay Redfield – *Night Falls Fast*. Vintage Books, 2000.

Jamison, Kay Redfield – *Touched with Fire*. Free Press Paperbacks, 1994.

Jones, Steven; Hayward, Peter; and Lam, Dominic – *Coping with Bipolar Disorder*. Oneworld, 2002.

McManamy, John – *Living Well with Depression and Bipolar Disorder*. Collins 2006.

Miklowitz, David J and George, Elizabeth L – *The Bipolar Teen: What You Can Do to Help Your Child and Your Family*, Guilford Press, 2007.

Miklowitz, David J – *The Bipolar Disorder Survival Guide*. The Guilford Press, 2002.

Paplos, Demitri and Paplos, Janice – *The Bipolar Child*. Broadway Books, 2006.

Thomas, J and Hughes, T – *You Don't Have to be Famous to Have Manic Depression*. Michael Joseph, 2006.

Townsend, Martin – *The Father I Had*. Bantam Press, 2007.

With more thanks ...

Sarah would like to thank her dad Jim, her sister Rebecca, her mum Rose, her husband Anthony and her three sons, Harry, Jonah and Luke ...

Dad – You told me once that I was good at writing and that's probably why I ended up in journalism. Thank you for that confidence boost and for all your unconditional love. I hope you're looking down with pride!

Rebecca – Not only do I love you (as I always have), I've come to admire you greatly. You've taught me so much and you truly are the living inspiration for this book.

Mum – You're a living legend. You are the strongest, bravest, most practical person I have ever had the pleasure of meeting, let alone loving. Rebecca and I are the luckiest daughters on earth.

Anthony – You deserve unlimited thanks for all your emotional support, tea-making, chocolate-buying and child-entertaining while I'm tapping away in the office. I love you so much. What would I do without you?

Harry, Jonah and Luke – You are my brilliant boys that make my life worth living. I love you all to Pluto and back and back again.

Amanda – Writing this book turned out to be an unexpected, life-changing emotional journey for both of us. How incredible it was for me to share it – long-distance – with such a kind-natured, good-humoured and talented friend. I've truly loved working with you. Oh how we've laughed and cried. When are you free for a spot of shoe-shopping?

Amanda would like to thank her parents Irene and Gordon, her husband Martin and her three children Ben, Hannah and Will ...

Mum – I want you to know that, above everything else, this book is written with love, because I love you so much and always will ... I could not have asked for a better or happier start in life than the one you gave me. When I was younger, I didn't realize how lucky I was to have you, but I do now.

Dad – You're Mum's rock and support, and you have always put her and everyone else first. Your love for her radiates out of you, even in the most difficult of times. I love you more than I can say, a feeling shared by my children who think you're a brilliant Grandad – and I think they're right.

Martin – I'm so glad I got on that train to Hebden Bridge with you 23 years ago ... You're the other half of my soul, and I love you endlessly. Thank you for all the help, support and encouragement you've given me, especially during the writing of this book – and for putting up with some frankly dodgy culinary moments.

My fantastic children Ben, Hannah and Will – I'm proud of this book, but I'm a million times prouder of you three. I love you all so much, you make me laugh, and being your mum is the best job in the world *ever!*

Sarah – My cousin and also my friend. I have loved the journey we've been on together – and it's not over yet (not while there are still shoes to be bought!) I couldn't have worked on this book without you and your calm, positive energy ... you're the warmest, most compassionate person I have ever known. Everyone should have a Sarah in their lives – the world would be a better place.

We would also like to thank all the wonderful people who have supported us during the 18 months it's taken to write this book, particularly Andrew Bates, Helen Boud, Lisa Jackson and Rona Jones.

Glossary

ADHD (attention deficit hyperactivity disorder) – a range of problem behaviours, such as poor attention span, impulsiveness, restlessness and hyperactivity, often seen in children

Adrenaline – a hormone secreted by the adrenal glands that stimulates and boosts motivation

Advocate – a volunteer who helps those with mental illness communicate their needs, explore their options and get things done

Amino acid – the brain's messengers found in protein-rich food

Antidepressant – a drug prescribed to alleviate depression

Antipsychotic – a drug prescribed to alleviate psychosis, mania and hypomania

Approved mental health professional (AMHP) – the new title introduced by the Mental Health Act 2007 (replacing the title of approved social worker or ASW) to describe a nursing professional who's trained and qualified to partici-pate in the decision to section someone

Atypical – a class of antipsychotic drugs

Bipolar disorder – a mental illness characterized by mood swings

CAMHS (child and adolescent mental health) – health services for those under the age of 18

Care plan – a list of action points decided upon and written down by the person with bipolar and their support team to plan for the future

Carer – a person who cares for a sick or elderly person

Chronic – persisting for a long time

CPA (Care Programme Approach) – a care plan specifically designed for someone who's been in hospital to ease their transition back to their life outside

CPN (Community Psychiatric Nurse) – nurses who support those with mental illnesses when they're not in hospital

Cyclothymia – where depressive and manic symptoms last for two years but are not serious enough for a diagnosis of bipolar disorder

Depression – a low mood and a loss of interest and pleasure in previously enjoyed activities

Diagnosis – the identification of an illness by means of symptoms

Diagnostic and Statistical Manual of Mental Disorders (DSM IV) – the fourth edition of a manual published by the American Psychiatric Association, used in the UK and US for categorizing and diagnosing mental health problems

Discrimination – unfavourable treatment based on prejudice

Dopamine – a neurotransmitter that transmits signals between nerve cells

Dual diagnosis – where a diagnosis such as bipolar disorder is accompanied by another clinical condition, such as alcoholism

Essential fatty acids – healthy fats such as omega-3, important for healthy communication between brain cells

General practitioner (GP) – a family doctor who treats people in the community

Grandiosity – the delusion of high rank or superiority

Hallucination – the apparent perception of an object, person or experience not actually present

Holding power – a legal process in place to allow a doctor to detain and assess a patient in hospital for 72 hours while they decide whether an application for a section needs to be made; a psychiatric nurse can exercise a holding power for up to six hours until a doctor can begin the assessment

Holistic – treating the whole person including mental, emotional and social factors, rather than just the symptoms of a disease

Hypomania – a persistent mild elevation of mood

Hypothyroidism – a condition where the thyroid gland doesn't produce enough of the hormone thyroxine

Index of suspicion – a list of symptoms and/or behaviour a health professional needs to look out for to make a diagnosis

Informal patient – anyone who agrees to admit themselves to a psychiatric hospital voluntarily

Insomnia – habitual sleeplessness

Mania – an unnaturally high euphoric mood

Manic depression – a synonym for 'bipolar disorder', although the term is less frequently used today

Mental health crisis resolution team (CRT) – provides 24-hour support for anyone experiencing a mental health crisis

Mixed state – where symptoms of depression and mania occur at the same time

Nearest relative – the patient's closest family member who has certain rights

Neuroleptic malignant syndrome (NMS) – a rare but potentially life threatening adverse reaction to neuroleptic/antipsychotic drugs

Neurotransmitters – chemicals that relay nerve impulses between brain and body

NICE (National Institute for Clinical Excellence) – an independent organization responsible for providing national guidance on the promotion of good health and the prevention and treatment of ill health in the UK

Nicotine Replacement Therapy (NRT) – gum, patches, lozenges or tabs loaded with nicotine for quitting smoking

Occupational therapy – the assessment and treatment of physical and psychiatric conditions using specific, purposeful activity to prevent disability and promote independent function in all aspects of daily life

ORAC (Oxygen Radical Absorbance Capacity) – a scale to measure the anti-oxidant (cell-protecting) activity of fruit and vegetables

OTC (Over-The-Counter) – medicines that can be bought at any pharmacy or chemist without a prescription

Paranoia – experiencing delusions of persecution

Personality disorder – a mental illness characterized by a severe disturbance of the character, logic and behaviour of an individual

Pharmacist – a person qualified to prepare and dispense pharmaceutical drugs

Prescription – a doctor's written instruction for medicine to be taken

Prophylactic – preventative

Protocols – official rules for a procedure or treatment

Psychiatrist – a person qualified in the study and treatment of mental illness

Psychologist – a person qualified in the study of the human mind and its functions

Psychosis – a loss of contact with external reality

Puerperal psychosis – a condition where symptoms of confusion, hallucinations and a total loss of reality can happen suddenly, often after childbirth

Quality and Outcomes Framework (QUOF) – a governmental 'points' system for General Practitioners (GPs) in the UK

Rapid cycling – experiencing more than four mood swings in one year

Schizophrenia – a mental illness characterized by delusions and retreat from social life

Seasonal affective disorder (SAD) – a type of winter depression characterized by the need to sleep and eat carbohydrates

Section – compulsory admittance to a psychiatric hospital or ward

Serotonin – a 'neurotransmitter' known as the brain's happy chemical

Stigma – a sign of disgrace or discredit, which sets a person apart from others

Suicide – intentionally killing oneself

Thyroxine – the hormone produced by the thyroid gland that controls the way the body uses energy

Toxin – a poison

Tricyclic – a class of antidepressants

Tryptophan – an amino acid found in certain foods

Ultra rapid cycling – experiencing monthly, weekly or even daily mood swings

Unipolar – a word used to describe depression where only low moods are experienced (not the high moods also experienced by those with bipolar disorder)

Withdrawal symptoms – the unpleasant physical and emotional reaction that occurs when an addictive substance is no longer taken

Index

Abbott, Paul 236
acceptance 54–56, 86–87
acupuncture 184
Adapin 82t
adrenalin 191
advance directives
    and advance statements 103–4
    meaning of 103–4
    putting in writing 104
    self-management courses 92
    witnessing 104
advocacy
    advocate, finding 117
    advocate, meaning of 116
    group and formal 116
    Mental Health Act (2007) 155
age, and bipolar disorder 21
alcohol
    antidepressants, effect on working of
        209
    bipolar diagnosis 209
    dependency 210–11
    harmful effects of 208–9
    high risk use 209
Alcoholics Anonymous 210–11
Alepam 83t
AMHP see approved mental health
    practitioner (AMHP)
amino acids 200–201
amitriptyline 82t

Anafranil 82t
Anderton, Sophie 236
Ant, Adam 237
antidepressants 75, 81–82t
    and alcohol 209
    for children 101
    and corticosteroids 212
    mania, risk of switch to 82, 101
    mood stabilizers, taking with 84–85,
        101
    over prescription of 48, 72–73
    SSRIs 80, 81t
    tricyclic antidepressants 80, 82t
antimanics see mood
        stabilizers/antimanics
antipsychotics/neuroleptics 75,
        78–79t
    neuroleptic malignant syndrome
        (NMS), risk of 80
    typical/atypical groups 80
    weight gain 89
anxiety
    obsessive behaviour 31, 32
    panic attacks 32
    paranoia 32
    symptoms of 31
Appleby, Louis 72
approved mental health practitioner
        (AMHP) 151, 162
aromatherapy 184–85

Ativan 83t
Attention-Deficit Hyperactivity Disorder
   (ADHD) 100
attorney, power of *see* Lasting Power of
   Attorney

Bacon, Jeremy 18, 90
Barnes, Caryl 95
Be . . . foundation 132
'Beating the Blues' CCBT programme
   72
benefits, entitlement to 230–31
benzodiazepines/anti-anxiety drugs
   75, 83
beta-blockers 212
Bipolar Child, The (Papolos) 101, 102
bipolar disorder
   Bipolar I 19–20, 23, 26, 31
   Bipolar II 20, 23, 31
   Bipolar III 20
   definition of 17
Bipolar Disorder for Dummies (Fink &
   Kraynak) 56
bipolar spectrum disorder 19
Bipolar Survival Guide, The (Miklowitz)
   120
blood pressure, high 176
British Association of Behavioural and
   Cognitive Psychotherapists 70
British Association of Counselling and
   Psychotherapy 70
Bruno, Frank 237
Byron, Lord 237

caffeine
   alternatives to 207–8
   effects of 206
   reducing intake of 206–7
calcium 196

CALM (Campaign Against Living
   Miserably) 132
Camcolit 76t
cannabis (pot, skunk, weed) 213–14
carbamazepine 76t
care co-ordinators 110
Care Programme Approach (CPA)
   170–71
carers
   psychiatric hospitals 157–61
   support groups 139
   see also family and friends, support
   for
causes, of bipolar 36–37
CBT *see* Cognitive Behavioural Therapy
   (CBT)
child, explaining parent's bipolar to
   honesty 223
   hospital stays 224–25
   listening 223–24
   not their fault 224
child psychologists 100
children, and bipolar
   childhood symptoms 43–44, 45
   diagnosis, difficulty of 43, 45, 100
   hospital treatment 101
   information gathering 102
   mood stabilizers *versus*
      antidepressants 101
   psychological intervention 101
   risk factors 38–39
   treatment choices 60, 100–101
   worsening situation, prevention of
      99–100
chlorpromazine 78t, 80
choline (lecithin) 196, 197
Cipramil 81t
citalopram 81t
clomipramine 82t

clonazepam 83t
clozapine 79t, 80
Clozaril 79t, 80
CMHT see Community Mental Health
    Team (CMHT)
Cobain, Kurt 238
cocaine (charlie, coke) 215
Code of Practice (Mental Health Act
    (1983))
  key workers 158
  occupational therapists 161
  patient rights 146
cognitive behavioural therapy (CBT) 60
  early warning signs, detecting
    66–68
  mood diary 65–66
  mood swings, setting up systems
    before 68–69
  negative thinking, as bad habit 64
  psycho-education stage 65
  relapse prevention 64–65
  seasonal affective disorder (SAD)
    99
  tools, equipping people with 63–64
community mental health team (CMHT)
  50, 61, 70–71, 108, 130–31
community psychiatric nurse (CPN)
  discharge planning meeting 170
  early warning signs, recognition of
    111
  family involvement 111
  holistic needs-based approach
    110–11
  medication, understanding 110
  nurse therapists (specialists) 111
  physical healthcare, promotion of
    111
  regional variations 111–13
  risk management 110

  support 110–11
Community Treatment Orders (CTOs)
  155, 172
Complaints Advocacy Service (ICAS)
  232
complaints procedure, aspects of care
  England 232
  gross professional misconduct 234
  in hospital 232–33
  private treatment 233–34
  Scotland 232
  Wales 232
complementary therapies
  acupuncture 184
  aromatherapy 184–85
  as beneficial 183–84
  homeopathy 185
  massage 185
  meditation 186
  reflexology 186
  Reiki 187
  yoga 187–88
computerised cognitive behavioural
    therapy (CCBT) 72
Concordin 82t
consultant psychiatrist 157–58
continuum of bipolarity 19
coping approaches, improving 246
Cornwell, Patricia 238
corticosteroids 212
Corvin, Dr 203
cough medicine 212
CPA see Care Programme Approach
  (CPA)
CPN see Community Psychiatric Nurse
  (CPN)
Craddock, Nick 19, 37, 40, 42, 47,
  229, 230, 245
creativity, and hypomania 25

crisis resolution team (CRT)
A&E/999 as alternative in
emergencies 115-16
crisis phone number, obtaining 116
information, provision of 116
NICE guidelines on 114
regional variations 115
role of 113-14
CRT *see* Crisis Resolution Team (CRT)
CTOs *see* Community Treatment Orders
(CTOs)
cyclothymia 20

Daw, Rowena 172
Daya, Shabir 201, 202
decongestants 212
denial 53f, 54
Denzapine 79t, 80
Depakote 76t
depression
and alcohol 208
in Bipolar I and II 23
childhood symptoms 43
diagnosis, of bipolar 47-49,
50-51
DSM IV definition 22
experiences of 23-24
family and friends, toll on 133-34
late-onset bipolar disorder 45-46
unipolar *versus* bipolar 22-23
Desyrel 82t
diagnosis, of bipolar
importance of early 50
insight, and pathway of care 52-54
mental health history 51-52
misdiagnosis 46-49
as positive thing 242-44
Diagnostic and Statistical Manual of
Mental Disorders (DSM IV) 22, 35

diazepam 83t
dietary changes
alcohol, cut down 193
brain, effect of nutrients on 188
breakfast, importance of for mood
193
caffeine, drink less 193
fish, eat more 190
food, and mood 188-89
fruit and vegetables, eat more
190-91
low-fat protein, eat lots 191
nut/seed snacks 193
processed foods, and mood 192
sugar, eat less 192
'The Mind Meal' 193-95
water, drink lots 193
see also nutritional supplements
Disability Discrimination Act (1995)
226, 230-31
discharge process, psychiatric hospitals
Care Programme Approach (CAP)
170-71
early warning signs, awareness of
169-70
discrimination, and mental health
explaining bipolar 218
workplace 226-27
Divalproex 76t
Donnelly, Peter 41
dopamine 191
doxepin 82t
Dozic 78t, 80
Driver and Vehicle Licensing Agency
(DVLA) 234-35
driving, with bipolar 234-36
drug treatments
acceptance, informed decisions
about 86-87

antidepressants 75, 81–82t
antipsychotics/neuroleptics 78–79t, 80
benzodiazepines/anti-anxiety drugs 75, 83
medicines, over-the-counter 211–12
mood stabilizers/antimanics 75, 76t, 77–78
prescription drugs 212–13
relapse, danger of 86
and weight gain 88–89
see also drug treatments; medication; recreational drugs

early warning signs, recognition of
cognitive behavioural therapy (CBT) 66–68
community psychiatric nurse (CPN) 111
hospital care 169–70
ecstasy (E) 215
ECT see electroconvulsive therapy (ECT)
Edronax 81t
Effexor 81t
eicosapentaenoic acid (EPA) 199–200
Elavil 82t
elderly people
diagnosis of 45–46
treatment of 102–3
electroconvulsive therapy (ECT)
consent, giving 97
as controversial treatment 95
effectiveness of 96–97
Mental Health Act (1983) safeguards 97
Mental Health Act (2007) criteria 155

NICE guidelines 60, 95
procedure 95
side effects 96
employer, informing about bipolar
honesty 227–29
legal position 227
stigma, of mental illness 225–27
workplace discrimination 226–27
endorphins, and exercise 182
Enduring Power of Attorney see Lasting Power of Attorney
environmental factors, and bipolar 36– 37
Epilim 76t
Equilibrium - The Bipolar Foundation 20, 57
essential fatty acids 190, 199–200
exercise
and bipolar highs 183
and endorphins 182
and reduced levels of depression 182–83
and smoking cessation 204
explaining bipolar
to child 223–25
discrimination, and mental health 218
shame, and mental illness 219–21
stereotypes, prevalence of 222–23
stigma, and mental illness 218, 219, 221–22

family and friends, support for
depression, toll of 133–34
mania, toll of 133
ongoing support, need for 134–36
relationships, strain on 136–39
tough times, coping during 133–39
unpredictability, dealing with 133

family and friends, support from
  education, importance of 120
  holistic treatment plan, devising 124
  household tasks 122
  as invaluable 118–20
  possible relapse, planning for 123
  regular patterns, sticking to 122
  signs of relapse, spotting 118
  unconditional non-judgemental
    support 123
family based home care, transition to
  245
family focused therapy 69–70
Fast, Julie A. 19, 124, 138
Faverin 81t
Fink, Candida 56
Fisher, Carrie 221, 238
fluvoxamine 81t
folic acid (or folate) 196, 229
food see dietary changes
Fry, Stephen 18, 221, 239
future, for bipolar disorder 244–47

Gamanil 82t
gender, and bipolar disorder 21
General Practitioners (GPs)
  lithium monitoring 106, 107
  mental health, and 'index of
    suspicion' 106–7
  physical check-up 107
  role of 105–7
  support 107
genetic factors, and bipolar 36–37,
  58
genetic testing, for bipolar disorder 41
glossary 268–72
Goodwin, Guy 74, 245–46

Haldol 78t, 80

haloperidol 78t, 80
Healthcare Commission 61, 233
healthy lifestyle, NICE guidelines 60
  see also lifestyle choices
herbal remedies 201–2
heroin (smack, gear) 215–16
'holding power' 150
Holford, Patrick 195
holistic needs-based approach
  110–11
homeopathy 185
hospital care see psychiatric hospitals
Hulatt, Ian 145, 167, 245
Hunt, Neil 220–21
hypomania 20
  Bipolar II 24
  creativity 25
  escalation into mania 26
  irritability 25
  light therapy 99
  WHO definition 24
hypothyroidism 36, 77–78

Ibuprofen 211–12
impramine 82t
incidence, of bipolar disorder 20
insight, and pathway of care 53-56
involuntary detention see sectioning
iron 196–97

Jamison, Kay Redfield 242
Jones, Steven 39, 62–63, 66, 246

Katona, Kerry 238
Ketter, Terence 50
key workers 158
Kinderman, Peter 63, 68
Klonopin 83t
Kraynak, Joe 56

Lam, Dominic 64, 91
Lamictal 76t
lamotrigine 76t
Largactil 78t, 80
larium (mefloquine) 213
Lasting Power of Attorney 231
late-onset bipolar *see* elderly people
lecithin 196, 197
Leigh, Vivien 239
Leponex 79t, 80
libido problems 33
life insurance, and bipolar 234
Lifelink 132
lifestyle choices
  caffeine 205–8
  complementary therapies 183–88
  dietary changes 188–93
  exercise 182–83
  herbal remedies 201–2
  medicines, over-the-counter
    211–12
  nicotine 202–5
  nutritional supplements 195–201
  onset/relapse, effect on 175–76
  prescription drugs 212–13
  recreational drugs 213–17
  sleep patterns 178–81
  stress (negative/positive), and mood
    swings 176–78
light therapy 99
Liskonum 76t
Litarex 76t
lithium
  double dose, risk of 87
  GP monitoring 106, 107
  hypothyroidism 36, 77–78
lithium carbonate 76t
lithium citrate 76t
Lithonate 76t

Living with Depression and Bipolar Disorder
    (McManamy) 35
lofepramine 82t
lorazepam 83t
Loving Someone with Bipolar Disorder (Fast)
    19, 124
LSD (acid) 216
Lustral 81t
Luvox 81t

magnesium 197
Maidment, Ian 89, 160, 205, 212
manganese 197
manic depression
  coining of term 17–18
  as preferred term 18–19
manic episodes
  delusions of grandeur 28
  duration of 26
  failure to disclose 47
  impulsiveness 27
  insight, lack of 27
  mania, symptoms of 26
  over-spending 27–28
massage 185
McCulloch, Andrew 188
McDougall, Tim 110, 113
McManamy, John 35, 73
MDF The BiPolar Organisation 18,
    20, 57, 75, 90, 133, 139–40,
    234
media coverage, positive 244
medication
  childhood symptoms 43
  forgetting to take 87–88
  resistance to 85–86
  see also drug treatments; over-the-
    counter medicines
meditation 186

Mental Capacity Act (2007)
    advance directives 103
    Lasting Power of Attorney 231
Mental Health Act (1983)
    detention, no right to resist 156
    ECT safeguards 97
    'nearest relative', definition and
        rights of 162–63
    patients' rights 156–57
    Section 2 process 154
    Section 3 process 154
    Section 4 process 155
    sectioning 47, 54, 151
    see also Code of Practice (Mental
        Health Act (1983))
Mental Health Act (2007)
    advocacy rights 155
    children, safeguards for 155
    Community Treatment Orders (CTOs)
        155, 172
    definitions, scrapping of 155
    ECT criteria 155
    'nearest relative', definition of 155
    patients' rights 156–57
    'treatability test' 155
mental health charities, support offered
    by 139–41
mental health nurse *see* community
    psychiatric nurse (CPN)
Miklowitz, David 62, 120
Miller, Michael 41, 101
Milligan, Spike 221, 239
Mind 75
    advance directives 104
    advocacy 116
    Community Treatment Orders (CTOs)
        172
    ECT 96
    smoking in hospitals 169

workplace discrimination 226, 227
mirtazapine 81t
mixed state, of depression and mania
    17, 30–31
Molipaxin 82t
mood stabilizers/antimanics 75, 76t,
    77–78
mood swings
    bipolar symptoms 17, 21–22
    early warning signs 66, 68–69
    getting help for extreme 50
    and stress 176–78
Moodgym 72
Morriss, Richard 57, 106, 107, 245
multipolar disorder 19
multivitamins 196
Murray, Robin 213

named nurse 158
National Director for Mental Health
    (Mental Health Tsar) 72
National Institution of Clinical
    Excellence *see* NICE (National
    Institution of Clinical Excellence)
National Suicide Hotlines 133
'nearest relative', definition and rights
    of 155, 162–63
neuroleptic malignant syndrome (NMS)
    80
neuroleptics *see* antipsychotics/
    neuroleptics
neurotransmitters 191, 200
niacin 198
NICE (National Institution of Clinical
    Excellence) guidelines
    acute episodes, long-term
        management 60
    children, diagnosis and treatment of
        45, 60

community mental health team (CMHT) 61
crisis resolution team (CRT) 114
drug protocols 60
ECT 60, 95
elderly people, treatment of 102-3
healthy lifestyle 60
official treatment guidelines 59-61
patients/families/carers, good relations with 60-61
physical monitoring 60
psychological treatments 62
rapid cycling 60
recognition, of bipolar disorder 106
relapse prevention 60
self-management courses 94
smoking cessation 203
team working 101-2
weight gain 89
nicotine see smoking
Nicotine Replacement Therapy (NRT) 203
nutritional supplements
amino acids 200-201
benefits of 195-93
calcium 196
choline (as lecithin) 196, 197
essential fatty acids 199-200
folic acid (or folate) 196
iron 196-97
magnesium 197
manganese 197
multivitamins 196
omega-3 supplements 196
vitamin B1 (thiamine) 197
vitamin B3 (niacin) 198
vitamin B5 (pantothenic acid) 198
vitamin B6 198
vitamin B12 198
vitamin C 199
zinc 199

Obree, Graeme 240
obsessive behaviour 31, 32
occupational therapists 161
O'Connor, Sinead 240
olanzapine 79t, 80
omega-3 supplements 196
Optimum Nutrition For The Mind (Holford) 195
over-the-counter medicines
cough medicine 212
decongestants 212
Ibuprofen 211-12
oxazepam 83t
Oxygen Radical Absorbance Capacity scale 191

panic attacks 32
pantothenic acid 198
Papolos, Demitri 101
paranoia 32
paroxetine 81t
Patients Advice Liaison Service (PALS) 232
Patients' Association 233
patients' rights
advocacy services, information about 156
psychiatric hospitals 146
right to vote 157
sectioning 156
seeking discharge 157
sexual abuse, protection from 157
Pemberton, Max 97
physical monitoring, NICE guidelines 60
Plath, Sylvia 240-41

Positive Mental Attitude League (PMAL)
182, 222
pregnancy
birth, relapse risk after 229-30
pre-conception 229
pregnancy 229
prescription drugs
antidepressants, and corticosteroids
212
beta-blockers 212
larium (mefloquine) 213
Rimonabant appetite suppressant
213
Roaccutane, and serotonin
production 212
Priadel 76t
protriptyline 82t
psychiatric hospitals
acute admission wards 143
carers in 157-61
discharge process 169-72
family and friends, relating to
167-68
high security special hospitals 144
'holding power' 150
hospital environment 146-48
improvements in 147-48
'informal patients' (voluntary
admission) 150-51
intensive care wards 143
medium secure units 143-44
mixed-sex wards 147-48
patient rights 146
privacy, lack of 146-47
private health care 149-50
pros and cons of treatment in
173-74
quality of care, inadequate 146
rules and regulations 144-45

smoking, allowing 168-69
stigma and stereotype 142
supporting loved one in 163-66
psychiatric nurses 158-59
psychiatric pharmacists 160-61
psychiatrists
choosing privately 109
NHS referral 108-9
psychological treatments
benefits of 62-63
cognitive behavioural therapy (CBT)
63-69
computerised cognitive behavioural
therapy (CCBT) 72
counselling 70
and drug treatments 72-74
family focused therapy 69-70
as first choice for children 101
funding, proposal for increasing
71
GP/community mental health team
(CMHT) referrals 70-71
group therapy 70
intense psychotherapy, effectiveness
of 61-62
NICE guidelines 62
obtaining 70-71
poor availability on NHS 71, 72
private treatment 70
psychologists 109
psychosis 29-30
psychotherapy, effectiveness of 61-62
puerperal psychosis, risk of 230

quetiapine 79t, 80
QUOF (Quality and Outcomes
Framework) points 106, 107

rapid cycling 22, 36, 60

reading, recommended 264–65
reboxetine 81t
recreational drugs
    cannabis (pot, skunk, weed)
        213–14
    cocaine (charlie, coke) 215
    drugs, getting help with 217
    ecstasy (E) 215
    heroin (smack, gear) 215–16
    LSD (acid) 216
    speed (whizz, uppers) 216
reflexology 186
Reiki 187
relapse prevention
    birth, relapse risk after 229–30
    cognitive behavioural therapy (CBT)
        64–65
    NICE guidelines 60
    symptom control, and relapse risk
        86
    see also early warning signs
relationships, strain on 136–39
Remeron 81t
resources
    Australia and New Zealand
        261–62
    Canada 259–61
    South Africa 262
    United Kingdom 248–57
    United States of America 257–59
    Worldwide 262–63
review meetings, attending 164–65
Rimonabant appetite suppressant
    213
risk factors
    children 38–39
    lifestyle choices 40–41
    relatives 40
Risperdal 79t, 80

risperidone 79t, 80
Rivotril 83t
Roaccutane 212
Rowett, Michelle 57

Sajatovic, Maria 45, 102
Samaritans 131–32
Scott, Jan 65
seasonal affective disorder (SAD)
    34–36
Secret Life of the Manic Depressive:
    Everything You Need to Know about
    Bipolar Disorder (Fry/BBC) 18, 52,
    239, 244
sectioning
    advance directives 104
    approved mental health practitioner
        (AMHP) 151, 162
    decision, parties to 151
    detention, no right to resist 156
    discharge process 170
    families, guilt feelings of 152–53
    incidence of 153
    involuntary hospitalization process,
        US 153–54
    meaning of 151
    'nearest relative', definition and
        rights of 162–63
    patients' rights 156–57
    physical intervention, and police
        involvement 152
    section orders, or 'involuntary
        detentions' 153
    sectioning procedures, types of 151,
        154–55
    as upsetting process 151–52
self-esteem 33, 39
self-harm 34, 44
self-help groups 139–41

self-management
  control, gaining more 89–90
  online 94–95
  research studies, and benefits of 94
self-management courses (MDF)
  action plans 92
  advance directives 92
  availability of 246
  complementary therapies 92
  coping strategies 91
  healthy lifestyle strategies 92
  participant feedback 92–93
  principles aims and objectives 91
  self-help programme, MDF 245
  self-medication 91
  support networks 91–92
  triggers and warning signs 91
Serax 83t
Serenace 78t, 80
Serenid 83t
Seroquel 79t, 80
serotonin 191, 198
Seroxat 81t
sertraline 81t
shame, and mental illness 219–21
Sinequan 82t
Slattery, Tony 241
sleep patterns
  and depression 179
  and mood 178–79
  sleep rules, good 180–81
smoking
  dangers of 202–3
  giving up 203–5
  in hospitals 168–69
  passive smoking 203
Social Security Administration (SSA)
  (US) 231
sodium valproate 76t

'soft' bipolar 20
speed (whizz, uppers) 216
SSRIs (selective serotonin reuptake
  inhibitors) 80, 81t
St John's wort (Hypericum perforatum)
  201
stereotypes, and mental illness
  222–23
stigma, and mental illness 142, 218,
  219, 221–22, 225–27, 246
Stoll, Andrew 199
Stowe, Zachery 229
stress (negative or positive), and mood
  swings 176–78
suicidal feelings, dealing with
  crisis situation, course of action 130
  guilt, letting go of 129
  professional help, seeking 130–33
  risk factors, knowing 129
  suicide attempts 126–28
  warning factors, recognizing 130
Suicide and Mental Health Association
  International 132
Sutcliffe, Andrea 47
symptoms, of bipolar disorder
  control of and danger of relapse 86
  less recognized 31–34
  mood swings 21–22
  and seasonal affective disorder (SAD)
    34–36
  symptom prevention approaches
    58–59
  variability of 21–22
Syrett, Michel 52, 53–54, 53f, 244

Taachi, Mary 65
Tai, Sara 59, 63, 71, 72, 100–101,
  118, 123, 245
team working 101–2

Tegretol 76t
thiamine 197
Thorncroft, Graham 218
*Through the Eyes of Young People with
    Bipolar Disorder* (Anglada) 102
thyroid problems, and bipolar disorder
    36, 77–78
Tofranil 82t
transcranial magnetic stimulation (TMS)
    98
travel insurance, and bipolar 234
trazodone 82t
treatment
    management *versus* cure 57
    medication plus therapy plus self-
        management techniques 58
    NICE guidelines 59–61
    personalized treatments 58
    preventative treatments 58–59
    Scottish Intercollegiate Guidelines
        Network (SIGN) 61
    World Federation of Societies of
        Biological Psychiatry (WFSBP)
        guidelines 61
    see also drug treatments;
        electroconvulsive therapy (ECT);
        psychological treatments; self-
        management
tricyclic antidepressants 80, 82t
    see also antidepressants
Tryptizol 82t

ultra rapid cycling 22
Unquiet Mind, An (Jamison) 242

valium 83t

valproate semisodium 76t
van Gogh, Vincent 241
venlafaxine 80, 81t
vitamin B1 (thiamine) 197
vitamin B3 (niacin) 198
vitamin B5 (pantothenic acid) 198
vitamin B6 198
vitamin B12 198
vitamin C 199
vitamins 190
Vivactil 82t
von Beethoven, Ludwig 237

Warner, James 157
weight gain 191
    carbohydrate cravings, reducing
        191
    drug treatment 88–89
well-known people, with bipolar 236–41
Wellcome Trust Case Control
    Consortium (WTCCC) 41, 58
Woolf, Virginia 241
workplace discrimination 226–27
    see also employer, informing about
        bipolar

yoga 187–88

Zaponex 79t, 80
Zimovane 83t
zinc 199
Zispin 81t
Zoloft 81t
zopiclone 83t
Zyban 205
Zyprexa 79t, 80